ALISTAIR FINDLAY has a BA (Hons) in Literatur University), an MA in Applied Social Studies Certificate in Scottish Cultural Studies, with University) and an MPhil in Modern P< Distinction (Stirling University). He has three lished by Luath, *Sex, Death and Football* (20~~~~~, ~~~ ~~~~ ~~~~~ *of John Knox* (2006) and *Dancing With Big Eunice: Missives from the frontline of a fractured society* (2010) and is the editor of *100 Favourite Scottish Football Poems*, recently published by Luath Press. A Social Work Manager for West Lothian Council until August 2007, he was awarded a Writer's Bursary by the Scottish Arts Council to produce *Dancing With Big Eunice* on social work and to edit a critical anthology of the poetry of Scottish Marxism. *Shale Voices* is now used as an example of 'creative-memoir' on a course run for Adult Learning at Edinburgh University. Teaching Ideas for use in schools have also been made available on www.luath.co.uk/ShaleVoices/Index.html and will also be made available to Learning and Teaching Scotland.

Shale Voices

A creative memoir of Scotland's
shale oil communities

ALISTAIR FINDLAY

Luath Press Limited

EDINBURGH

www.luath.co.uk

First Edition 1999
This edition 2010

ISBN: 978-1-906307-11-0

The paper used in this book is recyclable. It is made from
low chlorine pulps produced in a low energy, low emission manner
from renewable forests.

Printed and bound by
Bell & Bain Ltd., Glasgow

Typeset in 10.5 point Sabon by
3btype.com

for my father, mother, brothers, cousins, nephews, nieces

Acknowledgements

I would like to thank Livingston Heritage Museum for access to Sara Randall's transcripts and oral history tapes for her study, *A Socio-historical Study of Scottish Shale Mining Communities*, Institute of Occupational Medicine, 1990, for the US Department of Energy final report on agreement no. DE-ACO2-84ER 60199 (West Lothian District Library); Sybil Cavanagh, Local History Librarian, for her talk, *The Shale Oil Industry*; Raymond Ross for his poem, *The Burngrange Disaster*, and the extract from his article, *A Century of Shale*, which appeared in Cencrastus, Summer 1994; (Raymond draws extensively on John MacKay's unpublished OU doctorate, *Social History of the Scottish Shale Oil Industry, 1850–1914*, West Lothian District Library, 1984); David Kerr's booklet, *Shale Oil: Scotland*, self-published, 1994, to be republished, 1999; George Garson for the extract from Jock Wardrope's interview in *No Idle Bread*, West Lothian District Library, 1992; John Kelly for photographs and text of the rent protest at West Calder during the 1926 Strike, and the poem, *Scottish Stalwarts*, by Sarah Moore, his grandmother; my brother, Alan Findlay for his short-stories, *Spug's Transfer* and *Painting the Scullery* which appear in revised form in *Football Boots for Christmas*, The Green-shale Publishing Corporation, 1999; Dennis O'Donnell for his poem, *The Bings*, published in *Two Clocks Ticking*, Curly Snake Publishing, 1997; Joe Corrie's daughter, Morag, for permission to print *Image O' God*; my own poems have appeared in the following publications – *Brithers*, Cencrastus, Autumn issue, 1992; *Out of History*, West Coast Magazine, No 16, 1993; *The Five Sisters*, ZED 20, Akros, June 1994; *Fitba' Cliché*, Chapman, Summer, 1995; photographs are supplied by BP Grangemouth, West Lothian District Library or myself unless individually noted; I would also like to thank Duncan Glen, Tom Leonard, Murdo MacDonald, Alan Jamieson, Raymond Ross and Tam Dalyell for their comments and various encouragements along the way.

I am grateful to West Lothian Council and to Young's Paraffin Light and Mineral Oil Company Ltd, part of the BP Group, for generously funding and supporting this book.

Contents

Preface to the 2nd Edition

It is a milestone in the life of an author, and no less of a book, especially a commemorative one, to have it re-published. *Shale Voices* was my first book, six years in the making. I had broadly three kinds of readership in mind while writing it: old shale-oil workers, their families and descendants; schools, particularly in West Lothian and Grangemouth; readers of social history and biography, interested to learn of an industry and a people that clearly had national and international importance for Scotland and the UK for a century or so before oil was struck in the North Sea. *Shale Voices* tells the story of a community with a way of life, a sense of being, now well and truly gone, though graspable, in some respects, through its re-telling.

The book was well reviewed on publication, and its combination of several genres – oral testimony set out like poetry, old newspaper reports, obituaries, reportage, family history, anecdote, short-stories, pictures, poetry and literary allusion – was noted, usually favourably, as here by Robert Alan Jamieson, poet, playwright, novelist and lecturer in Creative Writing at Edinburgh University:

> Shale Voices *was, to my mind, one of the outstanding books of 1999 – an idiosyncratic collection of many forms of writing, from reportage and local history to short stories and poetry. All in all, it is an elegy to a lost way of life, yet critical and studied; tragic, yet also funny and deeply warm. Its hybrid, 'cultural studies' format may have made it a difficult work to classify, or indeed promote, but it remains a fine example of how the individuality of the artist can be made to interact productively with community and locality.*

I, of course, agree with all of that! The question of what to 'call' *Shale Voices* – biography, history, literature – has since been resolved, at least to its author's satisfaction, by a colleague of Alan Jamieson at Edinburgh University, Helen Lamb, who uses it as a text for a course she runs entitled 'Blood-ties: Creative Memoir'. One of the innovative features of the book frequently remarked upon, which pushes it towards being considered in literary terms and not simply as biography or history, is the laying out of the oral testimonies in lines, designed to capture the dynamics of speech, but which often reads like poetry. This was particularly well discussed by Professor John Foster, probably Scotland's foremost labour historian:

Alistair Findlay's Shale Voices *seeks to ensure that the industry's people, as well as its waste tips, survive. Findlay records their voices, as sharp and red as the rock they worked. In his Introduction, he quotes the Scottish socialist poet, Tom Leonard: 'Any society is a society in conflict and any anthology of a society's poetry which does not reflect this is a lie'. The book's achievement is to reveal the mining villages of West Lothian as communities that are alive in Leonard's sense. It is no mere archive of recordings. Findlay reconstructs the big families of the miners' rows, their often distant origins in the Highlands and Ireland, their work histories and struggles. Their voices are also, in a strange way, freed. Findlay, himself a poet, lays them out on the page as poetry: to capture the 'dynamics of conversation'. The result is to recreate the directness, simplicity and power of everyday speech. Today, if we want to hear the authentic voices of Kilmarnock's miners we can read the novels of William McIlvanney. John Byrne's 'Slab Boys' preserves the anarchic wit of Paisley's young rebels from the 1950s. In a different way, the shale mining communities of West Lothian will continue to be heard through* Shale Voices.

John Foster's review appeared in the *Morning Star*, but I was pleased to have the book equally well received across the whole political spectrum: Billy Wolfe thought he detected elements of Lewis Grassic Gibbon's *Sunset Song* in it; Dennis Canavan pronounced it 'required reading' for all New Labour MSPs; John Stevenson recommended it to white-collar trade unionists; and Tam Dalyell urged it on America and Australia, which have shale mining histories of their own, and massive deposits of it still in the ground, should the black-oil ever run out. Indeed, I can recall only one begrudging reviewer who wondered why 'the history' of the industry had been placed at the back rather than the front, but I believe he was an economist! I have, however, in this new edition, altered the structure of the book by bringing Sybil Cavanagh's historical sketch forward into the centre where it can act as a 'bridge' between the oral testimony and my father's history and local journalism which then puts what has gone before into a wider social, cultural and historical context.

And so, now that we know what to call it – a 'creative memoir' – and with a brand new cover, *Shale Voices* may perhaps find the wider readership its publisher still hopes is out there, and its author too. This opportunity is due to BP providing yet more funding to allow the book to be re-published, and in the process a copy will be given away to every senior school in West Lothian, Falkirk, Grangemouth and Bo'ness. I am immensely grateful to them and also to Sean McPartlin, Assistant Headteacher of St Margaret's Academy, Livingston, for finding the time to produce teaching notes/ideas for the book's flexible and imaginative use in the education setting. Teachers and pupils can access these notes at www.luath.co.uk/ ShaleVoices/Index.html

Finally, I have been gratified, indeed sometimes overwhelmed, by the responses I have had from *Shale Voices'* most informed readers: old shale-oil workers and their families. Some of this was fed-back to me through home-helps, occupational therapists and care staff in residential homes and the like, whom I come into contact with through my own occupation of social work in West Lothian. However, I still receive letters and photographs, sometimes from far-flung parts of the world, asking for, or giving me, more information about some of the characters or aspects of life mentioned in the book. They write as though I knew them all personally, the way my father did, and, as Tam Dalyell remarks in his Foreword, I can think of no better epitaph. Indeed, this has been beautifully expressed by one of the 'voices' who features in the book itself, the award winning poet and critic, Dennis O'Donnell, himself a West Lothian 'character' as defined by my father, one who knows and encompasses the flavours and values of the area, and whose appreciation of *Shale Voices* I am pleased to accept on behalf of all those whose lives it depicts and remembers:

> It is a vast compendium that includes documentary journalism and history, photographs, diagrams and sketches, reminiscence and poetry. But mainly, it is the voices of the people who grew up in the rows under the huge pink shale bings and who toiled in the mines and refineries. These voices flit through the book, like ghostly conversations heard in scraps and fragments, talking of seams, hutches, carbide lamps, the Burngrange disaster, strikes and soup kitchens, quoits and tossing schools. They are the voices of miners, oil workers, wives and children, summoned from a past long erased, and they have the hypnotic fascination you would expect from hearing the dead talk. They are the voices of Addiewell, Seafield, Broxburn, Pumpherston and Roman Camp – nowadays all villages and towns sleeping off their moment of history, but once vibrant and living. ... The mines are long closed. The oil works too. They've even taken away most of the bings that were the industry's colossal cenotaphs. There is, in Livingston, a museum to the industry, and that's good, as far as it goes. But, in 'Shale Voices', Alistair Findlay has given the area, the industry and the ghosts that still bewail its passing, an imperishable monument: the people themselves and their memories.

Alistair Findlay
Bathgate
February 2010

Shale Voices

One of the voices in this book belonged to my father, a shaleminer for over 20 years, who later became a local journalist and then editor of the West Lothian Courier, in which capacity he wrote extensively about shale and its people – characters – he would have said.

> Memory is not simply personal: the memories which constitute our identity and provide the context for every thought and action are not only our own, but are learned, borrowed and inherited – in part, and part of, a common stock, constructed, sustained, and transmitted by the families, communities and culture to which we belong.[1]

This study began as part of an Edinburgh University course on Scottish Cultural Studies. It attempts to convey some of the social and personal experience of working and living in the shale communities of West Lothian from the later decades of last century to around the middle of this century. It contains poetry, speech, anecdote, personal correspondence, reportage, fiction, folklore, family memoir and obituary.

> Ask first whose history, what are its limits? Take your eyes from the stage: listen for the voices from the dark, listen to the mingling of the voices in and out of history.[2]

History belongs not only to those who made it, but to those who inherit it. The first priority is to set it down. The second is to make it available. Only then can we argue about it later. Either way, the result will be what the Dutch poet, Hans Faverey, calls 'against the forgetting'. In the collective and individual experience called human memory, the past and the present inhabit each other. This book might then be said to have been written as much for those who will read it, as for those it was written about.

Alistair Findlay
Bathgate
November 1999

Foreword

Every year, from 1951 until 1962, there was a small ritual in the House of Commons. My predecessor, the late John Taylor MP, who became Opposition Deputy Chief Whip under Hugh Gaitskell, as Leader of the Labour Party, would move an Amendment to the Annual Finance Bill which gave effect to the implementation of the Budget.

John Taylor's Amendment was worded in the arcane, legalistic language that was required in those days.

In effect, he asked for special consideration to be given to remitting tax on oil derived from shale, which was necessarily more expensive to produce than the oil from the well-endowed oil fields of the Middle East and Venezuela. Every year, Conservative Ministers expressed polite sympathy but declined to do anything to help.

In candour, the finger of criticism in this matter should not only be pointed at the Tory Government from 1951 to 1964. John Taylor's predecessor, George Mathers, MP, had endeavoured to gain fiscal advantages for the shale oil industry, but had been met with equally polite but negative sympathy from Labour Treasury Ministers. And this was in spite of support from a man, who had been both Minister of Fuel & Power and Member of Parliament for West Lothian, Emmanuel Shinwell.

When I was elected in May 1962, following the death of John Taylor, it was already too late! The last shale mine in West Lothian, and indeed in Britain, had been scheduled for closure, and there was no chance of a reprieve. I do not pretend for one moment that, if I had been elected any earlier, I would have fared better than my predecessors in gaining Treasury support for the shale mining industry. The whole atmosphere of the time was such that Governments accepted there was an endless abundance of cheap oil and it was only economic good sense to put the padlocks on the old shale mines and consign the industry to the past.

No-one can know for certain, but I suspect that had the world oil crisis for the early 1970s occured a decade before in the early 1960s, decision-making in relation to the shale oil industry in Scotland would have been very different. Prices would have been more competitive. And Governments might well have taken the view that any home-based sources of oil should be protected, even if it meant some degree of subsidy. Further more, it is my personal recollection that, even after North Sea Oil began to come on stream, the cognoscenti of the industry thought that there could have been a place for shale oil, and its important by-products, such as industrial wax, in the economy.

Hindsight is a marvellous thing, and with hindsight it was a terrible mistake to close the shale producing pits before they were exhausted, and indeed not to open one or two new pits to keep the expertise of the shale miner alive.

At the Labour Party Parliamentary Selection Conference, held by the West Lothian Constituency Labour Party in March 1962, I won the very important five votes of the Shale Miners' Union. The decision to support me, I subsequently discovered, was their last official political act before they were disbanded.

After I was elected, and I had got to know him very well, I said, late at night, to Joe Heaney, the last Secretary of the Shale Miners' Union.

'Joe, why on earth did you and your Union support me rather than the official NUM candidate, Dan Kellachan?'

Joe replied: 'Well, I'll tell you. It wasn't for your political views or talents. The reason was simple and self-interested. Dan was 63 years of age. You were 29 years of age. I wanted someone who would be able, for 20 years or more, to fight the compensation cases of my members, who had been injured in the shale mines, and would have no Union to go into battle for them.'

I was very touched by this. And for years, I regarded it as one of my priority tasks, myself, to go into detail on shale miners' injury cases, and to take endless trouble to ensure that they were not deprived of their due. The truth is that in one way it was easier to win compensation for shale miners than for coal miners, because the coal miners tended to suffer more from silicosis, pneumiconiosis and chronic bronchitis than from injury. The shale miners, particularly from shallow pits, like Whitequarries and Deans, tended to suffer from really nasty cuts inflicted by the brittle nature of the shale, that resulted in permanent damage.

Few men were more knowledgeable about the shale miners and shale mines than Bob Findlay of the village of Winchburgh, the outstanding editor of the *West Lothian Courier* for a quarter of a century. During my first 16 years as a Member of Parliament, what Bob Findlay thought and wrote was of maximum importance to me as Member of Parliament. He was one of the great editors of the *West Lothian Courier* – or any other local newspaper in Scotland. He wrote pungently. He was no respecter of persons. He always had a point of view, unpalatable and uncomfortable as we all found it from time to time.

He was, above all, a great great newshound. To my dying day, I will never forget Bob Findlay turning up at every significant meeting or happening in West Lothian, cloth cap nonchalantly poised, the same hard-wearing mackintosh, cigarette dangling out of the side of his mouth as he scribbled notes to enhance his wonderful memory.

The whole life of West Lothian was reflected in the pages of the *Courier* in those days.

It is the source of the greatest pleasure that the author of this Memorial in Letters – so much more relevant than any Memorial in Stone – should be the son, Alistair, of that editor, who chronicled so much of the shale mining communities in their latter stages, and the grand-son of a shale mining family. No-one has more impeccable credentials to perform this task than Alistair Findlay.

My reading of his draft confirms the expectation that he would perform the task with imagination, flair and scholarship. My wife, Kathleen and I are particularly touched by the choice and the emphasis given to poetry.

I do not exaggerate when I assert that Alistair Findlay has added a basic source material to the study of Scottish History that is invaluable and will be of great benefit to future generations. Scotland owes him a debt of gratitude for undertaking this work.

Tam Dalyell MP
November 1999

Hearing the voices

Teaching Ideas for Schools

When Alistair Findlay's *Shale Voices* was published by Luath Press in 1999, it became immediately the most comprehensive and authoritative source for the history of shale mining in West Lothian. Taken in combination with the excellent exhibition at the Almond Valley Heritage Centre in Livingston Village, it tells the story of a crucial and formative era in local history.

However, it is much more than that. The importance of *Shale Voices* for local people, and especially school pupils, is that it captures the authentic voice of West Lothian in an era that is on the edge of being out of reach. Here, faithfully recorded, are individual memories, conversations, newspaper articles, short stories, poems and factual accounts that don't merely record the provenance of those strange alien pink mountains on our landscape, but evoke the lives of the people who produced them, and who, in so doing, for a brief period, made this part of the Lothians 'the oil capital of the world'.

It is a time that will already seem strange to our 21st century children – when their homeplace appears to have been lodged somewhere between Houston in Texas and the Wild West, while still retaining its own unique brand of 'east meets west' central Scotland.

In its pages they can find, in many cases, the authentic voices of their ancestors or their neighbours. For others, incomers from other parts of the country or furth of Scotland, it will be a partial explanation of how their adopted home came to be the way it is today.

In providing the *Teaching Ideas Booklet* – available at www.luath. co.uk/acatalog/Shale_Voices.html and through Learning and Teaching Scotland – we hope to encourage teachers and their pupils to dip into *Shale Voices*, to use it as the source book it is, but also to use it as a springboard to new writing, study and research; to put into practice the wise dictum that only through understanding the past can we confidently shape our future.

The booklet does not lay out lesson plans – each teacher knows best the needs of their class. However, hopefully, the ideas suggested to various departments in the following pages will instigate an examination of all that the book offers and a body of work that not only fits in tidily with 'A Curriculum for Excellence' but also provides local, social and historical relevance to pupils' studies at all stages in primary and secondary.

There is a rich seam of material to be mined – let these pages serve as the miners' lamps!

Sean McPartlin
Assistant Headteacher, St Margaret's Academy, Livingston
November 2007

SCOTCH PETROL

Wholly manufactured in Scotland in our own refineries.

———

Containing the whole output of Motor Spirit from the Scottish Shale Industry.

Beginnings

At its height, which was early this century, a quarter of West Lothian's population was dependent on the shale oil industry. Apart from a few surviving bings and miners rows, there is little to suggest that it was here that the world's first oil industry began. A few statistics might help indicate the extent of the role that shale played in the economic, social and cultural life of the area: between 1850–1962, over 100 shale mines were in operation; in 1866, James 'Sir Paraffine' Young built the largest oil works in the world and a new village at Addiewell to service it; seven shale mines supplied the works, which occupied 70 acres, the foundation stone being laid by Young's friend, David Livingstone, whose African exploits were largely funded by the profits from shale [Livingstone in fact called the western branch of the Lualaba River, the Young River]; between 1860–1900, the population of Broxburn, a major centre for the industry, doubled every decade, rising from 600 in 1861 to 5,898 in 1891.

Almost overnight, therefore, West Lothian was changed from a mainly agricultural-textile district into a klondyke of pit-villages and speculative oil works – 38 starting up in 1864 alone, the year that Young's patents ran out. Work brought labour – an influx of migrants, primarily from Ireland and the Highlands, forced out by famine and years of clearance. The Irish brought with them different traditions and a revival of Catholicism to the district: in 1845, there were three Roman Catholic families in Bathgate – by 1855, they had built their own church and could support their own priest. Until then, the names in West Lothian's Parish Registers had almost invariably been local, Lowland, Scottish and Presbyterian. As one local history puts it:

> In the course of less than half a century, West Lothian was transformed from a small, rural, homogeneous population to a growing, industrial, multi-ethnic one.[1]

Young's Paraffin Light and Mineral Oil Company Ltd,
Addiewell Works, West Calder, c. 1850s

The founder of the shale industry was a Glasgow chemist, James Young. In 1850, he took out patents in Britain and America for processes which obtained oil from bituminous coal [then shale] by first distilling it at low temperatures and then refining it further by distillation and chemical treatment. In 1851, Young and his partners opened Bathgate Chemical Works which initially produced 900 gallons a week of lubricants and naptha solvent for use in the paint and rubber industries. By 1854, it was producing 8,000 gallons a week of 'paraffin' and associated oil products, developments detailed in David Kerr's booklet, Shale Oil: Scotland:

> Dwellings in Bathgate were the first to benefit from the new oil [burned in specially adapted lamps]. Before long one quarter of the lamp oil used in London came from the Bathgate Works. ... By 1861, five tons of wax were being produced each week at Bathgate for sale to candle manufacturers. The impact of the brilliant light from the new candles is hard to imagine now, but at the time the achievement was likened to having coal gas, compressed into a white stick![2]

This image of Bathgate bathed in 'brilliant light', years before London, may itself help to illuminate the scale of the industry which was about to engulf the area, and the massive growth in townships, labour and profit that was to follow. Expansion continued until the First World War, and then came the Depression and the long drawn out struggle to retain industry, jobs and communities. Final closure occurred in 1962, the remaining refining operation being transferred to the BP plant at Grangemouth. This, of course, was light years removed from the early, staggering, period when Addiewell Oil Works employed 1,500 men, including 400 miners, and an army of other skilled trades. Sybil Cavanagh summarises all of this in concise fashion in her article at the end of the study.

* * *

The social and cultural history of shale can no longer be got by listening to the previous generation – to the kind of stories my father never tired of telling. So much is beyond recalling, and we are now left to imagine from the fragments that remain the immense presence shale once had in determining West Lothian's social and industrial history. This study intends to explore some of that through the words and lives of some of those who lived through the period. John Aubrey, one of the earliest chroniclers of other people's lives, and who was thought rather curious by his contemporaries for wanting to do so, sums up the spirit in which this book was originally taken up:

> In whatever way history is written, it is good; and though this be writt as I rode, at gallop, yet the novelty of it, and the faithfulness of the delivery, may make some amends for the incorrectness of the Stile.[3]

Dear Auld Niddry Raws

Oral transcript: unknown resident

nae mair tae hear the hutches
timmin ower the tips
nae mair tae go oan the auld haey-cairts
tae oor annual trips
nae mair tae hear the auld pug's whussle
or the works horn's blaws
nae mair tae see the auld lums reek
in dear auld niddry raws

nae mair tae gaither at the coarner there
nae mair tae jig and dance
or listen tae the auld yins tales
o how they fought in france
nae mair tae wander up the brae
tae jist staun there and pause
or linger oan the memories
o dear auld niddry raws

NIDDRY

There are 96 houses owned by Young's Mineral Oil Company in Niddry. Some 88 houses consist of room (12ft x 13ft), kitchen (12ft x 13ft), scullery (7.5ft x 6ft) with sink. There is a dry closet and coal cellar to each house. A wash-house is provided a few feet from scullery door, where gravitation water is obtained for domestic use. Small gardens are also provided. There is a good drainage system. Refuse is removed twice weekly. Many of these houses are over 40 years built. Two houses have been converted into games and reading rooms. The total number of houses in Niddry is 118, and the population is 690.

Submission by the National Union of Shaleminers
to The Royal Commission on Housing, 1914.

1994: Site of Niddry Rows, which ran along each side of the road

Niddry: A Shale Rows, 1875 – 1960

A transcript from the oral

Alistair Findlay

the laddies helped tim the lavvies
– shunkies – they wir cried
a board wi' a hole in it
an a bucket

if ye'd nae paper ye used a bunch o' gress
or a doaken
ay
they'd say
ye'll laugh
        but ye'll no pu' gress

we ken whaur you come fae
you come fae Niddry
ye've the mark o' the pail oan ye

an o the roars o'it

if ye gave cheek ye goat beltit
an that wis yir nixt door neebers
if ye telt yir ain
ye goat anither yin

that's how we learnt respect

mind ye
the weemin hud a hard time o'it
keepin the hoose an the weans
clean an fed
they'd make the porridge in the mornin
an pit it oot oan the windae ledge
tae cool
then dae thir ither course
the ashes
the grate

it wis
the days o' the parish

they'd gie ye a chitty

but if ye hudnae a hole or
the soles o' yir bits hingin aff
ye goat nuthin

it wis
        the silent films

Tony Jordan played the organ
an when the cowboys galloped
thir hoarses
he'd play William Tell

then they closed the mines and
the oil works and then the war

    but
the people
       o the people
wir great
       in the rows – thir wir

th'Lyon	th'Birds	th'Kyles
th'Menzies	th'Mairs	th'Foxes
th'Broons	th'Balls	th'Banns
th'Cormies	th'Devlins	th'Neils
th'Buchans	th'Quinns	th'Flinns
th'Semples	th'Kellys	th'Hoggs
th'Mallons	th'Boyles	th'Morgans
th'Barrats	th'Clarks	th'Cannons
th'Brands	McEwans	McCormacks
th'Nichols	th'McGees	McWilliams
th'Feelies	th'Duffys	th'Finnigans
th'Newtons	th'Laceys	th'Cochrans
th'Wodecks	th'Byrnes	th'Printies
th'Daltons	th'Scotts	th'Stoddarts
th'Riders	Mary McGuire	th'Nugents
th'Allans	Barney McBride	th' Hannigans
th'Gormans	th'McLaughlans	th'Thompsons
th'Murrays	Big Gundy Hendry	th'Campbells
McCullochs	Brogansth'Donnellys	th'Roaches
Johnstones	Russellsth'Douglas's	th'Fairies
Andersons	Aitkens th'Duncans	th'Martins
th'Cairneys	Nellie Carsteelie	th'Paris's
th'Bailleys	Mary O'Hara	th'Fowlers
Donoghues	Sandy Post Old Lou	th'Tweedies

as I come down past niddry
amidst the moonlight pale
cathedralled there
by burned out stars
       they're gone
          who raised the shale
       they're gone
          who raised the shale

Shale Talk: ordinary discourse

I shall discuss some of the background to this study, beginning with Niddry, a shale mining rows built between Broxburn and Winchburgh in the 1870s by James Young's Mineral Oil Company during the shale oil boom last century. In 1914, Niddry had a population of 690 and 118 houses. It was demolished some 30 years ago. It and the people who lived and worked there have now, quite literally, vanished from view. Derelict buildings survived perhaps until the 1950s/ 60s here and in similar places – such as Oakbank (near East Calder) or Durhamtown and Paulville – both coal mining rows at Bathgate, where my family moved to from Winchburgh in 1953 – around the time of the great post-war transfer into newly built council houses.

Yet these old communities continued to inhabit the lives and sentiments, indeed, the identities of shaleworkers and their children – whether they had actually lived in them or not. No third generation Scottish exile's childhood in Nova Scotia or New Zealand could have been swaddled in more tales of their homeland than mine was on moving to Bathgate, aged four – from mining village to housing scheme – an unwitting participant in what was in fact just one more migratory experience in the lives of the Scottish working class.

This study probably began there.

Addiewell: Livingstone Street c. 1909

Addiewell: site of Livingstone Street c. 1990

I remained uncertain as to what form this study might take until I came upon 'The Fountain' – a community project in Londonderry – by Leon McAuley, who describes his work thus:

> I've never liked History – its so predictable, with its predictably constant wars and famines and droughts. And what I like least about History is that it has things the way they are today. Things today are not, as we all know, what they used to be in days-gone-by. They never are. In days-gone-by things were very, very good indeed. The hours were long, and you worked hard, but the summers were green and the days were golden. The people were poor but they were happy.
>
> I like people though, individuals, ordinary people. And ordinary people, along with equally unpredictable phenomena like earthquakes and volcanoes, are the makers of History. They make it by being implicated in the events that are recorded in the History books. They are the ones who call people to arms, take up the call to arms; who starve and who feed the hungry; who die of thirst and who invent ways of irrigating the land. They make it too, just by living, by going on about their business, simply by being there... The ultimate concern of the artist is to marry content, whatever that may be, and form. There was no shortage of content in The Fountain – nor is there, I am convinced, in any other community – and what was required was a form that would transmit that content effectively.
>
> The oral form in which the content was given to me had an innate vitality, character, and rightness. Each conversation had its own dynamics. The major problem in producing the text for the book was that the rightness and dynamic of speech are not the rightness and dynamic of written prose. While, at first sight, the text might seem, in its layout, to have aspirations towards being poetry, it should soon become clear that it is simply a way of representing, accurately, the dynamic of conversation. Not that that means it isn't sometimes closer to poetry than Poetry.[1]

In this study I have adopted Leon McAuley's approach and layout in terms of transcribing the oral histories of the retired shale men and women who were interviewed and recorded by Sara Randall for a health study in 1984.[2] The forenames, dates of birth, occupations and places of origin of individual speakers, where known, have been supplied in order to help readers 'locate' for themselves their various backgrounds and perspectives. I have tried to keep as faithfully as possible to the actual content, order, idiom and unbroken sequence of words and ideas contained in those passages selected.

It is quite a shock to get your own cultural heritage handed over to you in a large cardboard box from the Livingston Heritage Museum and to hear the voices, idioms, expressions, syntax and the demotic which shaped you, back there in front of you – and not just spitting in the back of the fireplace either! This is what I think McAuley means when he says that the oral form and content has its own 'innate vitality, character, and rightness.' And this is what I have wished to retain at the heart of this study.

The poem, *Niddry – a shale rows*, actually precedes my coming across either Randall or McAuley, and it arose from my listening to the tape of an old resident of Niddry whom I have been unable to identify. After listening to it, I found myself shaping it into a poem in a manner which is not the case with regard to any of the oral histories – which are offered here basically as straightforward 'soundbites', reproduced and rendered as faithfully to the original oral passages as I could make them.

*   *   *

I grew up with stories similar to those told in these oral histories, which I heard repeatedly from my father or uncles or old miners pattering in the pub or the welfare or at weddings or funerals in the Coop Hall. It is thus one of the purposes of this study to help tell these stories in a way faithful to the people it is about – which is what my father aspired to and attempted in his own way and times. In my father's conversation, locality, language and labour were virtually indivisible. A letter he wrote to me shortly before his death in 1978 captures this natural flow:

> I note that like the Arabs you are thinking of folding your tents yet again and stealing quietly away. Maybe you are trying to beat Tory Tam's record. Tam came from, you'd never guess it, Winchburgh! In those days among the miners and farm servants you could fall out with the gaffer one day and be in a new house and a new job the next. Some of the reasons for leaving the jobs were positively ludicrous. A man would move 20 miles for the sake of an extra bob or two a week or because the farmer wouldn't give him another fancy birler for the

horse's collar. Tam was the cantankerous type forever warring with the gaffers. He was also an expert pit repairer who could get a job anywhere. His wife told me that one year they flitted no less than 11 times. Not surprisingly she got that she just wouldn't unpack, and kept the crockery still in the tea chests.

My father was a correspondent of the local. 'Reclaiming the local' is Tom Leonard's view of 19th century working class writers writing about the 'ordinary', the substance of lived lives. His comments seem relevant to many of the texts, both written and oral, presented in this study:

> Much of the poetry [writing/utterance]..is..descriptive of work and poverty, with no separation between writer [speaker] and persona, no 'distancing' of emotion. None of the stuff is cosy. It's got nothing to do with those execrable sentimental nights out with bathos-laden songs about the slums I left behind me. It's as likely to upset the same type of people today as it would have upset a hundred years ago. And by that I don't mean it's all anti-establishment... But these poems [writings/utterances] are not held worthy of serious consideration. They name names, articulate opinions, would carry the argument into the living-room. And for this they have been hospitalised in the oblivion such deviance deserves. But there's another view, and it's a view I want to put across here. Such patients are alive and well, and they have a multitude of things to say about the Present as well as the Past. Locality by locality, A to Z of behind-the-counter library stock, old newspaper by old newspaper, people must go on with the work of release.[3]

Poetry, reportage, speech – contain views of the ordinary that are maybe already lost to us. Few shaleworkers kept diaries or felt themselves important enough to record their own thoughts or feelings in personal journals and the like – the usual source of social and cultural history – which is perhaps why the lives of women and the working class remain largely 'hidden'. Shaleworkers did write, of course, if only to local newspapers, though they were more often written about – observed, reported, praised, arrested, condemned or vilified – and all in ways that have been preserved in the literary and cultural forms of their day – chapbooks, kirk session records, local newspapers. And much of it is still there, awaiting our attention.

As if to confirm these remarks, I then came across an old newspaper report on Peter Johnston, a carter from Bo'ness, a writer of vernacular 'verse', who worked in the Lanarkshire coalfield in the mid-1850s. My father's grandfather, and those flocking to the new shale industry, would no doubt have warmed to the gentle humour of Peter Johnston's poetry:

West Lothian Courier
Saturday January 2, 1886
A Homely Song Writer

There died the other day at Bo'ness, an old carter named Peter Johnston, and though unknown to fame outside his immediate circle, he was the author of numerous songs and other poetical pieces some of which would have done credit to men of greater pretensions. Many of his pieces were connected with his work among horses during a long life-time, and it is remarkable the amount of inspiration an unlettered man like Johnston drew from what would appear at first glance a very prosy subject. His verses are mostly impulsive and written in commemoration of some incident in his career. A piece entitled 'The Toom [empty] Halter' is a combination of pathos and humour, describing his experiences in horse dealing. He begins with a good horse and 'swops' one with another till – 'Noo the toom halter is left in my han' '.

Times, which were always hard with him, were exceptionally so in 1856, and not having a horse of his own he got employment in one of the Lanarkshire coalmines to look after the horses. Trade unionism was strong at the time and he was not 'stationed' when a note from the Secretary demanding his entry money was handed to him. His reply was characteristic. We quote from memory:

> Dear sir, your note last nicht I got,
> To me twas roughly handed;
> To God the praise! for I can raise
> The bill whilk it demanded,
> Were I as fit a' claims to clear,
> Daylicht I ne'er wad shun it,
> Nor in a hole lurk like a mole
> Wi' a licht upon my bunnet.
>
> I on the hardy turnpike road
> Wad listen tae the lintie
> Wi' licht formed by the hand of God,
> An' heid an' side room plenty.
> But as I'm here the dree I'll bear,
> Sae tell your coal craft gentry
> That when declared a stationed man
> I'll frankly pay my entry.

This is as fine an example of working-class poetry as one might wish to obtain for the period – part of what Tom Leonard calls 'the voice of ordinary discourse' – and therefore unlikely to have found its way into standard 19th century volumes of 'poetry':

Any society is a society in conflict, and any anthology of a society's poetry that does not reflect this is a lie. But poetry has been so defined in the public mind as usually to exclude the possibility of social conflicts appearing. The belief is widespread that poetry is not about the expression of opinion, not about 'politics', not about employment, not about what people actually do with their time between waking up and falling asleep each day; not about what they eat; not about how much food costs. It is not the voice of ordinary discourse, contains nothing anyone anywhere could find offensive, above all contains nothing that will interfere with the lawful exercise of an English teacher going about his or her duty in a classroom.[4]

It was not until the turn of the century that modern poetry, like modern writing in general, began moving closer to speech and to the depiction of contemporary life:

> The Modernists, working at the beginning of this century, took Wordsworth further, wanting poetry to have the virtues of prose and to assimilate in its imagery and subject matter as much of modern life as it could – 'words that had not been used in poetry before'.[5]

There are many words and expressions used by these shale workers as part of their everyday speech and working lives that would have both intrigued and delighted many of the great modern writers and poets earlier this century: words such as 'strum' (fuse), 'cuddy-brae' (counter-loaded hutch) and so on, which seem to me to resonate with sound. A modern reader might well find the virtues of poetry – and of 'good literature' – in many of these texts if qualified by the following statement:

> All bad literature aspires to the condition of literature. All good literature aspires to the condition of life.[6]

As Leon McAuley suggests, the layout of the stories is intended to capture the dynamics of conversation rather than aspiring to the condition of 'poetry'. Poetry was originally spoken, of course, rather than written, and the vividness of some of these oral testimonies is similar to what figurative language attempts to achieve in conventional poetry. Before coming upon these oral histories, I had indeed looked at various volumes of local poetry hoping to uncover some kind of direct, contemporary 'voice'. I read *The Poets and Poetry of Linlithgowshire*, edited by Alexander Bisset in 1896, and my heart sank. Not only were James VI and Mary Queen of Scots included as 'local' poets – being one time residents of Linlithgow Palace – but the poems therein reflected Georgian Romanticism (sentimental poems about birds, trees and Nature). I was hoping for a more proletarian voice of the kind present in the poetry of Janet Hamilton[7], who lived in, and wrote about, the 19th century mining communities of Lanarkshire, a district adjacent and very similar to West Lothian:

Juist noo there are mony wha rin to an fro,
An knowledge increases, abune an ablow;
The yird's like a riddle, pits tunnels an bores;   [earth]

Whaur bodies, like mowdies, by hunners an scores,   [moles]
Are howkin, an holin, an blastin the rocks;
An droonins an burnins, explosions an shocks,
An a' ither meagries, amang us are rife: [troubles]
Oh, mony's the slain in the battle o' life!
It's Mammon we worship, wi' graspin an greed,
Wi' sailin an railin at telegraph speed,
Get gowd oot the ironstane, an siller frae coal,
An thoosans an thoosans draw oot o' a'e hole.
Wi' oil shale aneath us, an fire-warks abune,
I think we'll tak lowe, an bleeze up to the mune.   [catch fire]

And so the purpose of this book is to provide some sense of the
shale communities and the people who lived and worked in them,
using as far as possible their own words and in whatever form these
are available – poetry, reportage, speech. Indeed, 'heightened speech'
is a classic description of 'poetry' and it seems an equally apt description of the qualities to be found in many of these oral histories and
their tellers: matter-of-factness, simplicity of expression, directness,
visualisation.

Given that my own interest in this study partly relates to language
usage, I was more than happy to come upon the following report by
my father on a local survey into 'shale talk' carried out on behalf of
Edinburgh University in 1952 by the headmaster at Winchburgh, Mr
George, aided by my father's Uncle John:

> Mr J.B. George, MA, Headmaster of Winchburgh J S School, assisted by
> Mr J. Findlay, has recently been employed on an interesting survey for
> the University of Edinburgh. He conducted an investigation into local
> language in an effort to discover words which were peculiar to this dis-
> trict. Apparently, however, the investigation was comparatively unsuc-
> cessful. Very few words, if any, were discovered which could be said to
> belong to this district. The reason advanced is that up to 1870
> Winchburgh was solely an agricultural district. After that came the
> development of the shale oil industry, which saw workers imported
> from other parts of the Lothians and from Lanarkshire and the West of
> Scotland. The Irish immigrants too, have played their part in the devel-
> opment of Winchburgh. Consequently, the local dialect is composed to
> some degree by words brought to the district by the workers who settled
> within the past seventy years or so. The original dialect has therefore
> been absorbed and lost. The real Winchburgh natives, whose ancestors
> settled here long before the birth of shale oil, and who might have been
> able to help the survey, are now passed on. We have to remember, of
> course, that although shale oil at Winchburgh itself only dates back to
> the beginning of the century, the works at Niddry and the shale mine at
> Glendevon is much older. Glendevon must be the oldest mine still in oper-
> ation in the shalefield. Reverting to the subject of language, the miners

of course have many words peculiar to their own trade which are handed down from generation to generation. None of these can, however, be claimed to be peculiar to shale mining. They came from the much older craft of coal mining and there seems little doubt that the original shale miners were wooed from the older industry. Time and usage have moulded a distinct craft out of shale mining, but it is still very closely related to coal-getting.[8]

Readers will no doubt judge for themselves, but I believe that in these stories the local 'voice' I was hoping to find when I first set out on this project is indeed present. But why not present it in the vernacular Scots used by the speakers themselves? Well, it is mainly because I feel that the local voice comes through the written English in such a way as to actually emphasise its distinctiveness. I was therefore glad to have this confirmed by Duncan Glen, a respected Scots poet and publisher, whose comments on 'right, right, socialists' – the second story printed below – is perhaps worth repeating here:

> the distinctive voice is partly as a contrast to the different rhythms of the verse... the 'English' words are used by your speakers with a Scottish (Lowland, and maybe Central Lowland?) construction – 'that's right socialist policy' as much as 'och aye' or 'ken'. Also, you register that a very interesting 'formality' can be part of a 'working man's' speech in certain circumstances – 'and they were conversing' and then the movement on to the Scottish form of 'with the likes of Davy Kirkwood', and then the very good contrast (in 'form' as well as the words) –
>
> > they were
> >
> > ken
> >
> > right, right socialists
>
> Again, 'quite regular' – a Scottish 'form' but 'quite' is utterly South-east England also – which is a different construction of a phrase, sentence and, of course, sound when spoken.[9]

The 'formality' noted by Duncan Glen seems to me a quite common feature of West Lothian talk, present in my father's speech and those of his generation. It might be confused with an 'educated' diction in that it could take a particularly measured or deliberate form. This, then, rather than a vocabulary of words peculiar to the area is what I think most informs my own sense of what it is that is most distinctive about the language used in these stories and by these story-tellers. An indication of how the outside world, in the shape of the national press, reacted to 'shale talk' some 50 years ago has been preserved for us by The Scotsman reporter who attended the Burngrange Mine Inquiry, held at Seafield Miners Institute, in March 1947. This happened to be the first news story that my father covered as a full-time journalist, though he surely would not have had the difficulties of 'translation' described:

'It was near the waste and Willie was going down the cuddy while Tommy was in the dook, Charlie was coming up the upset and Peter was in the split. Alec was away to the stoop and Hughie was talking to the benchers. Jimmy was inbye, and Johnny, who had his glenny, chapped for the rake.' That seemingly incomprehensible statement is offered in the guise of an imaginary conversation among Lothian shale miners to illustrate the puzzlement of strangers attending the Inquiry into Burngrange Mine explosion. It was natural that the shale workers should use their own familiar trade terms in giving their evidence, but the results were somewhat disconcerting to the uninitiated. Hardest worked man at the Inquiry was the official shorthand writer, but, unlike the reporters who had to watch the clock closer than the traditional apprentice (although for a different reason), the high speed calligraphist could afford to wait until the end of the day for personal enlightenment on the cryptic phraseology.

The mineworkers called upon to testify – having taken the oath while holding a copy of the New Testament – had one estimable quality in common. They may have spoken too rapidly and too softly for the acoustics of the large hall, but all, without exception, displayed a composure not frequently encountered in ordinary court procedure. There was a quiet, manly confidence in facing an array of questioners and, apart from lapses into technicalities, a simplicity of statement that seemed strangely detached from the events they were describing. It was only those familiar with life below the surface of the earth who could visualise from the matter of fact speech the grim reality of the experience.[10]

And so, I have selected passages from the 80 or so oral histories collected by Sara Randall in 1984, using in the process about 25 different speakers, chosen on the basis that they not only told stories relevant to the social history of shale and the times, but did so in an interesting and engaging way, using language and phrasing which is both vivid and reflective of local speech rhythms and language construction. The extracts chosen have had to pass the linguistic and cultural tests of looking and sounding 'right', at least to me – a native of West Lothian.

Perhaps, in the end, the hardest part has been deciding what to leave out.

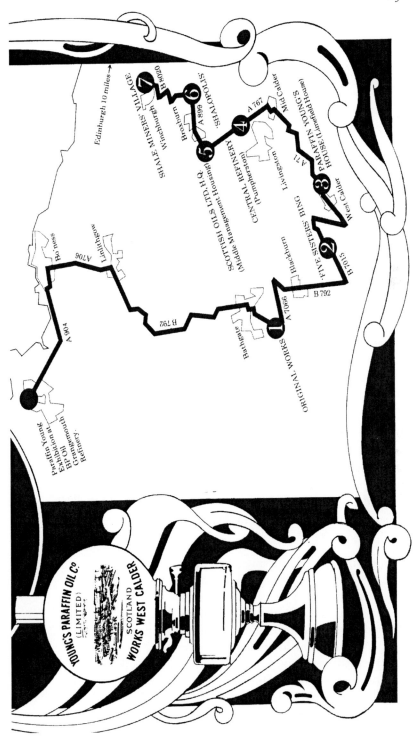

Edinburgh 10 miles →

7 SHALE MINERS' VILLAGE
B 8020
Winchburgh
Broxburn
A 899
6 'SHALOPOLIS'
A 767 Mid Calder
5 SCOTTISH OILS LTD. H.Q.
(Middle Management Housing)
4 CENTRAL REFINERY
(Pumpherston)
3 PARAFFIN YOUNG'S
HOUSE (Limefield House)
Livingston
A 71
West Calder
Bo'ness
Linlithgow
A 706
FIVE SISTERS' BING
Blackburn
2 B 7015
B 792
B 792
A 904
Bathgate
A 7066
1 ORIGINAL WORKS
Paraffin Young
Exhibition at
BP Oil
Grangemouth
Refinery.

YOUNG'S PARAFFIN OIL CO.
(LIMITED)
SCOTLAND
WORKS WEST CALDER

The Bings

Dennis O'Donnell

I

The slow wheels that grind away
the ugly and new to ivied beauty,
have barely touched West Lothian's bings,
these vast, red buttes of shale,
colossal heaps of layered husks,
gouged long ago from the guts of the earth.

Grass has tinged their lower slopes
in a stab at grafting Nature's skin
on to their rawness. They stand here still,
silent, fiery witness to all
 the century-long, dogged dredging
that amassed these monumental hills.

Old men who hang about cross and corner,
idling away the days that are now,
once ground and drudged in tunnelled labyrinths
far below the peaceful woods
and green fields of quiet West Lothian
blasting and howking at oil-yielding shales
and piling these mammoth memorial barrows.

When the last miner came up to the light
at the end of the last shift in Westwood,
thirty million tons of shale
were left entombed in the graves of an industry
choked to death by the niggardly hands
of successive governments in distant London

II

The 1860s: – the Company thrived,
Young's Paraffin Light and Mineral Oil,
from making wicks and fuel for lamps
to triggering the bonanza of oil from shale.
The prospect made boom towns of rural villages
that dovered in the long Victorian summers,
and townships sprang up around the mines
and oil works. Their names still ring on the ear,
the dinning hub of a labour that's lost:
Broxburn, Addiewell, Three Mile Town,
Seafield, Pumpherston, Roman Camps

Carts drove from Camilty mill
Down country lanes to bright main streets
delivering gunpowder to Co-op stores,
sold in blue bags direct to the miners.
Ponies drew hutches of shale to the surface.
Bars, hotels and boarding-houses
started up in the lee of the bings,
the mounds of spent red oxide blaes
that grew from nothing to 200 feet
and more, in under 20 years.

And wrung from the bowels of the earth each year
were twenty-five million gallons of crude.

III
In the 1960s, shale mining died
and 4,000 men walked from the pits.
The subsidy from London had dried to a trickle,
that subsidy earned in the First World War
when West Lothian's oil fuelled the Navy.

The workings stop. The men move away.
The miners' rows fade to ghost towns.
And these mountainous bluffs, pyramids of silence,
are levelled and landscaped, taken away
to lay the highways that by-pass the county.
Now, in the light of the western sun,
the bings that are gone, like those that remain
part of our geography, part of our history,
are soap-smooth mesas on a level plain.

The Five Sisters – West Calder

we realise ourselves in the dialect of our upbringing

[heard on the radio]

Mining Talk
Wife of electrician, born 1907, Breich

Oh I could give you a good laugh
from beginning to end,
right enough.
About all the mining talk we heard.
Getting up at 5 o'clock in the morning,
and lighting,
trying to light,
a fire,
a range.
We'd no electric cookers.
No gas cookers.
No nothing.
Trying to light a fire.
Trying to boil a kettle.
Trying to put a frying pan on,
to fry their breakfast.
Making up pieces.

There were three of them going into the pit then.
And then my brothers would be saying,
you haven't forgotten everything,
before you went out,
my piece box,
my flask,
my carbide,
my lamps,
my self,
    – cheerio mother!

You haven't got that on there!

Have you got that on there?

Right Right Socialists

James: engineer, born 1908, Oakbank

'I was kind of political minded,
at that time.
Couldn't get me near enough a communist meeting,
for to go to,
and that sort of thing,
ken.

Ken,
when you're young,
and you landed in a village that's struck,
right off the register,
in a backwater,
and no work,
its the best education you can get,
really.'

       'So you had leanings
       towards communism?'

'Oh no, no, no.
You just wanted me to say that.
No.
But I mean,
that's right socialist policy.

And then,
of course,
for the size of it,
it was a great community,
Oakbank,
you know,
because they had men in there,
and they were conversing,
with the likes of Davy Kirkwood,
and all these men.
They were,
ken,
right, right socialists.

And they used to bring them through there,
quite regular.
And the meetings were always packed,
at that time.
And they had a Burns Club.
And they had men in there that was,
they must have had,
an awful lot of knowledge.'

That's your graith

A = *James: drawer, born 1903, Winchburgh*
B = *James: drawer, born 1918, Winchburgh*

A- 'Well, I started with my father,
and I was learning how to be a miner,
how to use a pick,
and how to stamp holes,
and put up trees,
and what not.
But, at the beginning,
it was nearly all... I had to fill hutches,
and the seam was only four foot nine high.
And I was six feet!'

'That was a small seam. What seam was that?'

A- 'Well, they called it the underseam. I couldn't
tell you what they...'

**'Yes, but in the Dunnet, you have the under, the
mid and the upper. You have three seams in one.'**

A- 'She knows more about it than I do!'

B- *'Aye'*

'It's alright, go on! It was the under.'

A- 'Well, that was the height of it,
four foot nine.
And then I went to the drawing,
drawing hutches,
on what you call a cuddy.
I suppose that you'll have heard of them too,
if you've been around West Lothian.
And I used to be skinned from there
down to my tail,
lifting it all,
catching on the roof,
there you are!'

'And what mine was that?'

A- 'Duddingston. Number Three.'

'Number Three?'

A- 'You're not wanting the bloody numbers!'

B- *'Aye, the old mine number one.'*

A- 'I didn't know that!'

B- *'I'm telling you. I worked it too.'*

A- 'We're getting instructed, after we've been
in them all our life too!'

'But talking about, you know, the facemen treating these drawers, what would make a faceman treat his drawer better? His religion? His politics?'

A- 'No!'

'Where he came from?'

A- 'No!
    The earnings!
    The earnings!
    You could be in a good bit,
    or I could be in a good bit,
    and I could produce more than what you
    could, so therefore,
    you were maybe getting it easier to lie,
    you maybe weren't using as much explosives.
    We had to buy our own explosives.
    The Laird of Cockpen down here at
    Hopetoun,
    he had ninepence a ton,
    and I had half a crown a ton,
    and I had to buy explosives,
    and tools,
    boring machines and drills, shovels, picks...'

'That's your graith.'

A- 'Aye'

B- *'Oh, she knows that too!
I think that we should have went to her!'*

A- 'And I said tools!'

B- *'And you were being polite.
That's what we called it, the graith.'*

'And he got ninepence royalty?'

A- 'Yes. Exactly.
    Now he's getting a bloody fortune
    off this tip over here,
    and also the tips in West Lothian
    that are under his land.
    He sold them over again.'

B- *'Aye. That should have gone.
He was paid for it as it was, you know,
when it was being produced,
and, well,
he lost no sweat over it.'*

Braes: Cousy & Cuddy
Alec: under manager, born 1909, West Calder

'You'll have heard of what was known as the
back balance braes?'

                                                                No.

'Well, that is the weight of say 3 or 4 tubs, full tubs,
going down – drew the empty tubs up, didn't require
any engine, and it was controlled by a brake, just a
wheel, with a rope round it about three times, and it
came down. The boy just stood at the top of the brae
and worked this brake, this brake which was round
the wheel. It brought them down.'

                              Was that what they called a cousy brae?
'A cuddy.'

                                                    A cuddy brae?
'That worked on a different principle.
That was worked on a different principle.
I could draw that if you don't understand it.'

                    Yes, I see what you mean. There are three empties
                              being pulled out. That is for balance?
'Yes, that is the balance. We called it a cousy, a cousy brae,
but what you're talking about is a cuddy.'

                                                        A cuddy?
'Aye, that was a dumb hutch which was filled up
with any kind of material to load it, and it worked
with a double purpose wheel, fixed to the stoop side
in the shale up at the top, and the wheel –
the rock came off that pin, and it came down round the
wheel on the cuddy, and up round another wheel
at the top – and whenever the miner's drawer
filled the hutch, he put his rope in his hutch
and shoved it over, and the cuddy came up
– the loaded cuddy came up and balanced the ...'

                                                    I see, yes.

'That's what you would call the mechanics of
some form of ...'

                              That's a pulley system, isn't it?
'A pulley system, yes. It's quite easy to draw it on a bit
of paper. And the cuddy only travelled half the
distance, you see, because it had only a...
it had a double rope.'

                                                  Oh, I see.

'It only ... it's hard for somebody...'

                    Yes, you would have to see it working, perhaps.

No Rats

Under manager, born 1909, West Calder

'In Westwood
there were no rats ever seen
except one
that fell down the shaft.
But it was polluted with mice.'

'But no rats?'

'No rats.'

'And Polbeth 26 had rats?'

'They had rats.
And the coalmine,
Baads coalmine,
it had rats.

And I can't remember
what was at Hermand,
what lodgers we had there.
But how do you account
for that fact?'

'Atmospheric conditions?'

'Well, that's what we used to think, but
that's... it's no... because..
There were ponies in Westwood,
and it was mice.
And there were ponies in 26,
and it was virtually all rats.
And of course,
that's where they all went,
was round about the stables.
You got them in the workings right enough,
because,
you know how miners take their piece,
dropping crusts and that.
The mice in Westwood,
they were everywhere.'

'Westwood was a pit?'

'Westwood was a pit.'

'And it had rats? It had mice?'

'It had mice.'

'What about Polbeth?''

Polbeth was a mine.'

'And it had rats?'

'It had rats.'

'I wonder whether that's the reason why?'

'Yes.
In Westwood,
the mice got down in the food for the horses.
But that always puzzled me, why?

But that could be the answer right enough.
That the rats got down on their own.
Down a mine.'

'Down a mine, yes.'

'Down a pit?'

**'No. Because, you see, if a rat went down, in a
hutch, it would be seen, and it would be killed,
automatically killed, by a man.'**

'That's correct.
Because Baads coalmine,
it was a mine,
and there were rats there,
not mice.'

**'Winchburgh and Duddingston, they were mines,
and there were rats in there as well.'**

'That's correct.
Yes.'

'And Burngrange was a pit, and there was no rats.'

'No.
That's what it's been.'

Wife Talking: Clash-me-doon

Joe: electrician, born addiewell; & wife

'Well.
You got a job as a boy.
And then you worked your way up.
And you got in here to the face.
And maybe became a drawer.
That was,
you had the faceman and the drawer
– you know what the drawer is?
He filled the hutches and took them out.
Well.
When you thought that you were eligible to take
the faceman's job,
well,
you looked for them,

you see.
And it was just like that.
But now,
in the coal,
in the mining,
they have training schemes.
They have trained men for training them,
and so on.
But not in those days.
You just worked.'

(Wife Talking)

'What was that wee man?
Is it his son-in-law?
Or is it his nephew?
Across there?
Mind she died?
He stays at Chapeltown?
What's his second name?
Mind wee... wee Doonan?
Mind we were at the chap Doonan's wedding?

'Oh aye, aye.
    I knew you were.'

(Wife Talking)

'That wee man.
You know his wife died?
You know the two of them's went?

'Doonan!
Aye, Mickey.
Micky Doonan.
But see,
he was in the shale,
but he was just. ...'

(Wife Talking)

'I thought that he was.'

'Aye, he was in the...'

(Wife Talking)

'He's up in the (inaudible)'

'But he was just working on the pithead!'

(Wife Talking)

'What about Mr Corstan?
Was he not in there?'

'He was in the coal!
And then, of course,

he was at Addiewell Work.
Anyone goes in there is there for keeps.'

(Wife Talking)
'There's lots of other...'

'Pat!
Pat would be able to tell them
about Addiewell Retorts.'

(Wife Talking)
'Right enough, aye.'

'Aye.
There's a wheen of stories that I could tell you
about them.
But I just can't mind them all.'

(Wife Talking)
'Was there not (inaudible)?'

'Have you heard the story of Clash-Me-Doon?
The farm?
You'll have heard that?
You've never heard that story?
There used to be a farm there?
Well.
That's what it was called.
It was called Clash-Me-Doon.
Apparently it (inaudible),
and
apparently, (inaudible)
and the farmer that was there said,
you are going to 'clash me doon'!
Aye.
And ever since that,
it has that name.'

(Wife Talking)
'I doubt that we'll need to start
digging for treasure then!'

'So.
That's what I say.
There's a farm underneath it.
Clash-Me-Doon.'

(Wife Talking)
'Its time we got the spades out
and started digging for treasure.'

Sundays

[Maria: Co-op staff, born 1901, Broxburn]

'Well, I'll tell you.
You got up in the morning,
and you were dressed in your Sunday best. Then,
Sunday school went in at eleven,
and then we went to it.
The church went in at twelve. Well,
you didn't need to go to the church unless you liked,
you see.
So maybe we just came home.

Well, you wouldn't have taken a ball in your hands.
There wasn't even, there were no newspapers,
and you wouldn't, oh, you wouldn't dare lift a newspaper.
Oh, nobody lifted a newspaper on a Sunday to read it.
No way! You see, it was the war that started all that.
Folk got they wanted news of the war.

Then, in the afternoon,
you were all dressed up,
and maybe a great big silk hat, and you,
with elastic below your chin,
and you had to keep that,
oh, lovely hats!
And then,
this kept the hat on,
and you maybe had on your white dress.
Well, you'll never guess where we all went!

Up to the cemetery!
Well, that's at Uphall, the cemetery.
Well, the cemetery was packed with people.
And the seats, you couldn't get a seat!
The people were all there,
all dressed up, you see.
Well, they maybe had somebody in the cemetery, you see.
Well, at that time, we had, well,
I think it was my grandmother.
And we went up and we looked at her.
And we maybe took flowers or something up.
But that's where we went on a Sunday afternoon.

And we went for long walks,
and we used to go a lot to Almondell. And we walked it.
And we had a basket with us with food and lemonade and that.
And oh, the crowds of children, you know.
We were quite safe, and it was lovely.
And then we had to trek all that road home again.
Oh, we enjoyed ourselves.

And sometimes on a Sunday,
that road on a Sunday,
it was packed out with walking on it.
Nobody walks now.
Nobody walks.'

Dentists

Maria: Co-op staff, born 1901, Broxburn

'No, there weren't any dentists in Broxburn,
because my father said that Dr Scott, that's his photo,
he had to do it.
And he came home one day and he was having toothache.
So he says to my mother,

'Don't bother making the dinner till I get my tooth out.'

And he went down to Dr Scott.
And he sat him down in an ordinary chair.
You got no anesthetic, no injection.
And he said that he pulled. And he pulled. And he pulled.
And he said, my father's name was William,

'Hold on William. I'll get it out yet!'

And he did get it out.'

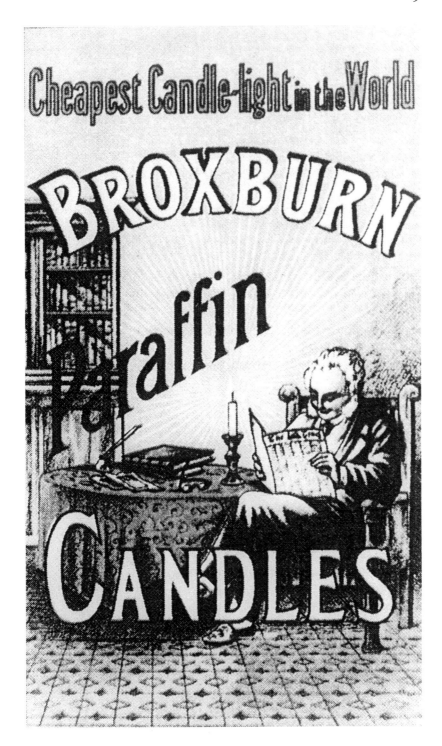

Children

Maria: Co-op staff, born 1901, Broxburn

'Oh, there were a lot of children died,
when I was young.
It was quite a common thing to see a cab,
you see it was cabs then,
and it was quite a common thing,
to see about four men in the cab,
and sitting with a wee coffin on their knee.

And there was one time, my mother said,
my sister was just a baby,
and there was an outbreak of German measles,
and I think it was pneumonia,
and she said, well,
my mother had a good idea of nursing,
my mother said,
that there were more children went to Uphall,
that's where the cemetery is,
my sister was about the only one that got better,
but, she said,
in those days,
pneumonia,
there was nothing but poulticing,
and you know,
it's a very weakening thing,
and, she said,
that she sat up all night,
and a neighbour came and sat with her,
to be with her,
and, she said,
when the doctor came in the next morning,
he said to her,
'you've got it lifted',
the pneumonia,
and, she said,
well there were people beside her,
and they lost two lovely boys,
with the same thing,
and, she said,
when they were up at the Uphall cemetery,

burying one,
the other one had died.
It was terrible, you know.
The children don't die the same now.
No.

'Ma' Moore's children 1920s
photo: John Kelly

Tarbrax: the fighting C......s

(note: 'C' refers to the family's surname)
Tom: a deputy (safety officer), born 1907, Tarbrax

And I was fourteen, between fourteen and fifteen,
when we came back to Tarbrax again.
That's where I started work.
My father was a shale miner practically all his days from he left
Ireland.
He was an old Irishman.
He was actually a tinsmith by trade, but he came over here.
A wild Irishman, a real wild Irishman.
But he came up to Tarbrax and I was born in Tarbrax.
He was hounded out of Ireland!
(wife talking) He tells everybody that!
(Tom) But he worked all – most – of his days in the shale.

But there were times, I suppose,
when he went to the coal and then back to the shale.
I don't know very much about the years before my time, you know.

Did you have water at Tarbrax?

There was everything at Tarbrax!
It was a real good place, Tarbrax.
There were nae dry closets up in Tarbrax that I mind of.
There would be maybe before my time I mean.
They were all toilets.
In fact, the way the houses were built,
there were a toilet between two houses, you see,
a flush toilet, outside.
You had to go outside.
And the new houses that were built, they all had inside toilets.
No bathroom, but an inside toilet.
They were great houses in Tarbrax, great houses.
All blasted down now.

So this isn't the houses that are there now?

Some of the houses that are there now.
See the top ones, the ones that we termed the new ones,
that was the last ones that was built. Well,
we stayed down on the bottom side of that.
There were rows of houses down on the bottom.
I would think about 300 houses altogether.
That's quite a big amount of houses, you know, way out in the hills.

I wouldnae say it was dusty and smoky but there was an oily smell
about the place, you ken?
Tarbrax there wasn't much smoke, just the smell of the retorts.
A really good healthy place to live because it was way up on the,
you know, one way in and one way out.
You had two miles to walk to the station before you started travelling.

And you were bound to be healthy because you were stuck in the
hills and you had to walk.
There were two churches. Well,
there was a built church and a hall church.
And there was two picture houses.
One was a travelling picture house that came to Tarbrax
and stayed there, and then there was one in the hall, you ken.
The hall was what we called the Institute, you know what I mean?
There was billiards and a reading room, all these things,
the dance hall and the picture house, you know.
It was a, really good, there were two chip shops, aye!
And then a Co-operative.

And then there were a big general grocer's shop
and the wee shops that you get.
A great wee place. A great wee place.

And did your father do anything to help in the house?

He didnae! Your father would,
if there was anybody sitting in his chair,
and he come in the door, they had to dive out!
And he'd sit there and 'Give me my pipe over!'
He was a great bold poacher and he used to sit there
by the fire and make snares and tie flies.
He had a shelf with all his flies and things on.
You darenae touch them.
My mother didnae dust them or nothing.
He was clever as regards to that, making flies and that for fishing.
You see, I don't know, men in these days.
My father wasn't just the only drunk.
He had cronies that he went drinking with as well,
you know what I mean?

Did he ever beat your mother when he was drunk?

And she wouldnae let anyone touch him.

Touch him? To stop him attacking her?

Mhm. And my brothers was all fighters, all boxers.
We used to be called the Fighting C......s!
And you had to – 'oh, no, that's your Dad'.
And only one brother hit him and knocked him out cold,
and 'oh, you've killed him, Willie, you've killed him!'.
But what can you do about it?
It was just the way of life, I think.
Well, he never actually beat me.
But they tell me that he leathered the older ones.
One of the oldest ones, I think he leathered him.
And he used to take him... you see, in those days, when the sons
become working age they'd take them into the pit to work with
them, and S had a tough time then.
But no me because I was always big, you see,
and 'fear not no man', you know.
And one time I must have got in his way and he done something
and I turned round to him and he says,
'no bloody son of mine'll lift his hand to me in my own house!
Get out of this!
And I says 'I'm not!'
When you look back on it,
we had some hard times.

Pitch & Toss
James: oilworker, born 1910, Winchburgh

'Aye,
well you just put your money in your pockets and stood.
It's just like the vandals today.
The police knew who was doing it,
but they couldn't catch them.
The police chased us one time.
The police wasn't too bad.
It was people.
One woman lived just opposite the bowling green.
She was a nosey old so and so,
and she was always complaining to the police,
and sometimes she would write a letter.
She never put her name on it.
The policeman says to me one day,

'we've got an anonymous letter from Mrs Nicholl.'

But there was one Sunday night,
when we had just started playing,
and the police came around,
and the ambulance followed close after that.
But ultimately they went away round the old work,
the Green Shale,
and they played there,
and nobody bothered them,
as long as you were away out of the road,
know what I mean?'

Quoits
Robin: drawer & mechanic, born 1905, Philpstoun

'About one of the most popular games with the miners,
at that time, was quoits.
You used to have them in every village,
and each village would challenge each other for prizes & cups.'

'Oh yes, there was a bit of gambling went on at the quoits,
and it was an old man's game, yes,
but some of the young boys that were well developed played it.
It was quite a heavy thing to throw.
You had to throw it 25 yards and hit the pin which was sunk in.
They put a white piece of paper behind it to help you aim,
and if you could ring it,

that was the highest points you could get.
If you could not,
you were out of the team.'

'The quoits weighed 4 or 5 lbs.
and they were loaded to keep them going straight,
instead of spinning.
If you did not throw them right they used to spin,
and they would not dig into the clay.
They dug holes in a field and had a fence all round it,
at the pavilion,
where you could go and sit with the men that were not playing.
The holes were about 2 & 1/2 ft. deep and filled with clay.
The clay round the pin was kept damp so it was soft.
When you threw the quoit,
it turned on its head,
just as it got to the heading,
and dug into the clay.
But if you got it to keep flat,
and it came down and landed on the pin,
you were a champion.
I think the last quoiting green used to be down at Fawnspark,
just at the end of the canal bridge.'

'1926, I think,
that the quoiting green shut down.
That was the last one, at that time.
The very last of them all was up at West Calder.
But in the shalefields down here,
it was about 1926 that the last one shut down.'

Pit-ponies
Dick: drawer, born 1906, Breich

'Well,
I had,
I had only two ponies,
that I know.
Victor and Douglas.
And Victor was the half stallion.
He wasn't right cut,
and he went mad,
you know.
You had to drive him with the long reins,
ken.

But the rest,
you let them go themselves,
ken.
Douglas was alright.
You could leave him standing and go away and he would be
there when you came back.
He wouldn't move.
And then there was one big,
Big Watty.
We had him.
And we had to..
You see,
he counted the couplings,
ken.
Maybe ten hutches on,
that was nine couplings,
nine jacks,
and if there were nine on,
he wouldn't take it away.
Take a hutch off,
and he walked away!
Aye.
We used to say that he counted them.
It was true.
They were wise.
They were wise enough,
the whole lot of them.

And there was another one.
What was its name?
Oh, I forget it now.
But you had to start it on a Sunday night,
starting with three hutches.
That's all it would take.
And then you could put on four,
then five,
then right up to ten.
It flew.
It flew round that road.
Talk about horses going on a racecourse.
You've never seen this.
Baldy, we cried him.
That's it.
Baldy.

But he was some..
He started with about three hutches,
and we piled them up every time too,
till he got to ten.
And it quietened him down,
after being lying off,
you see.
But every other night after that and he was alright.
Sunday night.
He was lying off,
maybe from Friday to Sunday night,
you see.
Fair desperate.
And he was a light horse too,
you know.
A light horse.'

The Japanese Shale
Adam: oilworker, born 1907, Oakbank

I'm seventy five years old and I went to Oakbank Oilworks
when I was fifteen and a half.
And my job was sanding the lids on the top of the retorts.
Now, the lids on the retorts were put on after the shale was in,
after the retort was charged with shale.
You put the lid on,
and there was thick dirty yellow smoke came out.
And I sanded the lids round about the edge to stop the smoke coming out, because the smoke was the actual stuff that they wanted,
the extraction out of the shale.
And they were going to lose a lot so I sanded them,
after they were filled right up to the top.

And the gaffer came to meet me and says:
'There's a chance of another job going on, Adam, if you want it.'
I says: 'Where is it about?'
He says: 'The sulphate is put up into a hopper,
and you are at the bottom with a bag and you put the bag in below
the thingummy, and pull the thingummy in,
about a hundredweight,
pull the bag off when you thought that it was about a hundredweight,
and took it over the scales and put it on the scales,
weigh it and, if it's too heavy, take some off with a scoop
till you get the right weight,

then sew it up with a big thingummy, steel needle with string,
you know, and burl it round about,
and you were left with two lugs,
and tie a knot on the end of the sting, like, you know, two knots.'

Wee Jimmy Cross was on that job along with me.
I think that Jimmy was, if I mind right.
I think that Jimmy was taking the bags off me when I sewed them.
And he had a two wheel barrow and he barrowed them across and
stowed them on a thingummy ready for dispatching, you know.
Aye.

And the sulphate of ammonia went all over.
I think that it was even exported, sulphate of ammonia.
Because it was great stuff, sulphate of ammonia.
All the folk in Oakbank had good leeks and onions and carrots
and everything. And it was all free, you know.
You would just fill up a bag in your pocket.
Aye, they were the days, boy!

> **You mentioned that the Japanese came across with
> some shale, over to find out how it was processed?**

Aye, I can mind of that fine.
And I should have a bit in the house here somewhere.
I'll need to look for it, unless it's been flung out.
I don't know, but I'm going to have a rake anyway.
It came across on a ship and it was loaded on to wagons.
And it come with the railway to Mid Calder Station
and shunted into Oakbank.
There was I don't know how many hundred ton or maybe
a thousand tons if it came to it.
Because the experiment with the Japanese stuff was to show them
and to prove to them what was the contents that was in that,
in their shale, the oil content, I mean.
After that, I mean,
you got sulphate of ammonia and wax and all the rest of the stuff,
you know.
What I was going to say about this bit that I have in the house
somewhere, that I could take an ordinary match,
put the shale in between my forefinger and my thumb,
and put the flame up to the corner of the Japanese shale.
And before the match burned my fingers the bit of shale was blazing.
And it proved that it must have been a high oil content in the
Japanese shale.
Because I tried it with the Scottish shale and there was no way.

You would need a candle!

The Japanese workers stayed in the hotels, as far as I mind.
I'd say in East Calder, the Grapes, and in Mid Calder,
the Torphichen Arms.
But I think myself that some of the kind of leading lights
of the Japanese would be in private digs.
And these Japanese fellows when they went back home,
whether it would be for leave or something,
they brought back to Oakbank for some of the women in Oakbank,
and some of the women in Mid Calder too, I would suppose,
linen and different stuff as a present for being so good to them.
And all the bairns in I would say Mid Calder and East Calder
and Oakbank and all over used to wave to them.
And they all waved to us back!
The bus picked them up at Mid Calder and East Calder
and took them up to the Oilworks.
And then it would take them down at night.
We were waving at night as well.
We thought that it was a great thing, the Japanese.

So you were just a laddie then?

Aye, I'm sure of that.
I wouldn't have been waving if I wasn't a laddie.
I don't think so, anyway! It's not that.
I mean, the Japanese are as good as me!
I've no religious bias or anything like that
or nationality, colour bars or nothing.
I mean that everybody's God's creation as far as I'm concerned.
We're breathing the same fresh air.
Oh aye, there was a bus load.
You see, there would be the chemists and actual workers too that
would go back there and do what they were doing at Oakbank.
They would have to be able to go back.
They also were men that would have to understand
the technicalities of the process, the retorts and the stills.

**And would you know if the Japanese had to mine
for their shale, or was it opencast at that time?**

We wouldn't know that, son! We wouldn't know that!
I doubt if it would be opencast unless it was something
they had found, an outcrop,
and had wondered about it and sent samples and, you know,
some of the British technicians maybe took it from there.
I doubt it would be opencast because when you come to think about

it, you hadn't the machines for opencast.
You had men with picks and shovels then.
But I have an awful feeling that it would be mining.
What they found first of all, I mean, it could have been an outcrop.
You get that with the coal. You get it from everything.

A shale crusher

And they sent for Sommerville & me again

Jock: drawer & pit-sinker, born 1900, at West Calder

'And I mind in 1939,
I was continually having a row with the gaffer.
for Westwood was overstocked with men.
You would get hutches to fill three days in a week,
and then the next three days,
you would get nothing.
I hardly had anything in a week –
you couldn't make wages with it.
Oh, many's the row I had with the gaffer.
He was wanting me,
when the hutches did come in,
to stoop them away, you know.

No, I said,
No, no, that'll not do, Tam,
you ken, wee Tam Brown,
that was the gaffer.

So just midway through 1939,
wee Tam Brown came down to see me in the mine
and says'

'How would you like to go to Hermand?
They're starting to sink a new mine up there.
Geordie Sommerville,'

'that was a man that worked all the stone mines
up at Burdiehouse and that,
on a lot of contracts,
and these things.
He said'

'Geordie Sommerville wants to ken
if you'll go with him to double-shift him,
to sink that mine?'

'Anything's better, I said.'

'Oh well, he says,
he'll see you on the pit bottom the night,
when you go up.'

'So I saw him and he says'

'Fine, Jock, fine,' he says.'

'Well anything, Tam'.
I cut out right through the clay, you know.
Your not on a seam to start with.
The seam's coming down that way,
and you're going down that way to meet it.'

'That's alright, he says.'

'We set off with a boring iron,
a big iron pointed,
and somebody was standing with a big pothammer,
and one standing cutting to give it a bit of a run.
Oh well, we done alright.
I mind it was Forbieson that was the manager at the time,
and he came up to try and get a contract with us signed.
Oh no, we couldn't sign it for that.
He said'

'I'll give you £14 a fathom
to sink that big mine
12ft wide and 9ft high
and laying the road across
and brick it.'

'So we had two brickies,
Wullie Mullholland and Geordie Morris,
to come when we were ready,
when we had about 12ft on each side.
I had three men on my shift and, eh,
Bruce Armour had three on his shift.
We got it down... about 12ft,
we went down to the founds,
for the brickies coming,
and I came out on the dayshift
instead of the backshift, of course,
two of us were on the one shift that week,
and we laboured.

I packed behind Geordie Morris,
and he packed behind Wullie Mullholland,
and the man on the surface sent down... you see,
I had two labourers sending down bricks and cement,
you know,
for thingummying it.

Oh, we done alright on that till we met,
I remember it went down like that.
It had a plug at the top, you see.
They surveyed it from the road across,
till they got the depth it was
down on the road measured,
and they gave us a gradient of 1 and 2 1/4.

Well, I think we went down about 50ft, I think,
on that gradient of 1 and 2 1/4,
when a rib came in the roof.
Do you know what a steel rib is?

Well, up on the pavement there was a steel rib,
about 3/4 to 1 inch thick.
But you couldn't bore it through even.
It was practically steel.
And that was what we always termed a pavement rib,
in the Duddingston.

So I remember the Manager.
He used to go up to Armadale twice a week to the golf course,
and always called in as he was coming down past.
And he came in the next morning.
We were firing shots at the time when he came in.
He says to me,'

                              'That's not...what rib is that, John?'

'I said, that's a pavement rib.
 He says,'

                                                      'It can't be.'

'I says, how can it not be?'

                                                    'Well, he says.'

'Well, it was all surveyed out and everything.'

                                    'Well, I'm not caring, John,
                                whether it's surveyed or not.'

'There's not another rib in the Dunny Seam, says I,
comparable with the pavement rib.'

'So it was going like that and we were into it...
Oh, nine steelworkers got it done, I think.
Sommerville got a place,
and three men to work with him.
I had a place and three men working to me.

When they were coming to us they were sinking that pit
up at Bosmains.
What was it you cried it?
They were sinking the pit anyway.
Two shafts down it, you know.
It was the Donaldson's from Fife.
They were the pit sinkers.
And they had one of the shafts down to the depth it had to go.
They had 950 ft to go down before they could connect it round,
you know,
and,
of course,
they sent for Sommerville and me again.'

A roof like glass

Jock: drawer, born 1900, West Calder

'What do you mean by the worst?'

'The worst conditions and the worst pay?'

'The worst paid was Westwood.
There were too many men in the pit.
They couldn't give you quite the money that you would want.
They would give you just enough to take in a day,
and then,
come the end of the week,
they would pour more hutches into you,
extra,
to make up for what you had lost over the three days.
Oh, a right rotten crowd of it.
A right rotten crowd.'

'And the best?'

'Oh, Twenty Six easy.
That's Polbeth along there.
That was the best easy.
Best in every way.
Well, there's only one pit better for shale,
pure shale.
Thirty Two.
That's the farm along at Limefield there.

It had a roof like glass and a pavement like glass.
Every other pit you worked with plates, you know,
to peel the shale off.
You never needed them in Thirty Two.
Westwood is only 9ft high,
8 to 9ft,
whereas Twenty Six and Thirty Two,
where you had this good roof,
you see,
you could just put your shots up to within a foot of them,
and that would clear it off,
the good roof.
All the rest of them were pretty scabby roofs.
You know,
flaky.

Westwood was the worst.
9ft high.
You would go in there,

9ft high,
and you would be continually pinching.
Pinching bits out of the roof that were flaking off.

They wouldn't let you put up crowns, you see,
that's stretchers across the top,
and fill on to one another.
But you would just use the top of the tree,
and they would just flake off,
all round the tree.'

'Trees' – wooden roof supports

Executed

James: faceman, born 1903, West Calder

'But there was a fatal one in Twenty Six.
The boy's head got,
I saw it too,
his head got cut clean off.
I saw it.
I saw it, after the thing happened.
Jimmy Robertson's drawer at Bellsquarry.
It wasn't with a shot though.
It was after they'd been fired.
The drawer went away in to start to fill this hutch,
and there was a thing had came down and got him on the head,
his head on the hutch edge,
cut his head.
His head was lying over the other side of the thing.
Aye, he was beheaded.
And this was from the roof.
Aye.
Well,
I expect there would maybe be about a couple of tons in it.
You'll know what that can do.
And it got his head on the side of the hutch,
you know what I mean,
and executed him.
And I saw this man just after it happened.
I guess,
once your in the pits for a long time,
you are,
you wasn't,
you know what I mean.
It looked gruesome,
you know.
You just get over these.
Aye.

I saw another.
Old Wull Scott from Oakbank.
He had left the shots,
and wasn't able to get down the end in time,
and put his strum,
and one lump came down and carried him right down.
That was Twenty Six.

Well, we could have all made accidents,
because you had to,
the likes of working in the pits,
we had to make our own wage.
You weren't on a set wage.
You had to make what you made,
what you got.
I felt that was a lot of,
you know what I mean,
the Companies were kind of irresponsible that way, taking risks, aye.
Oh aye.
I took them my own self sometimes,
there you are.
There was nothing happened.
Just lighting shots.
Fourteen shots I've lighted at a time.
You're only supposed to have lit three.
But the Company let it go,
because it knew it made things worse for that man to make a
wage,
because,
when you fire three shots,
you can't get in for reek,
especially if you're up headings,
you know.
You can't see what you're doing.

So,
if you're allowed to fire fourteen,
the air is just clearing it just the same,
maybe a wee bit more time,
but it's making it easier for them too.
Aye,
they played the game the Company's way,
there you are.
They closed their eyes to it.
Aye.'

The stone, the coal and the shale
Robert: drawer, born 1914, Brigend

But there was no comparison, no comparison,
to the shale and the coal.
The shale was heavy, beast work, you know.
The coal, well, it was a different type of work,
although it was dangerous.
When I was in coal the first run that I was up
I was putting in packs in the splint.
It was four feet high.
That was an awful difference to six feet when you're used to six feet,
you know.
Then I went to stone mining and,
although the work was heavy in parts,
but not near, not near as heavy as the shale, you know.
It had to be fast because we were cutting ground with stone mining.
You were cutting ground.
We were paid piece work, you see, paid on the cutting,
driving the road through to the new shaft.
It was fast work.
You never walked.
You never walked when you were at the face in stone mining.
You trotted.
You never took any more than five minutes to your piece.
You always took your piece when the full face was packed to allow
the reek, the smoke, to get that out the road.

And that was the difference.
Now, this is the difference between the coal and the shale.
Now, the coal was nationalised of course when I was in it.
The contract was explained to us by the undermanager.
And the contract was settled between the National Union of
Mineworkers and the Management that it would be 7/6d a foot.
And we couldn't believe it!
7/6d a foot for brushing the pavements!
And it had to go on for about a mile!

We sat down and we thought about it and I said to the leading man,
I said 'Look, if we bore holes straight down into that pavement a
        foot and a half all the way back, three or four feet across but
        keep them away from the girders, and we go about twenty
        yards and fire the whole lot at once, I'll go and get the blast
        shovel in and we'll lay the rails for the blast shovel,
        and we'll clean it up in less than half a shift!'

Niddrie Castle Oil Works, Winchburgh

I said 'With Jigger picks and hand shovels we'll never make wages,
     but at 7/6d a foot it's going to be a fortune!'

And wee Johnny Girvan was the leading man,
and he says 'Listen, Rab, you know the state of those girders',
he says, 'we'll blow them up!'.

I says, 'I don't think so! All it needs is half a spy of jelly in
     each hole, ignite them, and it slackens it all and',
     I says, 'the blast shovel will do the rest.'

And we did that and we finished that contract in a fortnight!
Do you know, I was coming here with £50 a week clear!
We finished it in a fortnight.

Now, the second week,
oh, they paid us the first week,
and the second week the Coal Board wouldn't pay us so we sent for
the Union chap. He came from Glasgow. I can't remember his name.
And he phoned Alloa and he got Trade Union leaders.
And he got on to the big brass and we got the rest of our wages.
They were going to take them up for a breach of contract.
That was the difference between the shale and coal.
One you got a contract and they thought that you were overpaid
they didn't cut it off you. But the shale was guilty of that.
It was the difference between a nationalised industry
and a privately run industry.

Burned

Dick: drawer, born 1906, Breich

'I got burned with gas.
I was lighting the shots,
you see,
and the fireman had left a quarter of an hour ago,
in front of me,
and I was lighting the shots a quarter of an hour after it,
and a wee pocket of gas had collected up in a corner,
and, of course,
we were lighting them when we shouldn't have been,
you know,
with this bit of strum.
Oh,
I was right round there,
and from there up to there,
burned,
all round my face and arms.

I was lighting the shots,
and I should have been using the caps,
you see,
and the pliers.
But you would never have got them done,
you know.
You were only supposed to light two at a time.
But you see what I mean?
You better cut that thing!

But I was lighting about six.
Och, I've seen a boy lighting ten after that,
up in Hermand.
Nothing happened.
He just got them all.
He cut the strum long,
you see.
I had the same.
But it was just the pocket of gas,
you see,
that's what done it.
I'll tell you,
I came down out of that heading quick enough!

My neighbour was on the level.
He was lighting other shots,
you know.
He was on the level and I was up the heading!
But they took me to the doctor,
and it was Twaites.
It was Doctor Twaites,
and he says,

'Oh, I can't do nothing. We'll just need to send you to
hospital.' So I went to the Royal Infirmary.
I was covered with gentian violet.
You maybe heard of it during the war?
That's what I was covered with.
I was like a darkie.
The wife didn't know me when she came in.
And when it started healing,
they had to cut this off with a pair of scissors,
you know.
But the nurse says to me,
away and have a bath like,
but don't wet your arms.
I looked at her and I said to myself,
how the hell am I going to do that?
Oh aye.
But when I came out I was bandaged from there to there.
Thirty nine bob a week compensation.
And John McArthur, the manager, says
will you sign that now?

I said to myself,
signing off compensation?
I said: Not me John.
I'm not signing off that!

They wanted me to sign off so that I couldn't claim any
more compensation.
But the doctor told me that these,
on the back of my hand,
are thin,
that skin is thin,
and it could burst any time.
You can see the marks there.
So I never signed off.
I wasn't getting a lump sum anyway.

I was only getting about thirty bob.
I didn't sign off.
But och,
I don't think that they would get anybody back to the shale
if they started it up again.
No, I don't think so. I don't think so.'

Tramps & Toffs
Harry: drawer, born 1918, Broxburn

'I started in the drawing,
filling hutches for four years,
and I was a spare drawer-cum-faceman.
If the drawer was off I was sent in to do his job,
or the faceman's job if he was off.
I did about 6 months of that,
and then I got put in a place of my own.
I had my own place at 24 years of age.
I was there from 1942-55.
That is when it closed down and I went from there to Westwood.
I stuck for four months and I packed it in
and went away to the coal in Fife, at Glenrothes,
and worked until it closed.
So, in all 15 years.
On average shale mining was harder but cleaner.
The conditions were better.
The coal pit some jobs were very hard,
but other jobs it was the conditions that made it hard.
The way I describe it is,
you're a coalminer and I am a shaleminer,
you're a tramp and I am a toff.
That is how I describe it.
No disrespect to the people.
When I was in the coal I was a tramp,
and in the shale I was a toff.
It was cleaner,
just the same amount of skill.
In fact there was more skill in coal,
more machinery, but cleaner.
I could come up the shale mine the way I am just now.
There is some men you thought never worked down a mine.
You work down a coal pit and you are black,
and that is the difference,
and conditions, plus the fact the coal,

I have worked in seams 3 feet high and about 1.1/2 ft water.
Not all the time.
There was some water in the shale but not to that extent.
The water in Camps mine they could pump it out within an
hour. Every 24 hours they would start this pump.

It was a dangerous mine that I worked in.
It had a bad roof.
You had to have plenty supports up.
Other shale mines the roofs would be standing and nothing
to hold them.
The likes of Dunnet in Westwood, the Dunnett 66,
that's the name of a section in the Dunnet,
it was amazing how that roof held up.
And then you got the same over here at Winchburgh.
I finished up there when I came back from the coal,
at Winchburgh.
I was only five months back when they completely shut down.
And over there you have seen trees standing, and you go and knock
them down with your hand.
They are rotten,
and yet the roof's still there.
You had what you call a crown,
a tree across and a centre leg on it every two feet,
and after a while you had to go back
and maybe put in others in between them.
The danger in the shale mining was what they call stooping,
that is,
you coming back and taking all the shale round about you.
You were retreating, and then the leg comes down and crashes.
I have seen a big pillar and you hear it creaking
and cracking.
So you get out, and the roof all closes round about it.
You get that warning.
But, at the same time, I was 15 years in that mine
and went up to Westwood and was only there 2 or 3 weeks.
But I will never forget.
It was the Saturday morning, and I went out.
It was creaking, and I would not go into it.
There was an old miner there who worked as a roadsman.
He said, 'it's alright son.'
But I just could not believe him after what I'd seen in the
Camps.

But, definitely, it was alright,
but I took an hour before I went into it.
I was very apprehensive.
It was just a layer of shale easing.
So I pinched it all down before I'd go down,
and I kept pinching it in.
So.
Oh, to me that was mining at its best.
Compared to the Camps, that was one of the worst mines
there was.

Different pits had different names.
There was 15 pit at Threemiletown at Linlithgow.
They say that was quite a hard pit, Totleywells.
But, all and all, Camps was just as bad as any No. 6.
I could get more shale from Westwood than I could from Camps,
because it was a smaller seam.
On average, if you could get 24 hutches of shale a day,
that is, between you and two drawers,
that was a good days work.
I could produce more than that up at Westwood because it is
a bigger seam, and less timbering to do.
That was what took up the time.
They called it a wooden mine.
There was more timber went down than shale came up, near enough.
I'm exaggerating a bit, but that is true.
If you stayed in Broxburn you worked in Broxburn,
very few moved about.
The only way would be if you were working with me,
and you fell out with me, and the manager would say,
'I'll get you a job in Winchburgh'.
That's the only way.

Checkweighman
George: drawer, born 1921, Winchburgh

'I can't just remember what I had,
but they had different things, some of them.
Some of them maybe had the lid of a bottle,
or something like that,
or maybe just a nail bent in two,
just out through the string or that.
And as soon as you put that pin,

you put that pin on,
before you started filling the hutch.
And when the hutch went up to the pithead,
the checkweighman just took that off,
and he knew whose hutch it was then.

And after you went up to,
if you liked,
when you went up at lousing time,
you could go up and ask the checkweighman,
how much?
It wasn't a case of how many hutches you put up,
but what the weight was inside them, you see,
how much shale that you sent up.

But the checkweighman,
he was paid by the miners.
They were right square.
Aye, well,
I don't know how they worked disputes out.
It was maybe up to the gaffer, or manager,
or whatever you liked,
to tell the pitheadman to watch,
to watch what they were sending up.
Because the manager was down every day.
He was maybe not down at the same section every day.
Well, at Glendevon,
there were a few mines at Glendevon.
It was just the one sort of big mine,
but it was what they cried six, seven and eight.
There were men working down No 6.
There were men working down No 7.
And there were men working down No 8.
So he would go down,
and he would see the circumstances of the place,
that you were working in,
and he would know what you were filling.
And if he thought you were filling maybe dirt or stones,
or that, he would just tell the pitheadman to check it.

And what they would do,
they would maybe take a hutch of yours off.
And maybe a hutch of somebody else's off.

It doesn't matter, anyway! He would take them off,
and take them out. There was a road out,
where they used to have a bing.
You could take them out and either runnel it,
or maybe just coup it,
and see what was in it.
And if there was dirt in it or that,
well,
you were called to question then!

A hutch reaches the surface and heads for the checkweighman

Thingummied: working the surface haulage
Wull: surface labourer, born 1939, Winchburgh

'I was just labouring,
only snibbling the hutches coming off the chain,
coming down from the retorts.
or you were snibbling the rake coming in from the pit,
when the boy brought it in,
then you brought that rake in,
and fed it through the thingummy to the chain,
that's where a boy,
my father,
worked,
he wasn't on the chain when I was there,
he worked up the top,
but he came to the chain eventually,
before he retired,
before he got finished,
and you shoved the hutch through the wee iron bridge,
and then the man,
which was a man,
it wasn't a laddie,
it was all laddies that worked the snibble of the hutches,
but when it came to the chain,
you had to throw the chain,
the hutch was built as such,
that there was a thing on the back of it,
shaped like that,
and you just pulled the chain on to that,
and of course,
the chain caught on to it,
it drew the haulage,
drew it up to the top of the retorts,
just like a grab,
that's it,
well, it was just a chain,
it was just a thing that was shaped like that,
with a 'V' in it,
it was thingummied,
so it would,
when the chain went in,
it caught,
you know,
well, that's where I worked,

the chain was put that way,
on the way up,
and there were a lot of good days alright,
there were some,
my father still talks about it yet,
a shift I had,
that I had to shove every hutch from the gavvy,
when it came off the chain,
coming back down,
to the other end of the lag,
in the snow.

A carbide lamp

George: drawer, born 1921, Winchburgh

'Well, you see,
a carbide lamp.
Do you know what I'm talking about?
It was only a wee thing on the top of your head.

When you were using the batteries,
you were carrying this thing about with you,
and, now, what is it?
I could be wrong in my way.
I could be wrong here.
But I think it was about thirteen and a half pounds
that they weighed,
and that was extra,
that you were carrying all day.
And you still had this bit on your light like.
You still had that on your head.

With the carbide lamp and that,
it was only a case of,
when your carbide was finished,
you just took the top off,
and filled it up again,
and a wee drop water,
and that was you away again.

Well, I would say the carbide was better.
Well, you hadn't much to carry with you.
And the thing was,
see when you got a new lamp,

a new carbide lamp,
I never knew of it going out.
Maybe I was going out with a hutch,
and there was somebody coming in.
I was dazzling them.
So, at the finish,
you got a great light off it.
But, nine times out of ten,
you had to blacken it.
You had to blacken your reflector,
to save you from causing bother with anybody else's.
If there was somebody coming in,
with their reflector glaring at you,
you couldn't see what you were doing, ken.

The electric wasn't the same.
Well, the electric,
it was more or less a sort of dull,
sort of dull.
I wouldn't say actually a dull mirror,
but it wasn't near as clear as what it was with the carbide.'

Shale from here to Ayr
Dick: drawer, born 1906, Breich

'I was a faceman in the Fraser,
the Dunnet field.
Well,
I started on the wooding first,
that was putting the crowns up,
and then they put me on the face.
It was a bad roof in some places then,
right enough,
you know.
If it had been a good roof,
I believe it would have been going yet.
Because there's shale from here to Ayr,
you see.
I've heard it often.
Shale from here to Ayr.
I mean,
you had it maybe twelve feet high and nine feet high,
and there was a good hard roof,

and it was only so far then,
just meal above that,
you know,
soft stuff above that.
You only went twelve feet wide,
you had to keep to that.
You had to tape sites,
but we used to tape ourselves just to keep it right.
Maybe two feet on one side and ten feet on the other side
of these sites,
you see.
And the fireman had to tell us to put up crowns and trees,
if we needed them.
But we knew ourselves,
really.
You know what I mean.
But there were some of them quite good.
I remember one fireman up there used to tape sites with
one string.
You were supposed to have three, you see.
But he used to have the one.
He was some fireman.
Aye, you had to line right through using the three strings.

A drawer loads shale onto a moving belt

Well, you put them up on the roof,
with maybe a wee clog of wood,
and then with a staple,
and hung the string down,
three,
and just lined the three of them right up.
And a boy on the top had his lamp,
you see,
and his lamp was shining through the three strings,
and you kept on moving them back and forward until you got that
site,
you see,
and you would say,
right,
chalk that,
and that's how you did it,
you see.
But Sanny Bradford,
one string,
I don't know how he did it.
Do you know Sanny Bradford?
Did you not know him?
He used to stay in Pumpherston.
Oh, he was some man.'

Half-a-crown extra for the faceman

James: faceman, born 1903, West Calder

'Well, I had a hell of a job getting to be a faceman.
They knew that I was outspoken.
And I started.
I was taking to do with the union when I went into the pits.
And there was me and two or three more,
you know.
We had a meeting.
And the faceman and the drawers carry on.
We decided to do away with it,
and make it equal pay.
So we had a wee job getting that thingummy.
But the Company gave in at the finish.
So, I always put that down to,
there were about four of us,
it was us that got equal payments in the pits.

Aye, I was all for that,
as a faceman.
Not everyone favoured it, aye.
Och no,
I got my books handed out of the window one Friday,
and never had asked for them!
I went round and asked the gaffer

'What's this?'

He says

'Oh, I thought that you were leaving.'

Now it was,
you know this,
it would have sickened you,
there you are,
what they tried to do with you.
Aye, well, it was us that brought it about.
It hadn't been.
And we brought all the other trade union secretaries over
to a meeting and explained what we were doing.
And it happened all over the shalefield after that.
Have you heard of Jock Wardrope?
Aye, well, he was the secretary of that branch over there.
And Pumpherston was Joe Heaney.
And there was one from Starlaw used to come to the meetings.
The four of us, aye.
We went to the management.
Aye, that was John Stein.
He was the General Manager.
Aye, we told him.
All these people that went were all facemen,
do you know what I mean?
And we told them.
On the Friday we wanted our wages put into two pay packets.
You only got one pay packet,
you see,
and you paid the man, the drawer, out of it.
We wanted two pay packets,
and the drawer to be halved.
And I mind of Jock Stein saying to me,
but wait till you hear this.
The faceman got half-a-crown a week,
no, a day,

extra,
for being faceman.
Now, I said to Jock Stein, I said

> 'Well, we want that half-a-crown.'

He turned round to me and says

> 'Oh no, that's not getting done. There's still going
> to be that half-a-crown for facemen.'

So I says

> 'Who's paying it? Are you going to pay this half-
> a-crown extra?'

He says

> 'No! It comes off.'

He wanted consent to having equal pay,
but there was still to be half-a-crown extra for the faceman.
He was still trying to keep it on these lines,
aye,
but he wasn't prepared to pay the half-crown.
This was for the faceman,
being in charge of the place and what not.
A lot of rogues, man.'

A faceman using an electric drill at Burngrange, West Calder 1951.
Note the steel pit props which replaced the wooden 'trees'

A Company Union

Peter: oncost, born 1910, Threemiletown

Were you a member of the Union?

Oh yes, all the time.
Och, it was a poor Union, very poor.
It was just a Company Union,
that's all that it was, a Company Union.

Did you have any grievances that you took to them?

Many! Don't ask that!
I remember once that I was working and I was put on a job,
and the man had ten pence a day more than me.
So I stuck out for the ten pence.
They wouldn't give me it. They wouldn't give me it!
So this day I went out and I says,
'Am I going to get that ten pence for the job?'
'No!'
'Well,' I says, 'I'm not going down!'
The War was on at the time but I said 'I'm not going down!'
So I went along, I went back to see the manager,
and he was an old coal manager and I said,
'I want to see you. I've a grievance.'
He said, 'So have I! You are the man that's on strike!'
I said, 'I don't think that I'm on strike.'
I said, 'I've a good grievance.'
So he said, 'Alright, you start work. I'll hear you're grievance and I'll
tell you when you come back tomorrow.'
So two days after it he came to me when I was working and I says,
'Have you and I not got something to talk about?'
'Oh aye', he said, 'I'll tell you. I'm going on holiday tomorrow.
I'll hear you when I come back!'
Says I, 'very good then'.
So away he went!
So after the holidays I got hold of him and I said 'Here, you and I
have something to speak about.
I'm wanting it settled!'
So he listened to me right enough. 'Okay, I'll see about it.'
So I got my pay on the Friday. Nothing there!
And so the next Friday I was out on the back-shift and my father was
in the canteen and he says,
'He's over there. You better go over and see him.'
Here, I missed him!
And it was a good job that I missed him because it was in!

I maybe would have made a mess of myself if I'd said things that I
didn't need to say if I hadn't seen it!
It was in! I had got it!

The filling and drawing
Jock: drawer, born 1900, West Calder

'In 1920, they started to renovate Twenty Six, Polbeth,
and they were eighteen months at it,
you see.
They ran with a rake of hutches,
four hutches at a time,
and then a double road
on carriages that only held four hutches.
And as four of them were going down,
four of them were coming up.

And then I worked on what they termed the oncost.
That was
doing jobs,
lining up cuddies,
laying roads,
laying crossings
and all these things.
You know,
I always thought that I was working harder than the men
that were filling the shale were doing.

I told the boss, Matt, the gaffer,

'I'm leaving this.
I'm going to get a job in the drawing,
filling and drawing.'

I was kind of head roadsman, you know, and eh,
I got on sweetly after that.
Done a lot of stuff and one thing and another,
you know, and then,
after being on it for about five years,
aye, five years,
four or five years,
I just thought I was getting it put on to me.

The man that was on the nightshift,
he would leave word with the gaffer,

'Get Jock to come out and lay up my cuddy tonight',
when he wasn't working, you see,
and he's needing a crossing laid.
All these things, you know.

And I said,

'To hell with this, I'm working harder here
than what the fillers and drawers are working.'

I mean, I was doing everything in the pit.
In fact, one week,
there was no under-manager there,
and I had to do under-manager.
And I had no certificates or anything,
but I had to see that everybody on the oncost
was working at their stations
and one thing and another.

And I've seen me going out to the pithead at night,
and
'oh, the magazine man's not out the day.
Go out to the magazine and fill the powder.'

And then you were down the pit and down the mine,
and there was somebody else not out,

'You want his job?'
And then I've seen me working there when I was on the
oncost.
Somebody would come along at 10 o'clock at night
to the house,
just after I was in bed,

'Come up to Thirty Two pithead the night, and do
pitheadman. The pitheadman's not out.'

Well, I said,
I'll come along if I'm getting the same wages
as I get down the pit.

So he agreed to that, and then I had to work on Twenty Six
in the morning.

I said,

'I want to start on the drawing,
filling and drawing.'

They were called rebels

Robert: drawer, born 1914, Brigend

There was never any light industry allowed in West Lothian because, you see, Mr Crichton and company didn't want any light industry in West Lothian.

He, they, the Scottish Oils at that time, they domineered the wage, the wage factor, in West Lothian. If light industry had been allowed into West Lothian at that time, the shale industry would have went short of manpower.

And it was only when the BMC came to Bathgate that we started getting some light industry into West Lothian.

The Scottish Oils could never have afforded it.
They would never have been able to afford it.
They would have been out of the game altogether.
Yet there was nothing for us to do here except go down the pit,
go down the shale mines.
And it was hard, hard work.
You came home at night, you were bone tired!
And yet, I've saw us coming out after an hour's sleep and going up to the football field and playing three hours at least.
Maybe not every night, you know,
just one night in maybe a week or something like that but, my god, it was hard work in the shale!

Anyone that had a flair for asking for their rights in the Scottish Oils, in the shale mines anyway, was never liked by the management.
They weren't liked by the management.
They were called, they were called rebels or something like that, you know.
And that was the whole sum of it.
Some of the Union Officers they seemed to go along with it,
but I didn't!
I never thought that there was enough backbone in them.

If you went up against Mr Crichton then you could look out,
I tell you!
I think myself he had an umbrage against our family for the simple reason that my brother stood against him in the local elections.
He almost beat him.
And he never even turned up for the count that day.
He only won by a whisker!
And it's surprising the number of people that voted for Mr Crichton because they were afraid of getting the sack.

Now, I'm quite sure about that!
That's how I felt at the time, and I still feel it now.
There's no doubt about it!
The Scottish Oils had the hems on the population in West Lothian,
in the shale mining area of West Lothian at least.
They had the hems on them and they were going to keep it there.
And it was only when light industry came to West Lothian that the
shale mines they had to pack it in,
because they just couldn't afford the wages!

I can remember my brother telling me as a matter of fact,
that my dad, I was only a youngster at the time, that my dad was off.
He got his toes cut across here, and he was in bed (inaudible)
and Mr Crichton came up to see.
He was working in No 4 up this way at the time.
He wasn't long in the shale industry at the time.
He lived down at the Scottish Oils houses at Brigend.
And Crichton came up to see why he wasn't at work!
He says 'I'm surprised at you!
A man like you should be up and at your work!'
And my mother put him out of the house!
'Mr Crichton', she says, 'the back of my hand to you!'
She says 'The back of my hand to you, Mr Crichton! Off you go!'
And she put him out of the house. That's true!
That was one reason why this family at least never had any love for
him, for Mr Crichton.
We maybe had a wee bit of feeling for Mr Keddie
because we had a feeling that Keddie
was a different cup of tea altogether.
But Mr Crichton!
We never had any time for him at all.

The Burngrange Disaster

Raymond Ross

deep down the dark crack of shale
splits the thought

the sudden flash it skelps
the waste edge length along
how could? how can?   almost quicker than
it will and has the choking flash
the open lamps that lit
burns out the breath

skull cracked one miner dies
the others   terrorised
their breath will out
where quick is slow
and slower than
gulps the life that
was that is that never will
not now not ever
in the everlasting second
is the hour
come round at last
in seconds flat
fall the miners
fourteen men
like scalded cats

fifteen dead
a village mourns   and more
eleven widows weep
a score and more of bairns
will howl and skrake like
falling shale
the dust will settle aye
it will and when
to drown in searing air
their bodies twist and tear
their jackets hang   their glenny lamps
that lit the darg   lit the firedamp

the seepage that was there was theirs
out from the hacking cough   despair
is resolution is despair   out from

the rasping throat death turns
the throttle on   a loved one's name
the final score   a bet we never placed
gambling on the seam   gambling on the edge
the waste   the gas   the firedamp

the water squelching boots
the simits soaked in sweat
and the quiet swell of tongues
an open mouth that mouths
I never meant   you never said   we never
talks now to the dark

the dust will settle aye
it will and when
remember well these uncouth men
that never lifted book or pen
that howked out rock from solid rock
what use to say the world's first oilmen
and light a lamp ironically
where their shadows never fall?

The Burngrange Disaster, 10th January 1947
(transcribed from an anonymous contemporary poem)

Alistair Findlay

friday night

      burngrange

fifty-three miners

      under

            ground

some heard

      the sound

            travel

or the cry

      run

            fast as you can

                  to the bottom

on the hill

      they made the count

            fifteen men still in

and some went back

      to a blazing section

while all the town stood round

            one out

                one dead

the water pumping down

      until

a fireman found

      thirteen miners

      the smoke still clearing

and the last one too

      taken out

            to a proper grave

Burngrange: Widows

'And as I say, well,
he went out on the Friday on the backshift,
and he would leave the house about two o'clock,
on a Friday.
Friday night,
when the sirens had gone,
my children were young,
and my oldest daughter had just started the school,
and the other one would be about three,
and I never thought anything about it.
You know.
I never sort of thought it was the pit.
And he should have been home about 11 o'clock,
and a neighbour and another friend came to the door,
to say there had been an accident.
The whole weekend,
I just sort of lived in hope that...
my brother-in-law and my father came through.
He was at Stow at that time.
He was an old man.
He came through,
and it was a case of everybody going to the pithead,
and there was no news.
And it was the Tuesday morning,
before they brought them out.
And there was that Rescue Brigade, you know,
from Coatbridge,
and everybody was so kind,
and so worried.
And of course they were all gone at that time,
but thankfully,
I don't think that they would do much suffering,
somebody said,
well, of course,
the death certificate was marked carbon monoxide poisoning,
and somebody said, you see,
that they didn't think that they would really suffer very much.
When they did bring them home,
they were unmarked,
they were so peaceful looking,
and that was one thing that we felt,

well, at least they didn't suffer, you know.
But there was all the trauma of that,
and the worry of Inquiries and men coming,
there was Mr Nellies,
I think it was,
the Union man,
and Mr Crichton and everybody,
and all the ministers of every denomination,
everybody was so kind.
But I think it took an awful long time,
before it just struck home,
what had really happened, you know.
He was forty one when he died.

Burngrange: Canaries

Alec: under manager, born 1909, West Calder

'Well, I'll tell you what happened.
It was the young haulage boy, and he was sitting there,
and out came Davie Muir with one full tub.
And I can't remember – it must have been the chap Rae –
I'm not very sure, but he came out with the second tub,
and that made his rake. He coupled them up,
and while he was doing so, he started play acting,
being a young boy. And all of a sudden – boom – the first
explosion. And they stopped, 'What was that?'
Off went another explosion, and the young boy,
Todd was his name, he got up and ran for the boys.

One of the drawers said he heard him telling the boys,
the faceman, but whether they had ignored it or not,
I don't know. Whether they had ignored the bencher.
But, naturally, you would have thought one of the two
drawers would have said, 'right, it's time.'

We always had a mine manager, his name was Mr Bowman,
and he was a man that believed in safety.
And he used to come down the pit, and he used to gather
all the men in the district round about him.
And he used to give them lectures on such things as that,
and what to do in the event of such an occurrence taking
place because, after all, it's a rare occurrence.

But there was one man,
he tried to put Mr Bowman's theory,
he tried to put it into practice.
When he knew he was trapped,
he wandered away and went into a closed area.
That was George Easton.
He went into a closed area,
and he fenced himself off and put screencloth up,
and tried to live on the oxygen that was lying in the area.
But it got him.

I wouldn't say he lasted much longer than the rest of them.
And he was in right at the very last place. But I can mind,
I went in with an inspector, and that's when they got him.

I'll always remember, we lifted Henry Cowie,
lifted him, and he was sitting. You've heard the old saying,
about miners sitting on their hunkers? Aye, he was sitting,
looking at his lamp.

We naturally thought we could just lift him up,
and put him in a stretcher, to lift him up this incline,
and then up to the level road, where you took them out,
and up to the pit bottom.
But that's how we had to lift Henry, straight up,
and took him into the hutch. One guy, big Tony Gauchan, we
straightened him up,
once we got him in the fresh air.
There's a bell for signalling, and he had come up,
and he must have stood talking to the rest of them.
Must have said, 'I doubt we're trapped.'
And he was standing, and he was holding on to this bell wire
as, well, seconds. Oh, it couldn't have been much at all.
Seconds, seconds.

I had read about it, and was lectured about it,
on many occasions – carbon monoxide – its affinity for blood
is 300 times greater than oxygen. So he's got 300, you know,
how you can't live – your blood can't be without oxygen –
but blood will accept carbon monoxide 300 times quicker,
300 times. So it doesn't take much to kill you. No.
I used to have it all off at my fingertips. 0.5% I think,
if I remember rightly, 0.5% breath for five minutes.

Oh, the chemists were never away from the place after,
but I never got around to asking them,
how much carbon monoxide was in the atmosphere.
The only thing, the only experience I had was,
we were sealing off this particular area,
where the explosion occurred, and it was a very nasty job,
you know. There were broken, being in a stooping area,
there were cracks here and cracks there. We had to try
and seal them up and I can remember Mr Keddie, the boss,
coming down to me and saying,

'I think you should go into the nearest point where these
men are working, and take a canary with you. And warn
these lads, and get them out as quick as possible, in case
there's any sign of carbon monoxide in the atmosphere.'

You see. Well, I goes in, sits down on this,
puts a nail on the tree, and hung up the canary,
and kept having a look at it.
And it wasn't to my – and I felt my heart going –
these boys walking backwards – and I kept saying to them,
'How you feeling? You feeling alright? Everything ok?'

Little did they know,
I was trying to feel how they felt in comparison to myself!
But, periodically, you see, they were getting away out
to the fresh air, and I was sitting there all the time.
And it wasn't until I was about to give up, Mr Keddie
came back in and said, 'everything going alright?'
I says, 'No, feel my heart, Mr Keddie.' He moved.
He took his footrule out his pocket, and plonked it.
And the canary dropped off the spar!
It was sitting on the spar dead.
How that was humanly possible,
I don't know!
And there it was. It toppled off down into the bottom of the cage.

'Take your time. Walk out there gradually, into the fresh
air.' He says.

I wasn't long out in the fresh air till I was ok again.
But there must have been a wee bit carbon monoxide got out.
And it had nailed the canary.

Some places they use a
mouse,
because a warm blooded
creature like that,
they've got a smaller heart,
you see.
And it affects these smaller
creatures quicker than us.
Whenever you see it affecting a canary or a mouse,
then you know it's time
you were in.
That's the reason, because
they've got this small
heart.
The smaller the bird, the
better.
Or the smaller the mouse, I
suppose.
They've a smaller heart,
and that would be effected
much quicker because, remember, it would only take
very little carbon monoxide to get you or me.
Oh, sometimes the canary can be saved too,
because the canary shows panic,
and it starts to flutter its wings about. That one,
it just sat on that spar.
I don't know.
But he stiffened up pretty quick.
And I just kept looking at him.
As long as he was sitting on the spar,
I was quite happy!
You see,
I didn't want to go over and upset the bird, you know,
and have it exhausting itself, you know,
when a stranger goes to a bird's cage,
and it starts to fly from one end to another.
But I didn't want to do that.
I was just quite content to have it sitting on the spar,
breathing the same stuff as me.
And sitting the same as I was doing.
He wasn't breathing, though, was he?'

No idle bread: Jock Wardrope

Faceman; president – National Union of Shaleworkers;
Labour Councillor – Seafield

Jenny Wardrope
photo: Ruth Hamilton

Jock Wardrope
photo: Ruth Hamilton

Jock: Well, as I said, I got actively involved with the unions in 1925. I was appointed president of the Seafield branch of the National Union of Shale-miners. I was only in the job a week when the strike come on – the big one! What we did first was to start up a soup kitchen. They were old wash-houses, and we made the soup in the old washing boilers. Sometimes the women folk would make big cloutie dumplings in they wash boilers as well. That year was the severest winter I think I ever felt. We couldn't get the cabbages nor the leeks out the ground, they were frozen solid. The local traders in Bathgate gave us bones and that to make the soup – ham bones, beef bones. We also sent parties out with accordions and collecting boxes all over the coal fields.

A soup kitchen, 1921 miner's strike, Whitburn

Did you work the soup kitchen, Mrs Wardrope?

Mrs W: No – no me! I run back and forwards
with jugs, that's what I did. Back and forwards
with jugs of soup. I was never in with politics, me.

Jock: Her father was an old Tory (laughs).

Mrs W: Aye. It's a long time past. This is what,
50 years married? We had no golden wedding.
Aye, says I, what's the good of taking presents,
for other folks is harder up thur me!

Jock: (itching to get on with the story) While I remember, I felt
ashamed of it too. First time I'd ever done it in my life, a begging can
round my shoulder, to a football match in Armadale, to collect. My
but I felt rotten. Begging from folk that were just as hard up. The
coal miner was just as hard up in 1926. Aberdeen were playing
Armadale, and we thought we would draw a lot of money. But it
wasn't damn many pennies that I got in that tin can. Forbye, some
of the cans never came back again, for the lads got drunk while they
were away for the day. You know what else happened? When we
were paying out the strike money, some members claimed they'd
never got their money. Well, we sat up there in that institute a whole
Sunday, looking for the money that should have been paid out, and
do you know where the deficiency had come in? There were names
on that list that had been away to Canada for years! Some were even
dead! And you know what else happened, the secretary had got a tip
for a runner at Newcastle – a 'certainty' – and he'd taken away the
union money and put it on this runner, a hundred yard sprint. We
had to bring him up afore the committee, and he had to pay it all
back in instalments.

Mrs W: What does a working man gain from the
likes of that!

Jock: When the strike ended, we lost the case and were left with no
union members. They had all dropped out. We had to start all over
again and build up the union after that. Funds were exhausted, and
we had to go chapping round the doors begging for money. When
they jaloused what we were after, the men would make off down the
road for a 'walk'. Wouldn't face up to us at all. Couldn't afford to
pay the sixpence a week.

I've heard that shaleminers were well looked after
by the company, compared to the coal miner.
Is that true?

Jock: Oh aye, they looked after us, right enough. The company built institutes and that kind of thing. We were far ahead of the coal in that respect. But, surely, they had it out of our skins just the same, paying the miserable wages that they had. The dividend that the Pumpherston Oil Company paid at one time to the share holder was around seventy percent! The average was about 50 per cent!

I became delegate to the executive and represented Seafield from 1931 until it shut down in 1962. In the early days, you had a lot of difficulty persuading the men to join the union. They were very conservative people who were awful loath to make bother. I had a lot of enemies then, and was fighting on the streets too – pulled the hair out of you, and kicked the door down when you were in discussing a grievance with the manager. We were in his room at the time when – BANG – other pony drivers came rushing in wanting to hear what we were talking about. They had the agent's car up-ended, going to tip it into the river Almond!

Why do you think the men distrusted those who were struggling to make working conditions better for them?

Jock: Fear! They were controlled by fear, the oldest weapon in the book. The managers would ask the men if he was a member of the union, and my they were delighted if they could tell them they weren't in the union. Most of them, if they got a man to work below the wage, the men would never say a word about it. They would put men in places where the seam wasn't regular, or bad clearment for shovelling. The contract system was so much per ton: a ton of shale – one and sevenpence three farthing for digging a ton of shale! To start with, apart from anything else, your tools and that, you had to pay out of your wage for the powder to blast that ton of shale! The men usually had a fixed wage. Sometimes they never made the wage, and some men just took whatever the company liked to give them. There was one woman come to me and she says: 'Listen Jock, I wonder if that man of mine is sitting on his erse all day because he never brings home a decent wage.' I says: 'Hey listen, Mrs Tait, I never got a report. And I know he's not getting the wage, but he's never come to me or seen managers or anything. He never went himself, to enquire why he wasn't getting made up.

I got the sack for interfering one time. They sent me 'up the road' (laughs). There was a wee laddie killed, you see, on these hutches. There was what we cried a 'jock' could tumble up the hutches if a rope or a coupling broke – they'd not run any further. But here, this wee laddie, instead of putting the 'jock' on before the engine man drew the hutches away, waited till they were drawing away and he run behind it and hooked it on. The rope broke, and he got killed.

Someone told me that the rope had been bad, what we cried a
'hedgehog' on the rope. I was enquiring about the state of this, when
the manager got to hear about it. I was coming up the pit head, and
I sees him walking up and down, and I thinks – my, he's surely in
good fettle the day – for I didn't think it was me he was waiting for.
'HEY YOU!' – that's how they spoke to you. 'HEY YOU. I WANT
A WORD WI' YOU!'– he says. 'What's this you've been doing inves-
tigating the state of the rope when the laddie was killed there?' Says
I: 'that's my job', says I, 'that's what I get paid for', says I. 'Well, I'm
just going to tell you that that's you FINISHED!', says he. S'i: 'Fair
enough then, I'll just go up and see Mr Caldwell.' He calmed down,
just like that. He said: 'By Christ, that's some job you're on. If I were
you, I'd give it up. I know what goes on at your meetings, and at the
street corners up here! I get all the information that's going on at
these, aye do I!' S'i: 'Listen sur! I won't give up the job. If you give
the verdict at what we decide at the meetings, I've nothing to do with
that, but I'm no giving up the Union job!'

It just showed you what lengths they would go to, to make you give
up. Aye, two pounds ten shillings, a year. I had all that abuse to stand
too, a paid delegate, two pounds ten!

Did you ever meet Shinwell in the early days?

Jock: I chaired Manny Shinwell's meetings here, from whenever he
was a candidate in the 1920s. I met him first though, when I was
eighteen or nineteen. He did his propaganding all round West
Lothian, and he came to live with a Broxburn man at the weekends.
Opposed to the House of Lords? My god, he was opposed to the
House of lords then! That's what sickened me. I cannot thole it,
accepting Lord Shinwell. He was so opposed to it in these days.
Mind, the man could speak. All that stuff about the gentry's horses'
stables being better than what the working folk were living in, aye,
a great orator – that's what held the people.

We went to see him in 1945, after the War. It was the cruellest visi-
tation I had ever been on (laughs ironically). We went to see him to
try and keep the shale industry going, because it was in decline by
then. We sat outside and the agent, Walter Nellies, was on two sticks
with arthritis. Jimmy McKelvie, from Broxburn, was organiser, and
he was pumped full of morphine for to keep him living, for to get to
London. The doctor says: 'You'll never make it McKelvie!' 'Aye,
well, I'll die on the road down then', he says. They took us into the
office down there, and we weren't half an hour in the place – not
even a cup of tea – when Shinwell told us that there was no hope for
the industry, and that it was antiquated. Aye, it was a cruel blow.

Nellies says to me: 'Do you know Jock, that's the worst treatment I've ever had. I never got that treatment from a Tory minister, than what we got from that man the day.' This was a cripple on two sticks, and McKelvie full of morphine – not a half hour in the place – after travelling all night too...'

Nellies must have been some man?

Jock: He was a great man, aye. He was a member of Bathgate Town Council, and it was him that introduced the big travelling grocery vans into West Lothian.

So then, after the War, the industry gradually died. It was gey hard to survive, I tell you. The wife had a hard time too. The women had a helluva time o'it.

How did you cope with this man of yours that was always causing bother?

Mrs W: Trouble every day, this one! (nods in his direction and laughs)

Jock: Seafield, of course, was a great Tory place. We had whole families of Tories here, droves of them. They'll be Tories till they die. We had cars would run voters to the poll, and these Tory cars would try to run us off the road into ditches. There were fights up the road there too (laughs). Aye, and all for two pounds ten shillings a year, sitting all night at the pit head demonstrating, just for the sake of showing that I was fighting for the working man...'

Could you tell me something about the great influx of Irishmen, who came over to howk the coal?

Jock: In they days, there were a lot of two-apartment company houses, and the women used to bring in lodgers from Ireland. Some of them had six, seven and eight lodgers living in a two-apartment house. The beds were three-shifted: backshift, dayshift and nightshift. The beds were never cold. Men were going in, as others were tumbling out.

Mrs W: Aye, they all had lodgers, and they only had a room and kitchen the same as me. And they had six lodgers. There were fights at night and everything, and we had to shoot out our necks about it at the hinderend.

Jock: I remember when I was a laddie, there was an old Irishman standing at the head of the mine. There was a mile of mine, and you could look down a good bit and see all these lights coming up in the bogeys. Anyway, this old chap comes forward when I landed. I had my lamp on, and he said: 'Hello son, what do you pay for that little teapot on your head?' S'i: 'Ninepence.' He said: ' Do you get a wick along with it as well?' S'i: 'You're looking for a bloody bargain! You'll just have to buy it off your wages, same as me.'

The management went across to Ireland and brought them over by the shipload, to cut down the wages. That was the purpose. You could pay the poor buggers anything at all.

Aye, I can see my whole life from this window here. You talk about blood, sweat and tears – there it is yonder, on that shale tip there. There's some of mine lying up there on that tip. The bings: men would walk out on the Saturday at one o'clock and weren't back home till the Sunday morning, hutches loaded with burning shale for these tips, smoke and burning, away up to the very top, men with rags bound round their hands, pushing away and tipping, with their heads bent over the hot shale, the buggers weighed a ton, heaving them up, with their heads on the trams, aye, dear god, aye – there were no idle bread.

WEST LOTHIAN COURIER – FRIDAY, APRIL 26, 1929

THE LATE MR M. O'HAGAN

A WELL-KNOWN TRADE UNION WORKER

The news of the death of Mr Michael O'Hagan, which took place on Wednesday morning, was received with much regret in the town. For some months Mr O'Hagan had not been enjoying good health, but he had always a cheery smile and bore his affliction with remarkable fortitude. During the three years he had been a residenter in the town Mr O'Hagan had gained the esteem of the inhabitants.

He was a native of Ireland, and more than 20 years have passed since he made West Lothian his home. Mr O'Hagan was perhaps better known for the part he played in organising the shale workers into a trade union. It is more than 20 years ago since he started the Scottish Shale Workers Association, which, in 1920, amalgamated with the Scottish Shale Miners Association. He became an agent to the National Union of Shale Miners and Oil Workers, and during the war took a leading part in the work of the committee in dealing with the supply of oil to the Admiralty. In the course of his work he came often into touch with the late Mr James Kidd, MP, and, although their political views were different, they were close friends, and Mr O'Hagan had a high opinion of Mr Kidd's worth and ability.

Mr O'Hagan was imbued with a love for public work, and was for some years a member of Uphall School Management Committee. In November last year he was an unsuccessful candidate at the Town Council election. It is three years ago since Mr O'Hagan gave up his activities as a trade union leader, and since then he has been carrying on a successful publican's business in the burgh.

He was a likeable personality, and possessed in a high degree that native wit characteristic of his race. He was fond of a joke. An excellent raconteur, he would regale his companions with his war-time experiences in London and stories of trade union personalities. He was a man of common sense and fair play, but was always ready to defend to the best of his ability what he believed to be a just cause. He is survived by a widow, three sons and a daughter, and his passing is mourned by a wide circle of people in the county. The funeral takes place today from Linlithgow to Uphall.

Michael O'Hagan

Robin: drawer & mechanic, born 1905, Philpstoun

I take it that the Union was not very strong then [1920s]?

No. The miners representatives at that time in the shale oil was a Walter Nellies in Bathgate. That was where their offices were. Walter Nellies was the President of the Shale Miners Union and Michael O'Hagan, a big Irishman, came across from Ireland in the First War. And he climbed on the waggon. And he was the agent around all the shalefields, going and trying to get the men into the Union, and then you are united, and force them, the same idea as they have now. Nellies was not so bad, but I used to wonder at this man, Michael O'Hagan. He was about the most illiterate man ever you heard, really. I will give you an instance: the 1926 strike, we had been out on strike for about twelve weeks and they were supposed to be negotiating. At that time each Company was supposed to be separate. It was not Scottish Oils. The way it was, they all amalgamated and each Oil Company getting the best they could, and they were negotiating with the Company for better conditions and better wages and, of course, the miners wanted them to push to get better wages and less working hours. At one time, you could go down the mines just when it was breaking daylight and stay until dark, depending on the man you worked for. You did not have fixed hours.'

.. But I remember at that time they always held the meeting for the James Ross Refinery, Philpstoun, at the local school and Bridgend School was the centre for Kingscavil, Bridgend and Philpstoun. They all met the Union leaders there. That Michael O'Hagan, he came – motorbike, sidecar, an old Royal Enfield, about eight horsepower. He had a stiff leg. What a job he had getting on that bike! I'll never forget that night. I was only in my twenties at that time. He came down and told them – 'Sorry men' – and this is how he put it, I can remember his voice yet, he said – 'You are up against a stone wall. You can say you are finished. You might as well go back on the terms you had, because your arse is out the window.' Honest! You would not have believed it. That was the type of agent they had in the Unions at that time.

The hole in the wall

Adam: oilworker, born 1907, Oakbank

**Were you ever connected with a Union when you
worked with the Scottish Oils?**

Aye, I think that I was in the Oilworkers and Shale Miners Union,
if I mind right!
And I wouldn't be right sure,
but it could have been old Michael O'Hagan.
He was the kind of leading light of it.
I can always mind of Michael O'Hagan saying to the miners,
and the oil workers as well,
if you ever see a hole in the wall,
get into it!
And Michael O'Hagan went into a pub in Linlithgow,
'The Hole in the Wall',
and that pub is there yet!

And why would he be saying if ever you see a hole in the wall ...?

It would be a term of something that he would be trying to illustrate
about the Union and the Companies, I would think.
If you ever see a hole in the wall – get out!
It could mean that if you weren't pleased with the Oilworks,
look for another job.
It was as simple as that.
But Michael did it.
He did it.
A thing that he said years before that,
he went into it!
Last week there,
I go into Edinburgh,
and take a train from Edinburgh to Linlithgow
and walk round about Linlithgow Loch.
It's better than sitting in the house.
And I was standing across the street waiting on a bus
going from Linlithgow to Bathgate,
and I looked straight across the road and there was the pub,
'The Hole in the Wall'.
And the men spoke about that often.
They said Mick done the right thing.
'The Hole in the Wall'.
That is true sir.
No doubt about that.

WEST LOTHIAN COURIER – JANUARY 27, 1956

'DEATH OF EX-BAILIE WALTER NELLIES TRADE UNION LEADER AND PUBLIC SERVANT'

Slowly but surely, time is removing the stalwarts of a past age, an age when public men and public servants were noted for their tenacity, enthusiasm and great zeal. Such a man was exBailie Walter Nellies, MBE, JP, former general secretary of the National Union of Shale Miners and Oil Workers, who passed away late last Thursday evening at his home, 'greenbank', Kirk Road, Bathgate. Mr Nellies was 77 years of age and had celebrated his birthday on New Years day.

Walter Nellies was a native of Kelty, Fife, the son of working class parents. Early in life he began to interest himself in social and political problems of the day. He early identified himself with the Labour Movement and under its banner sought and won election to various local bodies on which he served for several years. He also served on the Carnegie Trust, the body whose charge it is to administer the huge funds left by the late Andrew Carnegie, the American steel millionaire, to promote philanthropic objects in his native town of Dunfermline and in the United Kingdom. It was work dear to the heart of ex-Bailie Nellies.

In 1924, he applied for and secured the post of general secretary to the National Union of Shale Miners and Oil Workers. This was a new post in a new amalgamation. Previous to that time the oil workers had had a separate union with the late Mr M O'Hagen, a famous character and wag, and still remembered in the shale oil area as general secretary. The amalgamation was inevitable, but was not achieved without protracted negotiation.

Mr Nellies brought a new dignity and a forceful personality to the new union. A handsome man, he paid careful attention to his sartorial appearance and he was also exact in speech, correct in his manners and at all times polite and respectful to friends and opponents alike.

SERIOUS TIMES FOR SHALE OIL INDUSTRY

The new general secretary was to find that his new job was no sinecure. These were serious times for the shale oil industry. In 1926, Scottish Oils Ltd., and its subsidiary companies, announced the closing dawn of a number of works and mines and several thousand workers were thrown idle. Those who remained were asked to accept a ten per cent reduction in wages.

This action by the companies was resisted and a stoppage took place. The sequel was that later a Court of Inquiry into the ramifications of Scottish Oils Ltd. was held. The employees and the union sought to prove that operations of the Grangemouth Refinery should be included in any assessment of the industry and that therefore the decrease in wages was not justified.

To Mr Nellies fell the responsibility of preparing the union's case and although the Court of Inquiry's investigations and report made no difference to the position, it was agreed on all sides that the general secretary of the union had done a masterly job. About that time, too he produced a booklet entitled 'Lest We Forget', which was a treatise on the economic history of the industry and is still recognised as one of the most exact and authoritative records ever compiled regarding the shale oil industry.

A period of depression in the industry followed and the process of decline was accentuated in 1931 when further closures of works and mines took place. The blow was softened to some extent, however, by the introduction of a spreadover scheme whereby employees worked three weeks and were idle the fourth, thus the work available was spread over the maximum number and 900 men who would otherwise have been unemployed were kept in the industry. There are those in the shale oil area who will tell you that these were the happiest days of their lives. A ten per cent increase in wages was paid and on the idle week, unemployment benefit was drawn. The result was that over the month, only a shilling or two was lost in cash and there was a week's holiday to compensate for that.

RETIRED IN

Mr Nellies therefore had a strenuous and unenviable task during a large part of his service to the union 'The hour findeth the man' however, and his services to the shale miners and oil workers will never be forgotten. When he retired in 1948 his valued services were summed up in the 'Courier' as follows:

'During all these years Mr Nellies has been a worthy champion of the men's cause. By his wise guidance, tact and outstanding business ability he has been instrumental in carrying through with a remarkable degree of success, a series of negotiations with the representatives of Scottish Oils Ltd., which has not only led to wage increases, but to important improvements in working conditions generally. So satisfactory has been his relations with the company that these negotiations have invariably been completed without friction while, from the men's standpoint, has obviated disputes, the success which has attended his efforts which might have led to strikes. Mr Nellies has also rendered yeoman service in other aspects of the union's affairs. By his capable handling of the many problems encountered in the course of the industry's many vicissitudes, and, at times, precarious existence, as well as his efficient husbanding of the union's finances, he gained the complete confidence of the men and as a consequence, his ambition of securing a 100 per cent membership has practically been realised. The progress made by the union, in terms of finance, during Mr Nellies term of office as general secretary, may be gauged by the fact that in 1924 the joint free balance amounted to just under £5,000, while today it totals in the region of £11,00,011.

PUBLIC SERVICE

Mr Nellies will also be remembered for his outstanding public service to Bathgate and West Lothian. His experience of local authority work began at the age of twenty in his native Fife, where he was a member of various public bodies in addition to the Carnegie Trust. A miner for the first twenty years of his life, he resided in Edinburgh for a short time after his appointment to the NUSM & OW Union before coming to reside in Bathgate in 1925. He entered Bathgate Town Council in 1932 as a Labour Party nominee. He had experience as convenor of most of the important committees of the Council and gave particularly valuable service as convenor of the Housing Committee. He retired for health reasons in 1944 after having held the office of Bailie for four years and but for his retiral would doubtless have become Provost of the town. He also rendered great service to the County Council as a representative of the Town Council.

Mr Nellies also sat as insured contributors' representative on the Court of Referees, and among other bodies he served in were the War Pensions Committee for the Lothians and various advisory panels of the Ministry of Labour.

Closely identified with the Labour movement all his life, Mr Nellies took a broad view of his public duties and served the community with an impartiality which won the admiration of all. In the Coronation Honours of 1937 he received recognition of his services by the award of the MBE and he was for many years a Justice of the Peace for the County.

WEST LOTHIAN COURIER – MARCH 18, 1966

DEATH OF FORMER COUNTY CONVENOR
ROBERT CRICHTON, J.P., C.B.E

Robert Crichton, Managing Director,
Scottish Oils   *photo: Mr Robert Crichton*

With the death late on Wednesday of Mr Robert Crichton, JP, CBE, DL, at his home, Castlepark, Philpstoun, Linlithgow, the county of West Lothian lost a man who was its leading industrialist and public figure for more than half a century.

Mr Crichton will be best remembered for his close connection with and work for the Scottish Shale Oil industry into which he was born. His father was manager and a director of Jas. Ross & Co., Ltd., Philpstoun, one of the pioneer oil companies which later merged into Scottish Oils, Ltd.

LEADING POST

Educated at Linlithgow Academy and Heriot Watt College, Edinburgh, he entered the oil industry straight from College and was to serve it for 58 years before his retiral. As long ago as 1910 he was appointed

General Mining Manager of Jas. Ross & Co., and later he was managing director. With the formation of Scottish Oils, Ltd., he was immediately earmarked for a leading post in the new organisation and was managing director when he retired from the industry in 1954.

He was also a director of Grangemouth Refinery and of British Hydro-Carbons Chemicals Ltd., and also had wide interests in the fields of industry and technical education. He was for ten years a Governor of the Heriot Watt College, Edinburgh and received the Honorary Fellowship in 1952, also a Fellow of the British Institute of Petroleum and first chairman of the Scottish branch of the institute, a former chairman of the Institute of Mining Engineers and also a former chairman of the Institute of Mining Electrical and Mechanical Engineers.

His record of public service was extensive and remarkable and he was for over 30 years a member of West Lothian County Council, for 10 years of which he was County Convenor. With the introduction of the National Health Service in 1947, he became the first chairman of the West Lothian (Bangour) Hospital's Board of Management and held the post until a few years ago.

KEEN CHURCHMAN

A keen churchman, he was Senior Elder of St Michael's, Linlithgow, and was one of those chiefly responsible for organising restoration work on the church and the replacement of the crown and its steeple.

Mr Crichton was indeed the Father of the oil industry in the Lothians and throughout its many difficulties and vicissitudes he never lost faith in it. Indeed it is true to say that but for his unflagging interest and enthusiasm the industry would have wound up long before it was in 1962.

He was a man of great faith and complete integrity, a kindly man and a generous man. Occupying a post of high responsibility and trust, he believed that it was his duty to look after the welfare of all those under him, including their families. In times of hardship, bereavement etc., many a family had reason to bless his name and these things he did in complete secrecy seeking no publicity or credit. Under his direction, Scottish Oils Ltd., set an example to the rest of Scotland in the field of social welfare for workers.

In politics, he was a conservative and perhaps the greatest compliment ever paid to him was by a Labour member of the Labour controlled county council who described him in all seriousness as 'the greatest socialist of us all'.

For his services to industry and the country, Mr Crichton was created CBE in 1952. Predeceased by his wife he is survived by one son and two daughters.

Philipstoun Oil Works, James Ross & Co., no date

THE MID LOTHIAN ADVERTISER & WEST LOTHIAN & LANARKSHIRE NEWS – SEPTEMBER 19, 1947

THE LATE
MRS SARAH MOORE

The funeral of Mrs Sarah Moore, JP, member of Mid Lothian County Council and Convenor of the Public Health Committee, which took place at West Calder on Saturday, was attended by members and officials of the County Council, by members of North and South Mid Lothian Divisional Labour Parties and by a great gathering of the people of the district for which she spent herself.

She had been a member of the Council since 1929 and her vivid personality with her ready wit and eloquence and her great fighting spirit, made her one of the outstanding figures in the Council Chamber.

Her untiring exertions in fighting for houses for the people were not confined to her own district but they brought into being the village of Moorelands which was named after her at the desire of the inhabitants.

Mrs Moore was also a member of the Licensing Appeal Committee for Mid Lothian and Peebles Hospital, of Saughton Prison Visiting Committee and of many others. She is survived by six daughters and three sons.

AN APPRECIATION

Many people residing in the Calders district and in the Lothians will regret the passing of the late County Councillor for Addiewell, Mrs Sarah Moore.

Mrs Moore was one of the early pioneers of the Labour Party and because of her long association with the movement formed a link between its early pioneering days, containing many notable figures such as Keir Hardie, Smillie and others, to the present. She has seen the Labour Party develop from a small force of propaganda to become the Government of this Nation, also the attainment of many of the main points of Labour's early programme; she has been with it and shared with it all the ups and downs of its stormy history; always loyal, ever steadfast in her belief in its principles from attack from whatever quarter they might come.

Mrs Moore's amazing energy and strength of mind, coupled with her indomitable spirit evoked recognition and respect among all sections of the community, political sympathisers and opponents alike. Those vital forces in her make-up, tempered with kindliness, generosity and a deep sometimes surprising understanding of human nature, combined to make her probably the most outstanding personality in the district.

She was seen at her best when aroused by injustice and was ever ready to assist, guide, advise and if necessary fight with all the passion she could command, to right a wrong. Her great spirit rebelled against those deep social and economic evils which were in a way the legacy of industrialism and so she strove towards the laying of a foundation upon which a better order of society could be built, containing in its structure, the material and moral environment necessary for a wider appreciation of the finer things in life, and, attendant with them the responsibilities of citizenship and an interest in the well-being of the community. How well she succeeded in paving the way for the attainment of that goal can be understood by all who worked with her in public life and in the labour movement.

Mrs Moore was the first Labour member to become a County Councillor from the west side of the County, and to attempt to recount in detail the devoted work she gave to the County would require an abler pen than mine to describe. Suffice it to say that for almost 21 years she represented the Addiewell Ward, and in this period only once was returned unopposed. This in itself speaks volumes, as does the fact that although first returned at a period not far removed form the suffragette agitation, Mrs Moore without any ostentatious display about equality of sex, asserted her right to recognition by the very force of her personality and by the knowledge she possessed of the movement to which she belonged and the needs of the people among whom she lived and worked.

No history of the Calders, dealing with the past 30 or 40 years, would be complete without mention of this remarkable woman, the part she played in the period of industrial unrest after the first World War, her activities as Councillor, her work on Committees of the County Council dealing with health, education etc, and not least, as an active member of the Labour Party. It can be said that embodied in the story of her public life is the story of the growth of our movement; that it inspired such outstanding figures was probably inevitable in that its message expressed the hopes and aspirations of the ordinary man and woman. Mrs Moore because of that deep understanding and leadership was able to translate those feelings into action.

We salute the passing of this grand old pioneer of the Labour Movement, having in mind the splendid example she set, of selfless service to the community, an example of service we may try to copy but will find difficult to surpass.

James McRiner

Scottish Stalwarts

Sarah Moore

We've heard of Scottish stalwarts
of Bruce and Wallace's might
who fought and died for freedom
and proved that might was right

we've gloried in their going
and sang their praises high
we hoped that days of dying
for Scotland had gone by

the broken and the maimed came back
to find not peace but this instead
the people they loved the best on earth
unclothed uncared for unfed

not even the right to work and live
not even the right to cry
against the fate that life has spread
only the right to die

but Scotland has her stalwarts
and tyrants soon will know
that the heroes of the coalfields
never the knee shall bow

they'll still fight on for freedom
that god's right hand did give
to prove that right instead of might
can in this land let heroes live

yes Scotland still has stalwarts
their birthright they never will sell
they are the heroes of the oilfields
and their stronghold is Addiewell

Addiewell once the centre
known as the Light of the West
ruined by a Persian adventure
o god it is no jest

o god where is thy godhead
thy mercy power and grace
that a coalition combine
can mock thee to thy face

can send thy image and thy likeness
to be crocked and scrapped at will
o Lord was it this thou died for
then Lord thy dying was ill

Sarah Moore: Councillor for Addiewell
Leonara Kelly: daughter, born 1904, Addiewell

'Ma' Moore,
well that was my mother,
and she was a councillor for 31 years.
She was the,
oh what do you call it,
the convener of Midlothian when she died, in 1947,
and she really got this place put on the map.
And that is why it is called after her,
is Mooreland,
and it was Dr Young in West Calder that really named it.
At first it was called various things,
and they finished up calling it Moorelands.
Anyway though,
I wasn't born there,
I was born in Addiewell.
And well, Addiewell was a very friendly place, old fashioned.
But I must say everybody was respectable, you know,
and neighbourly,
very much so,
and well,
the Catholics – I was a Catholic –
but we had to go to West Calder school.
And it was a walk to West Calder, you see,
but my mother didn't send us to West Calder.
Some of my older brothers went to West Calder,
but she sent us to the public school – just across the road.

The education authority didn't recognise Catholic schools
until about 1920, and until about that time, the congregation
kept the Catholic priests, Catholic teachers.
But however,
I was educated at the public school in Addiewell.
I think Addiewell was actually built about 1884–85.
The school was built – the date was on it, it's off it now –
but it was above it: 1888.
And it was built then.
That was the public school.
The Catholic school wasn't built until,
well I was 12,
it would be 1916,
that was the first Catholic school.
It was the first Catholic school up until then.
But the older ones in the district went to West Calder school.
There was a good few who went,
but there was never any bigotry.
There was no bigotry.
The Protestants went in at 9am and got a half-hour's
religious education,
and we went in at 9.30am, you see...'

'I have a map of Addiewell.
It's a phototype thing,
but it gives all the streets. All the streets were named after,
Dr David Livingston,
all these,
the man that made the Glenny lamps,
I have them all on the map there.
But there was Bank Street, Cross Street and Watt Street,
and Davis Street and Stevenson Street,
– were all called the High Rows –
and Livingston Street.
And they thought themselves a wee bit high.
And the Low Rows.
The Low Rows were
Graham Street, Simpson Street, Campbell Street, Baker Street.
But Faraday Place,
that still stands.
that was the top area, you know.
Well, we were in line with Faraday Place,
so we were considered in the High Row too.

But there was no running water,
and there was no toilets...'

'And we borrowed a day in the wash house,
otherwise you had to wash in your living room,
or outside, if it was dry.
You would just use a tub and a stool and a wringer,
and it was the old fashioned way.
There was no such a thing as persil or things like that.
You got a soap powder in the Cooperative – it was 2d –
and you washed.
And then I mind these great big long double blankets,
but most people tramped on them,
with their feet...'

'And there were big greens,
but my mother was a keen gardener,
and she got her garden.
It went from the house right down to the hall wall.
And the woman next door gave her her garden,
and she grew flowers and she grew vegetables.
And my father built a hot house and she took up everything,
and she was a great cook.
And when the strikes were on, I mind,
Dr Young came out and asked my mother if she would go
and make the meals for the school children,
to come into school and be fed in West Calder.
And this was during the strike, yes,
and she went in and made the meals.
She had her two elder sisters helped her and all,
another two women,
and they made the meals and fed the children, you know,
just fed the school children ...'

'There was nothing in Addiewell actually,
but we once had a picture house that came in for the winter,
or two winters,
and you got in for 2d. And my mother she didn't believe in
the pictures, unless it was something educative.
But I was more interested,
although I was a Catholic.
The Hallelujahs used to come round with a tent.
The Hallelujahs.
These Hallelujahs were preachers.
They used to hold a tent,

and I used to love to go up and sneak into the tent,
and sing all the hymns.
And we sang all the hymns,
only this time I was nearly finished,
they gave a prize and I got a nice badge – 'Jesus loves me' –
hidden in the inside of my coat,
so as they wouldn't see it.
I never let on about the Hallelujahs and when I went home,
my mother said to me,
'where have you been?'
for I was dry,
and here it had poured with rain.
I didn't know that,
and I was sort of stranded,
and just said I was speaking to this girl in the wash house
on my way home.
But she didn't allow us to go to the pictures,
unless she thought it was something that she thought
was missing – or something like that, you know.
But there was a cinematicar that came 2 or 3 times a year
to the hall. And then she didn't believe in that either,
because she thought it wasn't safe,
there wasn't enough fire-escapes.
And they used to stand with a big engine outside,
just outside our doorway, and it worked from inside...'

'But there was an awful lot of Irish people that came.
It was the Wee Rows that they stayed.
They came from Ballamar and Ballameny and that,
and all these Irish people.
And they were the ones that were sort of,
well I don't say they were looked down on,
but other Rows were mixed,
sort of thought themselves superior.
But there was no – you never heard any quarrelling.
There was one man used to come up with a drink in him,
and he used to shout – he was a Catholic –
he used to shout for this football player – 'Johnnie Walker' –
and Johnnie Walker got him a suit of clothes for a present.
And then another Irishman used to come,
and he used to be going to fight everybody...'

'There were no toilets in Addiewell.
The women had to use poles or pails, you know.

But the men went to these places outside.
They were just dry toilets,
and they went in.
Some of the women in the other rows used to sneak in,
when they weren't looking. But there was no closet.
We got one.
My father built one because the policeman got one,
at the end of the street.
So my father built one.
He built two porches onto the rows and gave us a back door.
And the result was,
he built a toilet.
And he got a pipe taken along the back,
and into the same pipe as the policeman's toilet.
And that was the only flush toilets in Addiewell.
It would be about 1929,
when Livingstone Street got water closets,
and the top houses got water closets.
So that was 1929...'

'Oh aye, there was a lot of poverty.
I can mind my mother was standing in the stair they lived
the top of,
and I can mind my mother,
and we'd a great big message basket,
and it had a lid and handle,
and I can mind of my mother putting groceries of every kind,
tea, sugar, and butter, all these things into it,
and she gave them to my two elder sisters and she said,
'now take them up and open F's door,
and just put that in the door,
close the door and come home.'
And my sister went up and put it in the door,
and didn't say anything, just left it.
'These baskets', I says, 'must be cheap.'
Many mornings she did that,
because my father had the big wages,
and if she knew of anybody hungry.'

Mrs Moore & The Duchess of Atholl: 1922 election

Gladys: teacher, born 1900, Galloway

'I remember the Duchess of Atholl coming,
one of my first experiences,
going to hear them at the People's Hall,
the Duchess of Atholl speaking,
and this Mrs Moore,
now there's a street in Addiewell named after her,
and she was an agitator,
brandishing all the books at the Duchess of Atholl meeting,
and very vocal and abusive,
but the woman had her,
very definitely had her,
experience.'

Women of the Calders: 1926 Miners' Strike

1926 Miners' Strike at West Calder – Protest outside Parish Office at decision
to cease payments to strikers' dependants. The demonstration, mostly of
women and children, was led by Mrs Moore, standing in the foreground;
her daughter, Leonara, is standing, centre, behind her.

According to Mrs Moore's grandson, John Kelly, the protest was
sparked when the chief clerk, Mr Duncan Hay, took it upon himself
to stop the payments. Mrs Moore immediately summoned claimants
from the surrounding villages by bell-ringers to march en-masse to

West Calder to demand their rights. Mr Hay duly recognised 'Ma' Moore as their spokes-person but refused to change his decision, whereupon, the protestors resolved to camp out in front of the office, and arrangements were made for food to be brought for a 'sit-in'.

The protestors sat throughout Friday and Saturday (returning each working day) and gathered in such numbers on Monday morning that Mr Hay sent for the police to quell a 'riotous mob', finding instead mothers and toddlers jokingly passing the time. The police began to usher them into an orderly queue, strong accusations being that the police pushed with such enthusiasm that one protestor fell and burst his head against the pavement. The sight of blood riled the crowd and the police used their batons which then resulted in some men overturning vehicles belonging to the beseiged office, and the police defending themselves from what they took to be a frenzied mob.

Witnessing these scenes, Mr Hay sent for 'Ma' Moore and on the grounds of public safety relented his position. Every protestor was instructed to attend the following morning for payment – 'thus ending West Calder's notorious baton charge!'

A 'riotous mob' of mothers and toddlers

Women of the Calders, 1926 Miners' Strike:

peaceful but determined 'sit-in' – akin to rent

strikes; a small part of women's 'hidden history'

One Every Dividend
A = born 1903; B = born 1905, sisters, both Broxburn

B- *'I believe when we were children there used to be the well outside. We used to carry the water to the wash-house when we were young because, mind, we had the pails of water in the lobby. The last thing we had to do when we were kids – bring in two pails of water for my mother, for the men going to their work in the morning. So they'd have their fresh water for going to their work in the morning.'*

A- 'Aye, the well was at the door.'

B- *'No. The water out the wash-house. That was after they did away with the wells. The wells were when we were very young 'A'. And then we just got water in the wash-house. We carried pails of water from the wash-house.'*

A- 'And I said to Jimmy, 'it's your turn, you should carry the water.'

B- *'He never did.'*

It was always the girls who did it?

B- *'Aye.'*

So the girls did a lot more work in the house than the boys?

A- 'Aye.'

Didn't you think that was unfair then?

A- 'No. We were just brought up like that.'

B - *'We just had to do it.'*

A- 'I mean, we had to clean the shoes for them.'

For your brothers?

A- 'Aye.'

B- *'On a Saturday morning we used to have to oil their pit boots and polish them up ready for the Monday morning for the work. The men never did anything.'*

How about washing their clothes?

B- *'Oh aye. It was hard work.'*

Were they greasy and oily?

A- 'Aye. Sometimes we got a 6d, I think, from Hughie and Jimmy.'

What sort of things would people do for each other?

B- *'Anything at all, just help, you know. The old wife that lived just two doors from us was the midwife.'*

Was she qualified or trained?

B- *'No, and neither was Mrs Waters either.'*

They just went to be with the women?

A- 'The doctors trusted them. They knew they were going to be there.'

Did the doctors go too, or was it just the midwife?

B- *'No. I think the doctor went too. Before I had my two, Mrs Crawford had to have a certificate.'*

A- 'The first time my mother had Mrs Crawford as a midwife was when she, (B), was born, because it was my granny brought the rest of the bairns all home. It wasn't a midwife then. It was my granny that did it.'

Did you hear much about women or babies dying in childbirth?

A- 'Seemed to be. Aye. For a while, years after of course, they tried the abortions, ken, the women in the house. There's a lot of the women died. So did the bairn.'

Who did the abortions, the women themselves?

B- *'I don't know who did it ?'*

A- 'I don't know. They had somebody.'

B- *'My aunty died. One of my aunties.*

Trying to give herself an abortion?

B- *'Somebody else gives it to you, somebody else. And there was another three women all just, all about the same time. All died.'*

And were they having abortions because they were not married?

B- *'No. They were married and they'd a family, and they didn't want to have any more. So, they were stopping them.'*

But the doctors never did anything?

B- *'No.'*

And it was well known that women gave themselves abortions?

B- *'Aye, then. They did it. I don't know what other places were like, but here they did.'*

This was the midwives?

B- *'No. They hadn't the midwife at all. It was some other*
body that did it.'

What did they have – medicines?

B- *'I couldn't tell you. We were too young to know. My*
mother used to try and keep everything back from us,
anything like that, but you know what kids are like.'

A - 'We'd to find out things for ourselves. She
never spoke about anything.'

B- *'No even when it came to our period times. She never*
told us anything about it at all.'

That must have been quite a shock?

B- *'It was a shock, aye. She just told me, she said – 'you'll*
have that every month' – and that was that...'

[later] Did you have to work long hours in service?

B- *'6.00 in the morning till 10.00 at night. I was used to*
it, and that was all. You see, I was the kitchen maid, so
I had to get up and scrub the front door-step first
thing in the morning, and give the cook her cup of tea
in bed, and get the breakfast prepared, and then she
got up and cooked it. And then, of course, the dinner
was always at night, you see. 8.00 at night for
upstairs. So you had the dishes to wash after that, and
then the maids for their supper after them, so I'd still
to wash up after them, so it was about 10.00 at night
before I'd finished.'

And you got one day off a week?

B- *'Yes.'*

**And did you always come back to your family on
that day?**

B- *'Oh aye, always come home.'*

What about smoking? Did all the men smoke?

B- *'Oh aye.'*

Did your father smoke?

B- *'A pipe. And my granny smoked a pipe, a clay pipe.'*

A- 'And she was sitting on the doorstep and the
minister came. Oh what a state she got into.
She was trying to hide it. He says, 'don't
bother Mrs L., it's all right.'

Did a lot of old women smoke pipes?

A- 'Yes.'

And women of your mother's generation?

B- *'No.'*

When you were children, most of your friends were from large families?

B- *'Oh aye. There were seven Docherty's, and the Simpsons', there were sixteen or eighteen Simpsons.'*

A- 'She was having one every dividend we would say.'

An orange, an apple & a hankie
Wife of a drawer: born 1910, Winchburgh

How did you entertain yourselves as women?

'Just sitting reading, or we used to make rugs in those days. John's mother used to be very good at it. We'd just sit blethering.'

Did you have 'hen-parties'?

'Never in time!

When anyone was getting married in those days, they used to put a flag up the lum. They were supposed to get a bottle of whisky for it, but it was beginning to be a business with some of them. They were getting round, you know, the same one's doing it, just to get the whisky. So people stop. No, you'd just the events of the year at that time – Christmas day. They've all died out – the gala day, the sports day. You'd the football on Saturdays, but it's all died out. Very few go to football now. But that was our life.

Even Christmas and New Year, if you gave presents, which was rarely because you couldn't afford it, it was only within your own house, but nowadays, everyone round about you, you're giving presents to all the nephews and nieces, it mounts up and mounts up. You never kept Easter, you know, with the chocolate eggs and things. You dyed your eggs and rolled them up at Niddry Castle. Nowadays they're coming out with massive eggs.'

Now as a child what kind of Christmas present did you receive?

'Nothing. A threepenny bit, an orange or apple, and a hankie. You hung your stocking up. You hung it up at the end of the bed, and that's what was in it, nothing, one of these, that's what we got. You didn't expect any more.'

And what would a man give to his wife?

'Nothing. She got his pay on a Friday!'

What about birthdays and things like that?

'Oh they passed. You didn't have the money. We never bothered.'

And what about anniversaries?

'No. And there were no Mother's Day or Father's Day or Any Day!'

25th Wedding anniversaries passed. The weddings were all in the houses, and the person had to pay for everything.'

That must have been quite an interesting day, a wedding?

'Oh, great days, great days. But they were all in the house. Very occasionally, somebody who had a few bob would maybe hire a hall, but everybody said the ones in the house were the best weddings.'

So who would you invite? People from the village?

'No. Intimate friends and relations. And it was always at breakfast. We were married at nine o'clock in the morning, at nine o'clock mass, and then we had a celebration. A lot of them used to get married at six o'clock at night, in their own church, and have their celebrations at night. Ours went on till night. We were in Ireland and it was still going on! And that was us sailing! They were good. 'Pour oots' were great. There was a lot of money scattered then, you know what I mean, saving all the coppers for weeks and weeks. They would throw them out. You'd skint knees trying to get them! They were great events, weddings... They were great days, I mean, there was something about them, looking back, but living through them, thank god they're away. We'd never wish them back for young ones to go through it.'

Finishing article

James: faceman, born 1903, West Calder

'So, is there anything further that you would like to say on your past experience in the mines and pits?'

'Aye.

There's only one thing that I would like to say, that I hope we don't go back to it again.'

'Is that how you feel?'

'That's my finishing article.'

Women: Working and Striking

The oral history on Sarah Moore and testimony by Jock Wardrope illustrate the key role women played in supporting any industrial action being taken by their menfolk in respect of their jobs, conditions and, above all, wages. These activities could vary from providing food to stoning or heckling 'blacknebs' (those men continuing to work during a strike), or 'rent strikes' which had begun in Glasgow during the First World War in response to unscrupulous landlords trying to evict the families of men fighting and dying on the Front.

The rent strike in 1926 at West Calder followed this tradition, the women, led by Sarah Moore, taking on local officialdom and creating a stramash. As her daughter, Leonora Kelly, describes, Sarah Moore and her two elder sisters and others were also on active kitchen duty during the 1926 General Strike;

'And when the strikes were on, I mind
Dr Young came out and asked my mother if she would go
and make the meals for the school children,
to come into school and be fed in West Calder.
And this was during the Strike, yes,
and she went in and made the meals.
She had her two elder sisters helped her and all,
another two women,
and they made the meals and fed the children, you know,
just fed the school children...'

In *A Century of Shale*, Raymond Ross describes how women were active in support of the 1887 Shale Strike at Broxburn, and in colourful fashion. Raymond also discusses the actual employment of women that began to take place during the First World War.

THE 1887 STRIKE

During the 1887 strike, a wages dispute which affected almost the entire shale district and which lasted some 21 weeks in the Broxburn area, where the men stayed out the longest, the Broxburn Oil Company presented 121 petitions at Linlithgow County Court on August 24 'praying for warrants to eject that number of families from their houses' claiming that the striking miners had left the company's employment on July 25 and, therefore, had to leave the company's houses. The solicitor representing the miners argued that the men 'did not leave the company's employment, they are there to work as soon as certain terms are settled.

The originators of the strike were the masters themselves and the men were prevented from working to the company at the rate of wages they formerly received'.[1]

After some families 'removed' themselves there were still 72 miners occupying company houses in early September and the building of a wooden shed to accommodate some of the families awaiting eviction was stopped by Lord Cardross, a shale royalty holder, who also owned the land where the shed was being built. The miners began to build anew at Stuartfield in the east end of Broxburn. This wooden shed was intended to house 40 families.[2]

The strike had the support of, among

others, the radical MP and writer R.B. Cunninghame Grahame. Christening himself the miners 'Justiceman', the liberal MP who was to become the first president of the Scottish Labour Party in 1888 and the first President of the National Party of Scotland in 1928, was cheered through the streets of Broxburn in a carriage pulled by the miners. In his speeches he characteristically took time out to call for Home Rule for Ireland and Scotland.

Over forty families were evicted on a cold, wet October morning though there was plenty of life in the women who treated the Sheriff-Officers and police to a rendition of:

Glory, glory! Hallelujah!
Hark the miners' lonely cry;
Toom yer hooses, run like blazes, [empty]
Plenty toom yin's overbye.

On being evicted from her house, one Irish woman, waving her daughter's green straw hat, cried for 'three cheers for the green' before dancing a hornpipe in the street graced with a few spirited 'hooches'. Another miner's wife, holding a picture of 'Burns at the Plough' told the uniformed commisionaires 'if Rabbie was leevin', he wad gar ye dance'[3]

Seven evicted families were eventually put up in the Stuartfield shed, a 'cold looking dwelling' as reported in the *West Lothian Courier* (20/10/1887), others being accommodated in a hall and in houses not owned by Broxburn Oil Company. A settlement was not agreed until November 28 which brought union recognition, a nine hour day and the restoration of a 2d reduction per ton – a significant victory for unionised labour in the shale industry.

Another strategy employed by the Broxburn Oil Company during the strike was the use of 'blackneb' labour, a move bitterly opposed by the striking miners who verbally harassed them. With some local 'blacknebs' refusing to leave their houses because of taunts and threats from the strikers, the company ordered some 1,000 men from the oil works to turn out and escort the 'blacknebs' to the mine 'on the penalty of dismissal'. This procession, led by the works manager at 5.30am, was followed by a crowd of 200 men, women and children, ringing bells, rattling cans and tin trays and generally giein' it laidie. Two days previously, a number of women had stoned the 'blacknebs' coming out of the mine after their shift and later on this day as the 'blacknebs' came out the police occasionally made a charge at the women and snatched trays that they were beating upon from them'. The morning escort for the 'blacknebs' gave rise to the following squib in the West Lothian Courier;

What went ye out to see?
A sight to make angels weep,
Man fallen so very low,
Into the quagmire deep.
Minions instead of men,
Over the ground have trod,
Licking the very dust
At the will of the master's nod.

What went ye out to see?
Heroes from sire to son?
Spare us such sights, ye gods,
Ere our day's work is begun.
Was there a Scotsman there?
The country should him spurn –
That cradled a Robert Burns,
Or the Bruce of Bannockburn.[4]

The active participation of women in support of striking men can be traced back to the 'first recorded dispute' at Addiewell in 1870 when they also stoned 'blacknebs', putting many to flight. A crowd, 200 strong, stoned 'blacknebs' at four pits in succession. When they arrived at the fifth, the manager got them to disperse on the promise that he would settle with the men, which he did.

WORKING WOMEN

Not only did women support industrial action but many came to be employed by the oil companies during the First World War to take the place of men called up for military service.

They worked in the candle works, in the sulphate houses filling bags with ammonium sulphate, in cooperage and joinery, filling oil drums and at the loading banks, and some even worked at the pit heads tipping hutches and the like:

'...women took over lots of jobs... emptying the wagons and pulling the hutches and doing lots of odd jobs ... on the bing and up the works... married women whose men were away in the Army. And younger women between 18 and suchlike used to be on top of the wagons, emptying them with the shovels and pulling the hutches into the hopper and suchlike. There was one young woman from Westerton and one from Broxburn... started on the pit head ... along with the miners, and I'm afraid they didn't have a very easy passage because the men resented them because they showed that they could do it.'[5]

On top of this the women did practically all the domestic work at home. Their lot, as Randall shows in some detail, was a far from easy one in peace time, never mind during war.

When you consider the overcrowded and generally very poor housing conditions, the lack of proper sanitation, the notable pollution of air and water by the shale industry, domestic life was a hard darg in itself from the 1850s until at least the 1930s.

Naturally enough, overcrowding, poor housing, a poor diet (though relatively healthy compared to some cities), lack of proper sanitation etc. took its toll. The only plus seems to have been a lack of rickets, very much a city disease.

Looking, for example, at a single page in the Bathgate Mortality Books which records the death of my own aunt at the age of 10 months from meningitis, other (common) causes of death, in a period spanning 1888 to 1918, are bronchitis, measles, pneumonia, peritonitis, consumption, asthma, tonsillitis and of course, 'premature' (13 days old) or 'childbed' (a 25 year old woman).

Raymond Ross

Footnotes:

(1) West Lothian Courier 27/8/1887
(2) Ibid 10/9/1887; 8/10/1887
(3) Ibid 15/10/1887
(4) Ibid 8/10/1887
(5) Sara Randall Shale Community Study: Interviews (n.d.) p55F

Pithead women workers and miners in working gear;
possibly Loganlea Colliery, Addiewell, pre-Great War?
Photo: John Kelly

The shale oil industry: a sketch

by Sybil Cavanagh

The shale oil industry forms what is probably the most important and influential part of West Lothian's history; certainly the most unique part. Shale deposits are found elsewhere in Scotland and other parts of Britain, but nowhere were they found in such concentration and quantity as in West Lothian, and nowhere else was there created such a large scale shale oil industry as there was for just over a century in West Lothian.

The usual date given for the beginning of the shale oil industry is 1850 but, long before Paraffin Young's time, it was known that certain rocks, if subjected to high temperatures, could produce oil. One person who noted this was Sir Robert Sibbald of Kipps, a man of many talents; he was Geographer Royal in Scotland and he wrote the earliest history of West Lothian; he helped to publish the first atlas of Scotland; and he lived in Kipps House, now a ruin, near Beecraigs in the Bathgate Hills. In his book, on Linlithgowshire he wrote: The coal in Bonhard and the Grange (near Carriden) is full of oil substance; I have seen it melt with heat and run out like pitch. Here, in a book published in 1720, is presumably a description of shale oil, so we can safely say that nearly 150 years before Paraffin Young, it was widely known that minerals could produce oil, but that before James Young, no one had come up with a viable method of producing that oil on a commercial basis.

Paraffin Young was himself an interesting man, what we might now call a self-made man. He was born in Glasgow in 1811, the son of a carpenter. He attended evening classes at the Andersonian College in Glasgow (what is now Strathclyde University), and he became friendly with another young man of humble origins, David Livingstone. They remained friends throughout their lives, and it was James Young's money which helped to pay for the search and discovery of Livingstone by Stanley, for the bringing of Livingstone's body home for burial, and helped to keep his widow and family after his death.

After college, James Young obtained work as an industrial chemist. In 1847, another friend, James Oakes, who was working in a Derbyshire coal mine, reported to Young that the coal produced oil. James Young went down to investigate and did manage to invent a process of producing oil which was commercially viable. However, the Derbyshire deposits was very small and the search was on for other coal deposits which would be suitable. Many samples were tested, and the most productive was found to be Torbanite – also known as Boghead Parrot Coal – and found on the estate of Torbanehill, between Bathgate and Whitburn. And so the scene shifts to West Lothian. In 1850, James Young and his partners, Edward Meldrum and a lawyer called Edward Bennie, began building the Bathgate Chemical Works near Durhamtown (now Birniehill), which was in effect the first shale oil works in Britain. Bathgate was especially suitable because there was a nearby supply of Boghead coal and surplus labour. Bathgate's traditional industry of weaving was in decline because of the competition of steam-powered looms, and there was a large pool of available workmen.

At this early period, elaborate precautions were taken to keep the whole process secret, in case industrial spies got in and pirated Young's valuable new process. A high wall was built round the site, and two heavy wooden gates were kept constantly guarded. The workmen were sworn to secrecy. A house was built for Edward Meldrum at the works so that he could closely supervise the whole operation – day and night. The building had few windows and those were very high up. *The Falkirk Herald* of 9 September, 1852, reported: These works have lately been erected at Boghead near Bathgate ...Being conducted as a 'secret work', little is known in the district regarding the articles produced in them, and less of the means by which they are produced. Indeed all that is known on the subject, is that in them there is used large quantities of the Boghead cannel coal. from which it is understood that oil and various other valuable substances are, by some chemical process, extracted.

James Young had been careful to patent his new process, and the various modifications and improvements as they were made. He was careful also to word his patents with caution, so that as little technical information as possible was available to his rivals. Other patents and mineral rights were bought by him, not in order to be used, but to prevent others using them. He granted licences to work his new process to only a few firms, and he embarked on a series of lawsuits to protect his patent. He and his partners were thus astute and even ruthless businessmen, and all of them made huge fortunes within a short space of time. Meldrum built himself a huge Victorian castle at Dechmont, now demolished, and he now has a primary school named after him, and his bust is on display in the Local History Room at Library Headquarters. Meanwhile. the deposits of Torbanehill mineral were being used up and Young replaced it with shale. Shale, he had discovered. had a smaller yield of oil than Torbanite, but there was almost unlimited quantities of it. In modern marketing terms, James Young had a product – oil – and huge quantities of it, but was there a sufficient market for all that could be produced? Young resolved this by increasing the uses of oil, and so creating a market.

Bathgate Chemical Works: 1850–1950s, James Young's First Shale Oil Works

The main demand when he began producing had been for lubricant oils, for oiling the machinery of the new industries of the Industrial Revolution – particularly in the textile industry.

A by-product of Young's process was lamp-oil, but it was smelly, smoky, unreliable and even dangerous. Apparently it was liable to burst into flames without warning. Young worked out how to improve it, got rid of the smell and unreliability, and began promoting it with a vigorous publicity campaign. By the late 1850s, Young was importing into Britain a new type of lamp that was made in Germany which no longer caught fire, and which could burn his oil. By 1860, lamp-oil was a more lucrative part of his market than the original lubricating oils. The secret of his success was not just the quality of his product, but the creation of a market for it.

Young's monopoly ran out in 1864, and other oil companies sprang up all over West Lothian and Midlothian, plus a few smaller shale fields in Fife and Lanarkshire. By 1855–6, it is estimated that there were 120 oil firms in existence. all hoping to cash in on this demand for lighting and lubricating oils which was a consequence of the Industrial Revolution and huge population growth of the 19th century. The American coal-oil industry was also growing up rapidly, but was very soon overtaken by petroleum. Shale had to be mined and processed to produce oil. Petroleum just gushed out of the ground, and needed only to be refined. It was soon to provide cheaper and very harmful competition to the Scottish oil industry.

But still in the 1860s, the American Civil War meant a decline in their oil production and exporting, and so for a few years Scotland's oil companies remained unopposed. Fortunes were made and lost. West Lothian folk had never known anything like it. In the parish of Strathbrock (Uphall and Broxburn), there were 650 retorts in operation or being erected in 1864-5, and it was estimated that £150,000 had been invested in the area. One can imagine what it must have been like – everywhere you looked mines being sunk; retorts being built; cottages being flung up; men from the West, the Highlands, and most of all from Ireland, flooding in to find work. The population of Broxburn doubled every decade – every 10 years between 1860 and 1900. [1861: 660; 1871: 1,457; 1881: 3,066; 1891: 5,898]

And not just in the Broxburn area. In 1866, Young set up his Paraffin Light and Mineral Oil Company, the largest oil company in Britain. A new village – Addiewell – was built to house the workers, with a model school and a works medical service. The oil works complex produced its own raw materials: refining agents, tanks, barrels, bricks. It produced lamps for sale and marketed them. The Company's labour force numbered 1,500 men. If you take it that each of these men had a wife and two or three children to support, then Young's Company (the foundation stone for which was laid by David Livingstone) had around 5,000/6,000 people dependent on it for their livelihood.

This huge and sudden expansion, this oil mania, could not last. Workers became scarce and so wages went up. There was an oil glut and so prices fell, and then many companies, especially the smaller ones, went out of business. By 1868, there were so many oil works on the market that they all could not find a buyer. Between 1864 and 1870, 30 firms went bust and, to compound the difficulties, the American Civil War ended in 1866 and so American oil began to enter Britain again in competition with domestic supplies. Thus we can see the early pattern of the shale oil industry: a slow start when Paraffin Young monopolised the industry; a sudden surge in the mid-1860s when his monopoly ended, leading to over-production, a slump in prices, closure of many oil works, and a levelling off to a more sensible number of companies from about 1870 onwards.

A quick resume of Paraffin Young before we move on: he bought the estate and house of Limefield at Polbeth around 1860 and lived there until 1867, when he bought the estate of Kelly, overlooking the Firth of Clyde. He died in 1883, wealthy, respected and full of honours, and he was buried at Inverkip.

The next 40 or 50 years – from about 1870 till about the end of the First World War in 1918 – was the optimum period for the shale industry. West Lothian was then the source of many products that were not available from anywhere else in the UK. Output averaged around three million tons of oil a year, and at its peak during the first 20 years of this century, 10,000 were directly employed by the industry. Again, if we take account of wives and children, about 40,000 (or a quarter of West Lothian's total population) was dependent on the industry.

In order to promote Scottish Oil in the face of American and Middle East competition, the main oil companies formed a joint marketing board, whose main success was to persuade the British Navy to change over from coal to oil in 1914. The main advantages of oil to the Navy included the fact that men did not have to be taken from active fighting duties during battle in order to stoke coal into the furnaces, and a ship could go for longer on oil than on coal before it needed refuelling.

By the time of the First World War, the number of oil companies had been reduced by closures and mergers to just five large ones, and

West Lothian Oil Company, 1883–1892. Staff photograph, c. 1890.
photo: William Marjoriebanks

at the end of the War, in order to eliminate wasteful domestic competition, they combined to form Scottish Oils, whose technical headquarters was at Middleton Hall at Uphall. The Companies were: Pumpherston, Broxburn and Oakbank Oil Companies, Young's Paraffin Light and Mineral Oil Company, James Ross & Co. and Philpstoun Oil Works Ltd.. The houses around Middleton Hall were built as a kind of garden city suburb for the company's managerial and white collar workers.

A 'rationalisation' of works followed. Additional and unnecessary works were closed and the workforce was cut from between 10,000 to 8,000 men. Britain, and in fact the world, was entering upon the slump of the 1920s–30s. The average wage per shift in 1920 was 19 shillings. By the following August, it had been cut to just 10 shillings per shift. Times were hard for all industries. In 1925, a miner's strike led to a lockout of the shale miners because there was no coal to fuel the retorts. Broxburn oil works, just north of the town. Never re-opened after closure, nor did Tarbrax oil works and shale mines. In all, one third of all works and mines closed down. Thereafter, competition for jobs because of all the redundancies meant that the oil companies could further reduce wages. Times were hard indeed.

In 1925, the Admiralty contract for the supply of oil to the Royal Navy ships was lost. The government had removed its war-time controls over foreign oil imports, and supplies of cheap oil were flooding in from the United States and the Middle East. In 1932, Philpstoun Oil Works closed, as did the Oakbank Oil Works and Refinery and Seafield Oil Works; and the industry went on to a three weeks on, one week off rota. in order to avoid further lay-offs.

From 1921, some foresaw and feared the end of the shale oil industry because of cheaper foreign oils. During the Second World War, when foreign oil was hard to ship in, domestic oil was again realised to be a valuable resource. Production of oil went up and, in a surge of confidence, new shale mines were opened at West Calder, Broxburn and Totley Wells near Winchburgh. Abandoned mines were re-opened at Philpstoun. and a new crude oil works opened at Westwood near West Calder in 1941. And, best of all, wages increased, and a week's paid holiday was introduced in 1939. But this was, nevertheless, the beginning of the end.

In 1945, Walter Nellies, General Secretary of the National Union of Shaleminers and Oil Workers, and for many years a Bathgate Town Councillor, wrote: exemption from excise duty must continue for many years to come, otherwise the industry would cease to exist as a source of oil. He meant that the government must continue to keep Scottish oil cheaper by exempting it from tax so that it could compete with imported oil on more or less equal terms. In the same year, Nellies led a delegation to the government to plead for the shale oil industry to be saved. The minister responsible was Manny Shinwell, and there was a sad irony in this, because in 1924 it was Shinwell who, as MP for West Lothian, led a similar deputation of shale workers to ask the government of the day for help for the shale industry. When Shinwell was approached as Minister for Fuel, he turned them down. George Garson's book, 'No Idle Bread', records (p6–7) how they were seen for less than half an hour and offered neither hope nor a cup of tea!

Over 100 shale mines had been in operation at one time or another, the average lifespan of a mine before it was worked out or abandoned being about five years. From 1910–1920, there were about 45 mines in operation at any one time. By 1926, there were only 13 shale mines in operation, and this remained the average number until the 1960s. The end thus came abruptly when the government withdrew its protection, so that domestic oil prices could not compete with foreign oil. The final closures came in 1963, when there was only 1,000 men still employed in the industry, many of whom found work in British Leyland at Bathgate and the new industries of Livingston New Town. The life-span of the shale oil industry had thus been a mere 113 years.

I will only make a couple of points about the technical side of the industry: shale is a laminated clay deposit, and very hard; it is usually dark brown or black and shiny, rather like brittle treacle toffee. Once it has been processed, its waste product – blaes – has the distinctive pinky-red colour of the shale bings. Coal is used to heat the retorts that melt the oil out of the shale, so that the two industries, coal and shale, were always to some extent inter-dependent.

Shale sounds to me an environmentally-friendly sort of industry, one book stating that: scarcely anything is ever classified as a waste produce in an oil refinery. The oil was re-cycled time and time again to extract different products from it, such as the following: petrol (marketed under the name Scotch), naphtha, fuel oil, lamp oil, lubricating oil, paraffin wax, candles, ammonium sulphate, paraffin coke, smokeless fuel, and bricks. Other items which contained products of the shale industry include paints, oil cloth, waxed paper, rubber, tapers, preservatives, insulating materials and safety devices. And since you can use up the shale bings for road bottoming, shale might well be considered one of the 'greenest' of heavy industries.

The effects of the shale oil industry on one community, Broxburn, was mentioned earlier but large areas of West and Mid Lothian were affected. The industry's two main centres were West Calder and

Broxburn, and both of these greatly expanded. Whole new communities came into existence, built by the oil companies to attract workers into the area, and house them. For example, there were villages at Oakbank, Westerton and Kingscavil near Linlithgow, which have almost totally disappeared. Oakbank's bowling green survives, and Westerton's school, which is now the Astor Motel, but those are the sad remains of once thriving communities. Once the shale mine or works that they depended on closed down, their fate was scaled.

This was a time when West Lothian's population changed drastically – not just in size but in origin. The names to be found in West Lothian before the middle of the 19th century are local, lowland Scottish names, almost 100 per cent Protestant. The oil industry growth, together with coal, steel and all the other then growing industries, attracted many immigrant workers – Highlanders cleared from their glens to make way for sheep, and very many Irish. Ireland had been afflicted with a series of hardships, culminating in their dreadful potato famine of the 1840s. Irish people were arriving in their hundreds of thousands at Liverpool and Glasgow docks, desperate for work, for a means of livelihood for themselves and their families. West Lothian's new and growing industries attracted many of them. Towards the end of the century, it became common for young single Irishmen to come over to West Lothian and work for a few years, or even a single summer season, in the shale mines, in order to make some money before marrying and settling down again in Ireland. Needless to say, a good many married and settled here instead.

One of these men. Patrick Gallagher, worked in the shale mines at Niddry around the 1890s and lodged in the Randy Raws at Uphall Station, where the beds were said to be never empty long enough to get cold. So impressed was he with the local Co-op store system that he introduced the Co-operative movement into Ireland when he returned there. He wrote his autobiography – Paddy the Cope – which is recommended as a fascinating and often amusing read.

The influx of Irish led to the revival of Roman Catholicism in West Lothian, which had almost completely died out since the Reformation. In 1843, there were three Roman Catholic families in Bathgate; by the mid-1850s they were able to build their own church and support their own priest.

Thus, in the course of less than half a century, West Lothian was transformed from a small, rural, homogeneous population to a growing, industrial, 'multi-ethnic' one. It may have been an exciting time of opportunity for the young, but it would also have been, undoubtedly, a bewildering and perhaps alarming experience for the more elderly.

And so, in closing, a final word about the miners, oil workers and their families. What sort of lives did they lead at work and at home?

As previously stated, shale is a very hard material and so it was generally mined by blasting. The miners had to supply their own gunpowder and tools out of their wages. Gunpowder was manufactured locally at Camilty Mill near Harburn, and sold through the local Co-operative stores at 6-1/2d a pound. People bought it in 50 lb quantities and stored it generally in the press, or under the bed. Women filled their men's powder tins each morning ready for the day's work.

In the early days, circulation of air in the mines was produced by a furnace at the bottom of the upcast shaft, but after the terrible disaster at Starlaw shale mine in the 1860s – when eight men died because the timber lining of the shaft caught fire – mechanical fans were introduced. The greatest hazards were the fumes following blasting, and charges which failed to explode. In both cases, you were supposed to wait for a set number of minutes in order to let the fumes clear, or ensure that the charge wasn't going to explode late. But inevitably, being paid by the ton, miner's were impatient to get on, and so accidents sometimes occurred. Other fairly frequent injuries were caused by falls of the roof, or the derailment or brake failure of hutches carrying shale to the surface. The worst ever disaster in a shale mine was the Burngrange Disaster in 1947, when 15 men died after a fire underground and a seepage of gas. But this, though tragic, was not a common danger in shale mines. Fires were much commoner in coal mines because of firedamp.

What about the rest of their lives – how did they live when not at work? What sort of housing did they live in? Well, almost all of them lived in rented accommodation, either private or, more commonly, company houses. You can still see good examples of miner's rows at Winchburgh and at Pumpherston. Most of the rows were built after 1860, so had to conform to some early government legislation on housing which ensured certain basic standards of space and decency. Few of us would choose to live in them today as they were then. Most had a room and kitchen, a scullery and an outside privy. In the early years of this century, most companies installed flush toilets, but I think that none ever had proper baths. Pithead baths began to be installed in most pits only after the Second World War, so practically every miner's wife's daily duty included getting out the tin bath, heating the water and scrubbing her man's back. Certain areas were reckoned to have better or worse housing than others. Tarbrax was thought to be slightly superior as most houses had inside flush toilets at an early date. The Old Town in Broxburn, and the Happy Land in West Calder, were renowned for their poverty.

Overcrowding was very common. Large families were brought up three or four to a bed. Taking in lodgers was a common way of raising a little more income. Widows, especially, turned to this as a means of livelihood, and might house six, seven or even eight lodgers. sleeping in two shifts, the night shift getting into the beds the day shift were rising from. For all that, shale areas were slightly better off than coal mining areas. one survey proved Armadale, a coal mining area, to be the second worst-housed town in Scotland – the worst being Kilsyth. 55 per cent of the population of Armadale lived in two-roomed houses and 21 per cent in single ends.

Until the 1920s, the shale workers were on average slightly better off than the average working man. A provident shale worker with a thrifty wife had a chance of maybe laying something by for the future, perhaps even buying his own house, or some other property which could be let to bring in some income. From 1921, however, the industry was in terminal decline, and wages fell steadily although hours decreased to a more reasonable level. Until the end of the First World War, the average working hours for oil workers was up to 10–12 hours a day. After the War, the usual was an eight hour day, and a week's paid holiday was introduced only on the eve of the Second World War.

With low wages, overcrowding, long hours and poor sanitation, health could not be expected to be very good, though studies have shown that it was in general no worse than any comparable working population of the time. The oil companies took a paternal attitude to their workers' health. Young's Company provided a company doctor, while others deducted 1d a week from wages to provide free health care. So in fact shale workers enjoyed better health care than most of the rest of the working population. As well as that, many miners and oil workers were members of Friendly Societies, such as the Ancient Order of Foresters or the Shepherds, the Oddfellows, the Gardeners or the Rechabites (which was tea-total). These operated as a sort of insurance scheme against ill health or injury, and ensured that a small amount of money would be given for at least the first few weeks absence from work.

And, last of all, a few words about the lot of the women who married into the shale industry. To me, their lives read like a fate worse than death: a constant struggle against poverty, to make ends meet. The man's concern was to earn wages: it was the woman's task to spread the money thin enough to pay the rent, food, clothes, fuel and everything else. It was even worse if your husband drank or was thriftless and you never got his full pay packet.

Large families were the norm well into the 20th century. In 1931,

West Lothian had the highest overall fertility in Great Britain, and the 8th highest marital fertility – which means they were among the largest families in the country. This was probably as a result of these mining communities being fairly conservative, where married women did not work; they stayed at home and raised their families. Large families were both a cause and a consequence of poverty. A large family ensured a good number of wage earners at least until they married and set up their own homes. But too many mouths to feed also caused poverty while the children were young.

And with so few labour-saving devices, all the women's work was backbreaking labour: everything needed to be scrubbed – floors, chairs, tables, steps; the grate had to be blackleaded and polished, while washing day sounds like absolute hell. You had to make your own rugs, you knitted the family's socks and jerseys, you turned your sheets sides to the middle; everything was hard labour. And if you had a family working different shifts, you had to provide meals at different times; you had to dry the miners' clothes, clean his boots, make up his piece box, heat the water for his bath – neverending toil. And at the end of the day, there was virtually no social life for women except maybe a walk up the bings with the weans, or a blether with the neighbours – the men had their pubs, and quoits and bowling, and working men's institutes, but no respectable woman could be seen gallivanting about, and certainly not entering a pub.

Taken all in all, older people may lament the loss of the mines, the mining communities, the sense of neighbourliness and community, but would anyone today really choose to return to the life of the shale workers during their 113 years of existence?

But, of course, it is a history to take pride in. It was an industry which had made itself efficient, and was productive, had skilled engineers, miners and workers, and was only killed off by foreign competition, international trade, and a government too committed to a free market economy. This is a particularly topical subject, given the news lately about the closure of the majority of Britain's mines – a viable industry going to the wall because of cheap foreign competition and lack of government support. Perhaps governments would do well to consider the lessons of the past before deciding the future?

Pumpherston Oil Company oil tanker, c. 1920
photo: West Lothian History & Amenity Society

Advertising poster for James Ross & Co, Philpstoun Oil Works

WEST LOTHIAN COURIER – OCTOBER 13, 1978

TRIBUTE TO KIRKTON LAD –
FORMER COURIER EDITOR BOB FINDLAY

Save for the occasional holiday or participation and attendance at sports meetings, Bob Findlay seldom ventured out in thought or deed from his beloved West Lothian. He was always acutely aware of what was going on throughout the county, why it was happening and who and what was responsible. He celebrated and acclaimed the achievements of the natives as his own and unhesitatingly condemned those who he considered had soiled its name; he was a West Lothian nationalist.

A native of Winchburgh, Bob was reared by his grandparents. By thirteen he was dux of the local school and a promising athlete, by fourteen he was keeping the house and attending the water pumps in the mine.

He often recalled that the 'Company' was very good to him at this time in that they gave him the only job he could possibly do which carried a wage compatible with his adult responsibility.

The pumps had to be manned seven days a week and so it was common for Bob to be the only person in the darkness. Nevertheless he was seldom alone. Jack London, Scott Dickens etc. were his constant companions. He resolved to emulate his boyhood hero 'Martin Eden' by becoming a writer; he learnt shorthand by the light of his lamp.

Right from the beginning he was fascinated by character and social relationship rather than philosophy and politics. The result was that in later years he was content to comment rather than prescribe.

Built like the side of a house he is still remembered by his peers throughout the county as a hard rampaging centre with the

'Nitten Rangers and Winchburgh Albion'. He was determined and fast rather than skilful.

His stories of the period, he was a renowned pub storyteller, tended to recount the big pivots he had rendered unconscious rather than goals scored.

The other great love of his youth was athletics. He had a national reputation as a sprinter with Shettleston Harriers. It was generally agreed that he could have taken the Powderhall Sprint if family 'principle' had not intervened. Indeed, he was the stable trial horse of many who did.

When he was past the stage of playing he served first Winchburgh Albion and then the West Lothian Juvenile Association as secretary for many years. A great believer in discipline, he instituted a system of punishment for field offences automatically imposed on the basis of the referee's report. He never did have much time for extenuating circumstances!

An ardent admirer of Burns, especially his love songs, Bob was very active in the Burns Federation and the running of the 'Lea Rigg'.

He entered journalism as local correspondent of the Gazette and the People's Journal etc. In 1947 he was offered the job of reporter in Broxburn for the Courier at £2 a week less than his miner's wage and twice the hours. His neighbour Dough Quale, has a spare pair of moleskins within the hour!

Although this marked the end of his direct dependence on Scottish Oils, he continued as a loyal and devoted servant the rest of his days. He took every opportunity to praise a company he considered an exemplary employer, factor and provider of social and recreational facilities. Under a host of bylines in the national press he wrote numerous articles on the history, development and background of a system which many others saw as more despotic than benevolent. Critics tended to be outsiders however, and probably Bob's sentiments were roughly those of the employees generally.

At Broxburn he relished his work as commentator as much as reporter. There was apparently a human interest story under every flagstone in Greendykes Road.

People who had never given themselves a second thought became household names while some of those who had never questioned their significance got less than reassurance.

Controversy raged in the columns on a number of different issues at different times and with careful nursing, some lasted for months on end. With his keen wit, and the privilege of summing up and determining when the issue was closed, Bob was seldom seen to be the loser!

In a bid to regain the balance of the paper which many still see as the 'Bathgate Courier', Bob moved to the head office as Chief reporter in 1953 and then shortly afterwards was made editor.

Many of the older Bathgate folk know him best as Kirkton Lad in his 'Bathgate Brevities,' a collection of parables, homilies and Fairway gossip. It was in this column that he revealed his greatest talent – the common touch.

This ability to appreciate the sentiments, aspirations and consciousness of people who appeared to others as merely dour was well demonstrated in the obituaries of the prominent and the not so prominent.

He considered the task of revealing the true worth and merit of the self-effacing his most important responsibility. It was a service much appreciated by those left behind.

Football was his passion rather than mere interest and he was not averse to using the sports pages to advance his particular favourites of the time. He was outrageously biased towards teams which he and his sons were involved in, but since they were involved with so many over the years, most clubs got some share of the limelight sometime.

An astute judge of the game, he enjoyed nothing more than recounting the feats and personalities of the junior world which he had made into household names. It made very enjoyable reading and it captivated the vitality and drama of the local scene.

Bob was intensely involved and interested in all aspects of local affairs and the positions he adopted was consistent with his basic belief in social democracy and Scottish Oils type paternalism. He was probably Tam Dalyell's most ardent supporter.

One issue which caused tremendous controversy and passion throughout Bob's editorship was educational segregation. He chose to ignore the strong feelings and resentments engendered in his determination to heal a society divided against itself. He was not particularly interested in any other aspect of religion. The Masonic Lodge and the Orange Order were also condemned on occasions as equally divisive.

Over three years ago Bob contracted a debilitating kidney condition and was unfit to carry on working although he did manage to contribute the occasional obituary, historical article and other more contentious items.

Earlier this year he suffered a stroke and was very slowly getting over it when he suffered another which brought his struggle to an end

He is survived by his strong wee wife, Isa, five sons who would have marched to hell for him and the grandchildren he loved so much.

Several years ago a local correspondent produced a lengthy piece for Bob's perusal on a 'worthy' who has recently moved to Livingston from Glasgow. It was pitched into the waste paper basket with the comment: 'How the hell can a man from Glasgow be a Livingston worthy. He doesn't know the area'.

The correspondent had not appreciated the fact that 'worthy' was the highest accolade the Courier could bestow. It was seen to mean someone who encompassed the flavour and values of a particular locality.

Bob Findlay was a West Lothian worthy.

Alan Findlay

Unmapped Workings

Born in Threemiletown in 1911, my father was brought up in near-by Winchburgh by his paternal grandparents, so becoming the third generation of his family to work in the shalemines. His parents did not marry and, so the story goes, his grand parents took him to live with them towards the end of the Great War following the death of their youngest son, his uncle George, who was killed serving with the 1st/4th Battalion Royal Scots in 1917.

My father's grandfather and namesake, Robert, was the Crowpicker (or Shale Inspector) at Duddingston mine, near Winchburgh, which my father went down when he left school at the age of fourteen – as most youngsters then did. He was a bright boy, but he turned down a scholarship to the Royal High School in Edinburgh fearing that his origins, despite the conceits of his family, would have made his time there quite miserable.

His grandfather died in 1927, and 'The Company', Scottish Oils, gave my father the only job a boy could do to earn an adult wage – minding the pumps at nights and weekends – thus allowing him to, quite literally, 'keep the house' for himself and his grandmother. It also allowed him time to read some of the most popular authors of the day – Patrick MaGill *Children of the Dead-End* and Jack London *People of the Abyss* are some that he spoke of. His father, also Robert, and his Uncle John, both lived in the same village and worked in the same mine, his father being an underground foreman at Duddingston No 3 Mine, and his Uncle John its clerk. The family first came to Winchburgh in 1905 from West Calder about the time that the Oakbank Oil Company built the village for the miners [in 1902] and the first all-electric oil works – the Niddry Castle.

My father worked as a shaleminer for over 20 years, becoming in 1942 the local news correspondent for Winchburgh for the *West Lothian Courier*. This happened, apparently, when it was discovered that he had been writing the reports rather than the local barber, who was the paper's official correspondent. In 1947, he was taken on as a staff reporter at the Broxburn office, moving to the main office in Bathgate as Chief Reporter in 1953, and becoming Editor in 1962. He retired in poor health in 1976, and died in 1978 before he could fulfil his long-held intention of writing a book on the shale industry and its people – characters – as he would have said. We can be sure that it would have provided many colourful insights into a generation and culture that used the term 'hard work' for what today most would regard as falling not far short of slave labour.

My father wrote extensively about shale and its people in his own

My father: Bob Findlay –
a journalist in the 1950s

distinctive style for over 35 years in the pages of the local newspaper in countless articles, reports, obituaries, comments and editorials – covering gala-days, Burns Suppers, Co-op and Council meetings, education, housing, courts, politics, industry, brassbands, football, cup-ties, Powderhall sprints, religion, police, masonic meetings, amateur dramatics, local history and local talking-points – some of which he would fuel occasionally by writing anonymously to himself – ie. 'Letters To The Editor' – ('name and address supplied'!).

He knew the area and readership well enough, of course, to judge what would interest or annoy them, and he was quite prepared to express the views of others – as he had done a few years earlier in Winchburgh when he was much called on by other young miners to write love-letters on their behalf to their girl friends. He also had a remarkable memory for particular matters and would claim, for example, that he could express the views of councillors and the like more effectively than they – which may suggest the extent to which his writing was often regarded as encompassing the essential values and concerns of the local community. His own remarks on the matter were conveyed to me in a letter just before his death in 1978:

> The Burns season is with us again. In my memory, the best Burns orator I ever heard was a man named Herbert Down, a professional elocutionist from Edinburgh. I went along one night in Broxburn to report him deliver the Immortal Memory at a Masonic Burns Supper. He was one of the fastest speakers ever I encountered. My shorthand just couldn't cope so I threw aside my notebook and listened enthralled. I have heard dozens of Burns orators who could quote Burns' work by the yard. Down was the only speaker who assayed Burns from the point of view of the latter's correspondence, quoting copiously as he went.
>
> After the 'Courier' report appeared I got a letter from Down congratulating me on the speed of my shorthand! I wrote back admitting that it was done from memory. He wrote again to say he found what I had told astonishing. Much of my report was verbatim. The 'Scotsman' reporter had told him that he just couldn't keep up with him. Actually, I could see nothing remarkable in it. His delivery, theme and thought processes were crystal clear and I had no difficulty at all in recording and repeating them.

I once astonished J.B. George, the Winchburgh headmaster, when I was
late in going for a report on the annual school prize-giving at which the
guest of honour was local councillor Wattie Scott. George said he
would give me three points, these constituting the main themes of the
speech. After my report had appeared, George asked me if I had seen
Scott to get a copy of his speech and was amazed to hear that I hadn't.
I told him that I knew Scott so well that if I knew the occasion and the
general gist of Scott's remarks I could anticipate what he would say.
The same was true of a lot of the public figures I had to deal with. I
used to ring up Provosts, Convenors etc repeatedly for New Year mes-
sages etc. As often as not they would tell me to go ahead and write the
speech myself. Later they would congratulate me on the fine speech
they had made!

My father's journalism, along with certain aspects of his family history, may thus serve to offer commentary on wider cultural themes
while still remaining true to the original purpose of telling the story
of shale through the voices of shaleworkers themselves. There can be
little doubt that my father cherished the shale communities and
sought always to project an image of them which stressed, perhaps
over-optimistically, their benevolent nature, though he also criticised
strongly their more obvious divisions – such as segregated education
– which he saw as buttressing sectarianism. He would no doubt have
agreed with William McIlvanney's denunciation of the pervasive nature
of sectarianism, especially in communities bordering West Lothian –
'as difficult to locate exactly as the abandoned and often unmapped
mine-workings that comb the area.'[1] Unnecessary industrial conflict
was likewise condemned, a view undoubtedly widely shared in the
shalefield. West Lothian was regarded, and often regaled by him, as
one large cohesive community – which might be seen in an article he
wrote in 1959 lamenting shale's imminent demise. It reveals his views
on the importance of an industry which was going to the wall and,
with it, a set of values he considered nothing short of exemplary:

The Shale Oil Industry: A Tribute and a Plea

Speaking at the Winchburgh Learigg
Burns Club annual supper, Mr R. Findlay
of the *West Lothian Courier*, said to an
audience mainly comprising men directly
or indirectly depending on the shale oil
industry for their living –

'I know of no industry or class of people
less deserving of the worries, hardships and
uncertainties of trade depression and
unemployment than the shale oil industry
and the people who live by it. Consider
your record. No strike or major industrial
dispute in the industry in all of thirty years

to my knowledge. Throughout two World
Wars and the no less uncertain years of
peace, employers and employees have established a record of loyalty, patriotism and
sensible industrial relationship which has
been at the same time an example and an
admonition to other industries, particularly
the coal mining industry.

'Socially too, your record has been good.
I believe that in some respects in this area
you anticipated and beat to the punch by
several generations, the Welfare State. There
is among shale oil people a social and com-

munity consciousness unsurpassed and probably unequalled in the whole of the country. I believe that the real tragedy of the decline of shale oil is not the loss of jobs – such excellent workmen will get others – but the breaking up, the slow but sure disintegration of a magnificent labour force and its attendant communities, the product of generations.

'Your industry does not seek charity. It merely seeks relief from a tax which is strangling it. When I think of the millions that have been poured out subsidising coal mining and other industries, it seems to me that the loss to the Treasury entailed by granting the tax relief shale oil seeks would be a small price to pay for the preservation of so much that is good, and the restoration of security and a measure of prosperity to an industry and people who have so richly earned it.'[2]

Here is the voice of the respectable working class and its preoccupations – the continuities of class, poverty, communality and cooperation – handed down from the middle of last century to my father, the third generation of his family to become a shale miner.

The melting pot of 'the pits' rather than the Labour Party was probably my father's most formative experience, a place where self-educated workers could discuss class politics as the obvious answer to an exploitation all had to endure – whether or not you were employed and 'respectable', had the 'arse out of your breeks', or were Catholic or Protestant. I believe my father understood this very well. He spoke of seeing 'paupers' wearing distinctive clothing working in the fields round about Linlithgow. Poverty was visible everywhere, while the work-house remained a spectre at the feast, such as it was, a spur to the kind of brute labour it was sometimes felt a privilege to have: Scotland in the 1920s.

Of his family, and following the death of his grandfather, the most dominant figure in my father's youth and early life was probably his Uncle John. There may have been important political and temperamental differences between them, my father being far more proletarian and Rabelaisian in outlook and design, but they shared many similar interests and activities. Both were founder members of the Learigg Burns Club (in 1930), my father acting as its Secretary for a few years and his Uncle John as its occasional Chairman. Both were keen on local history and folk-lore and might well have written books on the shale industry.[3] Both were in their chosen fields exemplary 'committee men' and administrators – my father in district juvenile football circles and the local Labour Party [he was local Secretary at the 1945 election of the Labour Government] – while his Uncle John held posts in the Co-operative Movement, Rechabites and so on. And, of course, both were strong minded individualists who offered no sanctuary to those foolish or unfortunate enough to get caught breaking 'the rules', though the creative application of 'the rule-book' was as prized as any art form.

Although my father was a good deal more proletarian and secular in outlook than the strict kirk and masonic pre-dispositions of his

The Findlay Family from left: Mary, Robert (Shale Inspector), Agnes, George, William, Uncle John, Elizabeth, Robert (my father's father), c. 1908

family, moral corruption and contamination were key concerns for both 'the brethern' and 'the brothers', so to speak, which fitted well with one of the defining features of the culture and the times – the achievement and preservation of 'respectability'. My older brothers can recall growing up in Winchburgh in the 1940s, for example, and knowing who it was, and who it was not, permissible to play with – which had nothing to do with 'race' or 'religion' as such. Those to be avoided were the idle, card-playing, dog-racing, pitch-and-toss fraternity of the poor, and their children. My father thus had as few compunctions as his family regarding the making of moral judgements concerning 'character' – who had it; who hadn't it; and who hadn't a hope in Hell of getting it.

So let none of this be overlooked when considering the case of my father's Uncle John, the clerk at Duddingston mine, who figures in one of the oral histories – apparently worsted in a verbal exchange with an old Irish miner whose rate he was trying to cut. Uncle John was a staunch Rechabite (tea-totaller) and strongly provident of 'the Company's' money, and he would not have been all that keen to hand over additional funds for the procuring of, by his way of it, the demon drink. Some needed saving, even from themselves: my father's Uncle John.

Minjy: my father's uncle John
William: drawer, born 1914, Winchburgh

'Some of the old boys would owe half their pay in the pub.
Aye.
Oh aye.
You used to get tick in the pub at the time.
Not that I ever got tick in the pub.
I knew them that had.
It was most of the old Irishmen.
They were all mostly old guys that came over,
during the hard times in Ireland.
As it was,
they started here.
But they were hardy boys,
by jove!
They were still working,
some of them,
well after they were sixty-five,
in the mines.
Oh aye.
They were hard workers.
Of course,
they were hard drinkers.
That's why they were hard workers.
Aye.
They lived hard.
And played hard.
And lived long.
There were some good long livers among the whole lot of them,
actually.
They worked hard all their days.
All the days that I knew them.

Anyway,

about the John Findlay case in the old mine.
That was over in the Duddingston mine.
Aye.
He was actually a clerk,
a clerk above the mine,
but he took it into his head,
that he was a manager!
And this old boy,
that was a labourer on the surface,

there was some trouble in the mine
– old bricks or something –
and this John Findlay says to him,'
          'Is that all you've done, Jock?'

'Aye, that's all that I've got done.
But why? – he says,'
          'I could have done more myself, he says.'

'Well, he says,
          you're the man for the bloody job!'

That was old Jock McLeary.
And an old worthy miner too.
But he had been off.
He had been retired out of the mines to the surface,
by this time.
But there were some quite worthy ones too,
right enough.
But, oh,
that Jock Findlay.
He thought he was the manager.
Och aye.

And he was minjy too.
He wouldn't give you two ha'pennies for a penny.
Aye.

He was minjy.

When his Uncle John died in 1963, my father listed in his obituary
in the *Courier* the following features:

> President Broxburn Co-operative Society
> Secretary East of Scotland Co-operative District Council
> Secretary of the Co-operative Wages Board
> District Chief Ruler Independent Order of Rechabites
> Past Master of Lodge Kirkliston-Maitland
> Treasurer Learigg (Winchburgh) Burns Club
> Founding Committee Winchburgh Bowling Club
> Member of two Amateur Dramatic Societies
> Local Historian
> Uncompromising in Public Life
> An Austere Idealist
> Brilliant Conversationalist[4]

Uncle John stares out of old photographs with Calvinist certainty, a
figure simultaneously impressive and oppressive, altogether formidable.

If one were to substitute the Labour Party and Local Football for the Rechabites and the Masons in the above list, you would probably have my father. The bit about 'uncompromising' seems to ring true of them both: family legend has it that his Uncle John tried to have him banned from attending Co-op meetings for writing reports in the paper which were critical of 'The Society'.

And I can hear my father laughing yet.

He might well have laughed too at the poem about the Co-op 'Special Meeting' in 1887, and the mock-heroic drama surrounding its chairman, Jamie Wark, one of Uncle John's worthy precursors.

Co-op Hall, Greendykes Road, looking north towards the
Albyn Oil Works c. 1914
photo: Douglas McIndoe

West Lothian Courier
Saturday, November 19, 1887

BROXBURN

Assembly – The fourth annual assembly of the Broxburn C.C. took place in the Public Hall on Friday, 11th inst. There were 70 present, and music was supplied by Mr Henderson's band, Mr J Wark acting efficiently as M.C.

The 'COP' Special Meeting

O was ye at the meeting lad?
We had some jolly fun, man;
I mean the 'Cop', an ere I stop
I'll tell ye when begun man.
I to the Public Hall gaed doon,
the seats were packed roon an roon,
And then I saw that very soon

Twad be a row, I'll tell ye how,
And soon I trow, gat up the low,
Aye, jist as shair as daith, man.

Our auld frien' Willie he was there,
And Law an twa three mair, man;
While planted richt, jist in oor sicht,
Was Jamie in the chair, man.
But losh he had an unco job,
I ne'er saw such unruly mob,
It baffles pen tae keep a log,
Or jot it doon, ye micht as soon
Flee owre the moon, in gas balloon!
The thing could ne'er be dune, man.

The miner chiels, the sorry deils,
Had taen it in their heids, man,
On certain grounds, some twenty pounds
Would help tae serve their needs, man.

But lad, it wisnae jist tae be,
For some had smelt a rat ye see,
And swore it wisnae theirs tae gie;
They micht as weel gang tae the deil
As try tae steal, for a lawyer chiel
Had gien them his advice, man.

The Ould Man, eloquent was there,
Frae Niddrie a' the way, man,
A regular trump, when on the stump,
And plenty aye tae say, man.
The chairman now he rose to tax,
'What was the raison he would ax,
His motion thus to treat so lax?
All this and more, and things galore
About the Shtore, he'd towld before,'
And raged an' shuk his heid, man.

'To crown the labours of a loife,
I've come this very noight, man.
To champion the mimbers cause,
And for them I will foight, man!
Is eloquence and all to shlip?
And disappoinments dregs to slip!
O cruel fate! if this the state
Of small or great, or hoary pate,
It's all a moighty chate, man.'

Appeals like this could hardly fail,
They drooned him wi' applause, man,
And backed him up tae haud the grup,
Nor yield in honour's cause, man;
The clamour noo was at its height,
They booed and yelled wi' a' their might;
While some they claimed the chair their right,

Nor doon would sit, but up would get
In frantic fit, tho' sides micht split
Wi' laughter at the scene, man.

The cuts were keen and close between,
They flew like sabre flash, man,
And some that nicht they got a fricht
That didna get a hash, man;
The chairman's hair it stood on en',
But that is naething new ye ken,
Mid taunts and jibes he weel could fen
That none might chase him from his place,
So hard's the case on Jamie's face
That hatchet ne'er could mark, man.

But now a lesson I would teach,
Before I close my song, man,
Tae tell ye a' I heard and saw
Would spin it unco long, man;
There's some sae keen tae catch the vote
Of what will please they sune tak' note,
And then adopt it on the spot,
Sae fond tae claim a liberal name,
The more's the shame, tae spiel tae fame,
Is a' the block-heids want, man.

Of Jamie's cheek they had enough,
And some his ruling spurned, man;
Confusion worse confounded still,
The meeting was adjourned, man;
Disgusted noo wi' what they saw,
The members rose and slipped awa'
Wi' smothered laugh, or loud guffaw
At sich a sicht sae weel they micht,
For grupped ticht they served him richt,
And that's aboot it a', man.

My father's father, Robert, was a more contained character altogether, a strong kirkman, Rechabite, elder and treasurer of Abercorn Free Church, for which he also served as hall-keeper. He was a keen Freemason and a Past Master of Lodge Kirkliston Maitland. He spent all of his working life in the shale mines, retiring as underground foreman at Duddingston Mine No 3, and serving for many years as captain of the local mine-rescue team.[4] He enjoyed football and walking, and often combined the two by walking along the canal bank from Winchburgh to Albion Park Broxburn to watch the local Juniors. He was treasurer of the local Yearly Society, a thrift society which served also as an insurance against loss of wages through sickness in the days before social security and the welfare state. One distraught claimant even fainted on his living-room carpet.

The yearly society's AGM was reported in the Linlithgowshire Gazette on 16 May 1930, as follows:

deposits amounting to £1,734 19s for a membership of 365, composed of 360 males and 5 females. The amount of sick benefit paid to members was £240 19s as compared with £271 12s last year, while the membership last year was 24 less. The amount paid for a single share was £2 10s, the double share being £5 2s 6d, as compared with £2 7s 5d and £5 1s last year.[5]

And every penny a prisoner!

My father's grandfather, also Robert, was a Shale Inspector for the Oakbank Oil Company, a 'Crawpicker', and therefore an agent for the Company who decided how much was shale or dirt (ie. 'craw') – for miners only got paid for the amount of shale they brought to the surface. In his social history of the shale industry up to 1914, John MacKay describes the roles of Crowpicker and Checkweighman:

Shale was weighed at the pithead and also examined for dirt by a shale inspector or 'crow picker'. Various Mine Regulation Acts provided for checks on the weighing apparatus and for the employment of the miners of checkweighmen or justicemen. Until the establishment of the union in 1886 there were no checkweighmen in the shale area. By the middle of 1887, the men's agent was able to report that eight had been appointed and to claim that they 'were the most important event in the history of your union.' Subsequent events afford proof of their importance and of the lengths to which the oil companies would go to prevent their functioning... the level of accuracy in weighing was also a source of disagreement. Up to 1886 most companies weighed hutches to the nearest hundredweight. If a hutch weighed ten hundred-weights and 110 pounds the miner received nothing for the 110 pounds of shale.

After the formation of the union most employers conceded that weights should be taken to the half-hundredweight. There were numerous disputes concerning the activities of 'crow pickers'. On occasion it was alleged that oil companies used the presence of small amounts of dirt to condemn a whole hutch and so avoid paying for the shale, which was then processed in the normal way. Thus, in 1887, 40 hutches were kept off the miners at Stewartfield in one day and 90 per cent of the material went to the retorts. ...

.. The Oakbank Company remained particularly opposed to recognition of the Union. Physical violence was not unknown. In 1888 John Wilson [the miner's agent] was assaulted by the Oakbank mine manager, Robert Calderwood, when attempting to speak to some of the Company's miners. This hostility was maintained throughout the period for in 1906 it was reported that "a fire-hose was freely used at Winchburgh last week to keep Mr Wilson and the miners' officials away from the Oakbank Oil Company's works where they sought to get a vote of the men taken on appointing a checkweigher'.[6]

The prospect exists that my great grandfather might have been on the other end of that hose (thankfully the culprit is not named), as the family removed from West Calder to Winchburgh Main Street, the 'Gaffer's Row', in 1905. He, my grandfather, Robert, and his older brother, Uncle John, are all shown in the photograph earlier on in the chapter and suffice to note, they were all 'Company's Men' – masonic, respectable, Presbyterian – and as such, part of that skilled working class self-improving tradition described by Robert Grey in his study: 'The Labour Aristocracy in Victorian Edinburgh' – as indeed was, and perhaps even more obviously, the miner's agent, Mr John Wilson.

Following Robert Grey's analysis, the labour aristocracy (ie. the skilled working class which emerged out of an amalgam of 'intelligent artisans', trade unionists, co-operators and labourites) which, while they sometimes appeared to ape middle class aspirations and values, were more often reacting simply to the realities of their own material conditions: to the trade cycle and the market-place, which made habits of thrift a matter of necessity rather than ideology; where money was put-bye in good times in anticipation of lay-off; where money was for investment in tools, in your graith, not accumulation; where temperance and sobriety helped distance you and your family from the abyss of poverty and unemployment which always surrounded you; where education promised self-improvement and escape; and where religion and the brotherhood of societies offered intimations of personal salvation even as you were being uprooted, herded together and your individual (not just your 'craft') identity submerged within 'the masses' – a new term denoting a kind of collective working class identity which the more skilled sections rarely felt, and which they were often to resist well into the next century.

These are no doubt complex matters to consider but, as Grey notes: 'it is only in local settings that we can hope to obtain some picture of the formal and informal institutions that shaped the social world of working-class people'.[7] Between 1832–1914, Victorian Scotland voted solidly Liberal and the bulk of the MPs returned to Scottish seats during the period has been described in a recent history as 'undistinguished'. The leading Liberals may have been of Scottish extraction, such as Asquith or Gladstone himself, (and one might also add, in respect of West Lothian, Lord Roseberry), but they were too pre-occupied with British affairs of state to concern themselves much with Scottish matters. This did not seem to bother their local constituencies since these were content to bathe in their reflected glory. Both local associations and the electorate were astoundingly compliant. In 1888, when Keir Hardy, a talented firebrand with well-established mining connections, stood in the Mid-Lanark by-election as an Independent.... he was heckled by miners in Wishaw and managed just 617 votes, 8.3 percent of the poll. Mid-Lanark returned instead a Welsh barrister who lived in Wiltshire – the Liberal candidate.[8]

It is as well to be reminded, therefore, of the social and political culture facing the new movement of organised labour at the turn of the century:

The fact that religion – in its various forms – was etched more sharply on the working-class psyche than the politics of industrial society affected all parties, but none more so than Labour. Until at least 1890 the most important expressions of opinion of the Scottish working classes were not trade unions but trades councils, friendly societies and the Co-operative movement... The most militant groups, such as the miners, were the most fragmented. Although there was a four month strike of the 70,000 strong workforce in 1894, only one miner in 10 belonged to a union: and they were dispersed through eight separate unions.... In retrospect, it can be seen that a battle had already been joined for the loyalties of the working man. But before the First World War, the diverse attractions of freemasonry, friendly societies – such as the Rechabites which had 27,000 members in Lanarkshire alone in 1910 – and the Orange Order were more than holding their own against the growing appeal of organised labour.[9]

This battle for the loyalties of 'the working man', during the last quarter of last century, may be glimpsed by glancing through the columns of local newspapers of the period.

West Lothian Courier –
MARCH 20, 1886

ORANGE SOIREE

An Orange and Protestant soiree was held in the Public Hall, Broxburn on Tuesday the 16th inst. There was a large and enthusiastic meeting. Bro. John Grow, VWD, presided. After the audience had sung the 100th psalm, and the blessing by the Rev. D.M. Henry, MA, the chairman stated that the object of the meeting was one which was well worthy of support, viz. that of defending the Protestant religion. He considered the time had arrived when we ought to show which side we are on. A leading statesman some time ago described the Protestant Church in Ireland as an apas tree that ought to be cut down, and a similar manifesto was issued a few months ago. He was of opinion that the leading statesman was undermining the Constitution. The extension of the franchise had given the Nationalists a power over the men of Ulster, the most loyal men in Ireland, and it was their duty to resist to the utmost any intrigues of Mr Parnell and his agents. Rev. T. Aiton, Livingston, next addressed the meeting. He stated that the large audience, not withstanding the inclemency of the weather, was an evidence of their earnestness in the cause. He did not remember a time when the political horizon of our country looked so dark, as he was of opinion that our greatest statesman, the one who holds the helm at present, had pledged himself to give Home Rule – or what had prevented the Marquis of Hartington from joining Mr Gladstone's Cabinet? However, he had never any confidence in Mr Gladstone and if he intended to spend two hundred millions to buy up the landlords by adding 9d to the income tax, we might soon be on the verge of a revolution, such as we have not yet witnessed.

West Lothian Courier –
APRIL 3, 1886

WEST CALDER

MASONIC CONVERSAZIONE

The lodge of 'Star of Addiewell and West Calder' No. 63, held their seventh annual conversazione in the lodge room on the evening of Tuesday last – Bro. Wright, RWM, presiding. The meeting was opened by the company singing four lines of the 133rd Psalm, after which the RWM pronounced the blessing. A service of tea, in Mr Thomson's usual good style, was then done ample justice to. The RWM, in short address, stated that it was a desirable thing that the brethren of 635 should with their wives and sweethearts meet annually. He regretted that owing to the hurried manner in which the meeting was got up, because of a desire to keep by the old custom of holding it in March, there was less time given for the preparation than what was necessary for a great success. He then dwelt on the tenets of the order, showing that the secrecy of the brotherhood was essentially necessary to its organisation, and provided for it a still more glorious future. During his remarks, he gave some very fine illustrations, showing the ancient origin of the order, tracing it to the earliest ages of Christianity, and said we were then as now under one Father and Master. The order of the masonry, he said, beat down hatred by the love that was taught within its pale. On the battlefield one of our present living generals, being at the mercy of an enemy, he gave indication of the order he belonged to – that he was a freemason – when the enemy, being also a brother, sheathed his sword and passed on.

The address was listened to with great attention. Songs were sung during the evening by Bros. Rankine, Burt, Hendrie and Barrons. A service of fruit caused a short stoppage of the musical part, but on its being resumed some very fine singing followed. Bro. and Mrs Burt gave a very fine duet, and Bro. Barrons gave immense enjoyment to the company by a humorous description of why a Roman Catholic could not be a mason, which was very amusing indeed. The usual votes of thanks, and the singing of 'Auld Lang Syne' brought a very enjoyable treat to a close.

West Lothian Courier –
FEBRUARY 28, 1885

WEST CALDER HALLELUJAH MEETING

We were so much encouraged by your kindness in inserting our last report, that we again launch our barque. We are led to think that good may thus be done when the living voice is silent in the grave. We had the happiness and real profit to hear on Sunday night Mr Faulds one of our local preachers. He took for his subject 'Christ and him Crucified', in which he drew the majestic descriptions of the harmonising simplicity and grandeur of the attributes of Deity. There can be no question as to the great impression he made on his hearers. The style in which he preaches is so picturesque, so glowing, so rich in anecdote and illustration, and almost terrifying in his appeals, as even to hurry the hearer onward by his feelings to conclusions from which his cooler judgement would dissent. He was followed by Miss Tiggart, who, we are sorry to say, is under orders to remove to another part of the vineyard. May she go in the strength of our Master with a fervent jealousy for the honour of God and the integrity of his word.

West Lothian Courier –
APRIL 28, 1888

LETTERS TO THE EDITOR 'NO IRISH NEED APPLY'

Sir, There is a rumour afloat (whether true or false, is not known to deponent), to the effect that inducements are being held out to miners in the West Calder district to go to Broxburn. They are said to be offered higher wages than are being made as a rule in the district, in turn for which they are to work every day; – that is, upset the rule of taking idle days. In many cases, a line is drawn; and in this case also a line is drawn, and it is said to be at 'Irishmen'. No Irishman can be taken among the favoured ones. Can this be true? And, if true, has it the sanction of the managers of Broxburn Oil Works? It is said that it has and with all submission, sir, I think it requires clearing up. There are reasons why the oil and candle company at Broxburn should be charged with boycotting Irish workmen; these I may trouble you with some other time.

Enquirer

LETTERS TO THE EDITOR
'WHY THE UNION DOESN'T SUCCEED AT PUMPHERSTON'

Sir – The reason why Pumpherston miners do not go in for the restriction policy is this. There are two seams here that can be worked by men who are not practical miners, the shale being blown out, instead of holed with the pick; these men are not fit to go and work where pick work is required, so they have to be contented with any wage almost that the Company's overman likes to give them. Of course there are some good miners amongst them, but they are treated differently because they are independent and can shift. There is another class of men who, when the men meet to discuss any grievance that they may have, or when any of the Union officials call a meeting of the men, are always ready to uphold the actions of the manager, or any other officials of the Company. The men referred to are men who do not work half time, and some of them not near that yet they can always spend more money than the men that are working. In fact they are about the fastest living miners that you will meet with. Some of the men are puzzled to know how they get the money to get on with, while others maintain that it costs the Company a good deal to keep up this party, who always manage to make a split amongst the men. Now I, as one that worked for some time in the mines in Pumpherston, am quite sure that as long as the Company are prepared to keep this split party the Union officials may give up Pumpherston for a bad case. I may add that the members of this split party are the very ones that can cry loudest when they are not getting on well, and I am further of opinion that the Company have to pay pretty well for all the dirty work that they get done for them. Could something not be done to make these men known throughout the country? They can not be all their days in Pumpherston, and they ought to be expelled from the society of honest working men – I am &c...

A Union Man

As Robert Grey indicates, the 'labour aristocracy' had their own network of organisations: friendly societies, craft unions, a literary society, a unit of 'volunteers', a church or chapel and often a temperance society. Their values were ones of fierce independence, savings and rigid family morality. They were neat in home and dress. It consisted of men with better pay, more regular earnings, with some control over the pace and organisation of their work, and over entry, usually through apprenticeship, to their occupation. And, of course, they could read.

William Donaldson's study of the local weekly press in late Victorian Scotland makes important points about its range and intended readership, mainly the upper working-lower middle classes:

> Some papers, of course, contained nothing but news. But many had a wider function, aiming to supply a whole range of recreational reading, much of it expressly Scottish in content. They published original writing: poetry, prose fiction, memoirs and reminiscences, biography, history, folklore and popular musicology in enormous quantities. Little of it ever found its way into book form. Above all, they used vernacular Scots, to deal with an unprecedented range of topics in all the major dialects of the language.[10]

To read the *West Lothian Courier* of a century or so ago is to be returned very directly to the days of Empire, when 'The Fall of

Khartoum' and the latest London murder by 'Jack The Ripper' were reported in full column lengths side by side with debates on Home Rule For Ireland and Speeches by Mr Gladstone, trade disputes, Co-operative meetings, Mutual Improvement Societies, Soirees for Rechabites, Hallelujahs, The Orange Order or The Primrose League (Tories), Masonic Conversaziones, Popular Lectures on Marriage, Fauna, African Missionaries, Socialism, Free Trade and Radical Addresses – the latter very often held in Bathgate.

The works of literary figures were frequently reviewed and discussed – 'Burns and Goethe Compared' or a biography of George Elliot – described in a column and a half in newspapers which were at least a foot longer and broader than most modern readers are familiar with. Some of the features noted by Donaldson are also evident in the 19th century *West Lothian Courier* – such as the serialisation of popular fiction, often written in the vernacular. The extent of the literary and 'educational' material the local press then contained is a revelation, voluminous local news coverage comprising direct and very full reporting of talks, meetings, lectures and so on, 'word' pictures taking the place of actual pictures or photographs. Evident too is a scrupulousness for allowing individual opinion to be expressed in a way that the tabloid press of today would not recognise.

William Donaldson considers that during the second half of the 19th century, the newspaper press was the main-stay of Scottish popular culture, not the London dominated all-British bookmarket. That bookmarket would tolerate vernacular Scots only in a diluted form and in a way that satisfied the English reading public's expectations which, by and large, wanted to ignore contemporary Scottish life and character. It was thus left to a new wave of working class papers such as the Dundee based *People's Journal*, described as 'half newspaper, half popular miscellany', and its editor, William Latto, to reflect every aspect of contemporary Scottish life.

Latto wrote in what Donaldson calls 'discursive prose' in a style which was imitated throughout the country. His particular creation, 'Tammas Bodkin', made him the most famous vernacular essayist in Victorian Scotland. 'Tammas', created in 1858–79, is elderly, childless, and married to a headstrong wife called 'Tibbie' with whom he has an affectionate if stormy relationship. Between them they comment on a whole range of contemporary issues as seen by a couple of shrewd well-informed upper-working class Scots[11], in the following manner:

> We are feared for oor road to India, but hoo has it come aboot that we hae sic a deep interest in a road to India? Hoo did we get a haud o' India? Was it no by the sword? Ay, an' aften by the maist ootrageous

proceedin's that were ever seen or heard tell o' in this world! We got India by murder, treachery, an' stouthreif, an' we hae the cheek to blackguard Rooshia for annexin' her neebors! What did we do the ither day in the Sooth of Africa? Did we no annex an independent republic ca'd the Transvaal? O yes, but it was for the guid o' the inhabitants. But that is juist what Rooshia says when she swallows up her neebors, an' she has as guid a richt tae say sae as we have. We winna hear o' Rooshia takin' possession o' Constantinople, because she wad then dominate the entrance to the Black Sea. But, of coorse, there's nae harm in Britain dominatin' the entrance to the Mediterranean by keepin' possession o' Gibralter. We've a perfect richt to clap oorsel's doon at Aden, an' so control the entrance to the Red Sea... But Lordsake, dinna let Rooshia get a grip o' the Dardanelles![12]

The above material might help shed light on a remarkably revealing correspondence which took place in the pages of the *West Lothian Courier* during a shale miners wages dispute in the Broxburn area in 1887, which lasted 21 weeks. 'Sanny McGlaister', a Company hack no doubt, entered the fray just as I was beginning to marvel at the extensive space being allowed every week to the miner's agent, John Wilson – not a man, it must be said, of few words. Mr Wilson advanced the miners' case by adopting the highest possible moral tone, quoting scripture by the yard and castigating the 'masters' as lacking Christian duty, often rounding off with a few quatrains of his own poetry which, unfortunately, was of the most dire earnestness.

The shaleminers union had only been formed the year before, and into the middle of this ferocious propaganda battle steps 'Sanny', a brilliant apologee for all 'honest' miners being led astray by Mr Wilson's 'noo famous apistolary correspondence.. for the purpose o' enlightenin' the whole ceevilised worl' tae the tyranny o' the shale companies.' Sanny thus comes bearing all the hallmarks of the *People's Journal*, not so much the anti-imperialist stance of 'Tammas', more 'Sandy's Notes on the Week' – described by Donaldson as typical of the first generation of vernacular political commentators in his adoption of a speech-based standard reflecting local usage, his sober matter-of-fact style, his moral seriousness, and the informed working-class perspective from which he views the world.[13]

Despite the worthiness of the miners' agent's case, there can be little doubt that Sanny's wielding of what Donaldson calls 'discursive prose' puts him in a different league. And contrary to his earlier protestations, 'Sanny' does indeed become 'ane o' yer legion o' weekly correspondents' taking his place alongside 'Observer', 'A Full Private', 'Working On In Hope', 'Hallelujah Bob' and the rest. These letters strike me as unlikely postcards from another age – vividly inventive, satiric and full of finely judged irony and slander.

West Lothian Courier –
AUGUST 20, 1887

SANNY McGLAISTER ON THE BROXBURN DISPUTE

Mister Editor, – As an auld reader o' the Coorier, will ye kindly aloo me a sma' corner o' yer paper for twa or three remarks I wad like tae mak'. For a wheen months back noo yer columns hiv been fairly inundated wi' literature frae Broxburn, and maistly a' bearin' on the ae subject – the miners' dispute in that district. Noo, I'm ane o' them that's in a sense affected (or afflicted) by this dispute, an' while I hiv nae great desire tae figger as ane o' yer legion o' weekly correspondents, an' as little intention tae propose ony new theory as a solution o' the diffeeculty, still I wid like tae see them that hae raised a' this bizz descend for a wee while frae their seeventh heeven o' romance an' try tae grapple honestly wi' the bizness on han'. An' whit has been the cause o' a' this great storm o' words? Sae far as my memory ser's me, up till aboot a twelvemonth sin', the miners in this district were workin' awa' quite contentedly without ony grievance, or, at onyrate, withoot ony knowledge o' ane. At that time a useless daidlin' body that could naither work nor want cam' tae the place an' set up as a preacher o' releegion, forsooth! Failin' tae mak a leevin' at that he tried his han' at shale howkin', but that wis owre hard wark an' less than ever tae his likin'. He then turned his han' an great abeelities tae the mair congenial occipation o's-teerin' up a discontent amang the men, wha, by formin' theirsel's into a union, wid be able tae redress a' their real an' supposed grievances, dooble their wages, drink whusky or brandy, instead o'common yill, an' gie him a canny job at a guid wage as their agent. But och, hock! 'the best laid schemes o' mice an' men gang aft aglee'. At the same time he fillishly took by the han' oor present secretar' of the M & WLMA, wha was then the first an' only original martyr o' the Broxburn tyrants, an' by sae daein' he sealed his ain doom; for, efter endurin' the infliction of Maister Wilson's eloquence for a very wee while, he fled intae a far country an' has never been heard mair tell o' (here at least). Left in possession o' the field, Mr Wilson lost nae time in settin' tae wark. An' hoo? After he was electit as secretar', to vary the monotony o' his occipation in organization, Mr John began his noo famous apistolary correspondence in your columns for the purpose of enlightenin' the whole ceevilised worl' tae the tyranny o' the shale companies. He writes as if the subject wis o' the maist absorbin national interest, as if the weelfare or doom of Europe dependit on the result, an' as if he was the author o' the only an' original 'Wealth o' nations', an' could only dail't oot tae his fellowmen in penny numbers for fear that a larger doze o' his profound learnin' an' knowledge micht overwhelm their puirer understandin'. Whit connection, I wid like tae ken, is there atween the Apostle Paul (sae often quotit) an' Paddy Flannigan workin' in the Hut mine? Whaur is the connection atween the Pyramids o' Egypt an' hawkin' shale at Broxburn? Or whit has the Queen's Jubilee in common wi' the reduction o' the shale miners' wages? It wid seem tae me that a' this letter writin' is intendit, no sae much tae advance the interests o' the puir miners as tae afford an opportunity for airin' John's profound knowledge o' a' things. He can discoorse maist learnedly an' eloquently on a' subjects ancient an' modern, sacred an' secular, financial, commercial, political, an' moral; but ae thing he seemingly canna dae, an' that is, tae lead the miners oot o' the diffeeculty he has led them intae. He's caused the men tae strike against wages that, even efter the reduction, wid be much higher than the wages in the west, an' wi' the idea o' preservin' his importance an' his place amang them, persuaded the men no tae attempt negotiations wi' their employers without his help, because it took him a' his time tae haud his ain wi' the maisters, an' they wid staun nae chance wi' them! Great criftins!!, tae tell a body o' men that, as a body, they were aboon the average intelligence, an' then almost in the same breath to say, in effect, that they are a drove o' numskulls an' maun submit tae be led by the nose by him! If they ha'e half the intelligence they are credited wi', an' that I believe the majority o' them ha'e, the miners should be able, blin'fold, tae read atween the lines an' see his drift. Noo that he an' his Executive (the latter a mere machine) ha'e got us a' thrown oot o' wark, he wants us tae sit still an' see oor wives an' families starvin', while he's tryin' tae gratify personal vanity an' daein' his oot most tae widen the breach atween us an' the maister. But accordin' tae the newspaper report o' last Monday's meetin' he has little 'method in his madness'. Seein' a' his heroic efforts were seemin'ly tae end in meeserable failure he had got some o' the ministers o' the toon tae mediate wi' the Broxburn managers, an' arrange for a conference atween employers an' miners on Thursday; but feelin' he was thereby bein' set aside, he couldna help launchin' forth intae a violent harangue, coonsellin' the men against resumin' wark seemin'ly on ony terms, an' actually pledgin' them against any compromise. This wid appear tae be an effectual closing o' the door against ony conference, but should that meetin' be held and an agreement come tae, we maybe sure it is withoot the help, an' against the wishes o' John an' his Executive. Its against the interests o' the paid agents tae let us get a peacefu' settlement; oor time o' trouble is their harvest; an' as soon's we're a' workin' again their 'occupation's gone'. But unlest we can change his ways and bring us successfully oot o' oor diffeeculty in a very short time, he had better look oot, for a new prophet has arisen – a second Daniel – or raither a second Johnnie, wha bids fair tae eclipse his tutor and leader.

Bein' a 'knowledgable' man, he is equally able tae ramble in the realms o' poetry, an' bein' also 'A Lover of Liberty', he maun vary his occipation an' employ his spare energies by settin' tae tae redd up a' local grievances.

I'm almost sure 'Lover' stretched a'e point a wee bit aboot the Catholic banner [see below p.127]; and then the rigmarole in his later effusion aboot payin' his afftaxes and the doctor is something terrible: near eneuch tae mak' the angels greet. Nae doot he meant it tae be a crusher, an' so it wis, for it wis a' crushed up in a jumble o' confusion an' impossibility, that it showed plainly that it had been a gey lang time since he had had ony personal experience o' payin' afftaxes. As for needin' the doctor, I think he's hardly past that yet. I doot ye're getting' saft a wee, Lover? At the same time the ignorance he displays is maist peetifu', an' as that may possibly render him a mair deservin' object for support by a certain section o' the men, John I had better guard his position. If ever his shoon get slack, he'll certainly lose them, an' withoot a doot John II will certainly mak' a bold attempt tae fill them.

Noo, sir, I ha'e far exceedit the boonds o' my request an' maun stop, but in concludin' I may say that if ye survive this infliction there may be 'mair tae follow'.

Sanny McGlaister

West Lothian Courier –
AUGUST 27, 1887

THE BROXBURN DISPUTE
JUMP, JIM CROW

Sir – Your correspondent 'Sanny' changed his name for the last three weeks, but now he changes his tune. He is like a certain animal; he will go any road but the right one. He thinks, I suppose, he hit me very hard, but the fact is he never ruffled a hair on my head, and as for John I and John II, I think they can take care of themselves.

I would like to see Mr Sanny taking his stand among his fellow workmen and, with his great eloquence that he is wasting in cold type, use half the same in showing the men the right road and, if possible, lead them to victory or at least to a fair settlement. Then, and not till then, will I say he is an honest man. But no, he will rather skulk about and give a stab in the back to his fellow man when he gets the chance. He is like the dog in the manger; he cannot eat the hay himself, nor won't let the cow who can. I, for one, if I saw my way clear before me and a better road, would stand up in the hall and speak my mind; but my opinion of 'Sanny' is – He cares very little which horse wins the race so long as he is the rider. In his long and very clever letter he never denied one word that I said but contents himself with what he thinks a grand personal attack. Flunky and all as he is the truth hurts him. Then with his usual cowardice, he has recourse to the base weapon, untruth, when he says John the 1st told the men, when they got their wages raised, they could drink whisky and brandy. Now sir, I challenge any man, friend or open foe, to say Mr Wilson ever used these words, but on the contrary he often spoke against drink of any kind; but if he ('Sanny') takes my advice he will write to the Times; that is the paper for him.

A page of the Times the Devil read,
And he cast it aside, Amen;
I'm the father of lies, the Devil said
But I'm d——d if I'll father them

John Wilson

Sir, in my opinion, Mr Wilson deserves credit at all events. The terms of his speeches and letters show that he has counted the consequences, and is prepared, if necessary, to fight for the independence, the honour, and the interests of the working man against whatever odds are brought against him. Whatever may be the official voice and action of the masters, the sympathies of all true lovers of freedom must go out towards Mr Wilson and the gallant little band that has rallied around him. Not unnaturally the conviction has been forced home upon the minds of patriotic workmen that they have quite long enough played the part of waiters upon interested masters favours and dependants at will on there policy: and that since it is lain there is none else that can be trusted, they try to work out their own salvation. We have a good cause and a leader who is willing to put his means and reputation to the touch to win or lose it all and it would not be the first time in history if struggles like these were found to work miracles.

O, shameful time when golden ore
Can make of Scottish men such slaves
That they now suck their kindred's gore,
Obedient to the call of knaves.

I remain, your etc.

A LOVER OF LIBERTY
(i.e. John Wilson)

West Lothian Courier –
SEPTEMBER 24, 1887

THE BROXBURN DISPUTE

Sir, – In last weeks issue Sanny McGiaister, acting as 'Observer's' bottle-holder, brings forward the proof of the 'facts stated by 'Observer'. It seems I have to read the 'Bathgate Pup', dated July 28th, where I will find 'food for reflection, and an Irish bull as well'. When Sanny had the 'bull' shown him, did it not cross his dense intellect that some Irish wag had baited a hook through the columns of the 'Pup' for the special benefit of gudgeons like himself and his gaffer? This, then, is the only evidence Sanny can scrape together – a penny-a-line report in the news column of an obscure rag of a newspaper – and which 'Observer' has not the hardihood to mention, when he can find a tool for that purpose in Sanny McGIaister. On the other hand, we have Mr Wilson's denial that the words spoken would bear anything like the construction put on them, and Sanny will search the correct reports in the West Lothian Courier in vain for a confirmation of his 'Pup's' report; and further, the daily press is silent on the matter, and that at a time when some of them would have been glad off such a titbit; in fact, leaving out those two small matters, the 'Pup's' report, and Sanny McGIaister and Company, we find nobody believes a word of it. Poor Sanny's meal barrel is about empty, and after all the dirty work he has done for the oil company devil a one of them offers to fill it, and he must needs come with a beggarly whine to the miner's executive, showing his rags and pleading for a tammy line. Could you not, sir, open a subscription list for this poor wretch, to keep him out of the workhouse or Larbert Asylum; he is booked for the last named if he keeps up the present pace much longer. Sanny does not forget his usual laboured and second-hand criticism of my language, which criticism smells strongly of the midnight oil, and is as flatulent as the contents of his meal barrel. Most of us are getting rather tired of Sanny's' pooers o' rhetoric', 'perorations', 'laurchin' oot, and the rest of the stale stock he has bought cheap; if he has nothing more original he had better keep them for dumbfoundering his wife and bairns. Sanny also compares me to a certain 'laddie' he knows; his own son and heir for a safe choice although he forgets to say so, and now he will allow me to make my comparison. But to whom can I compare the incomparable Sanny McG.? To a slavering old humbug who, for the last eight weeks, has been churning in the depths of a black heart a diabolical compound of malice, spite, envy, low cunning, and all uncharitableness, and spewing the mixture over the miner's representatives, whose boots he is now prepared to lick if they will only give him a tammy line. Now, Sanny, keep in your natural position, and don't get up on your hind legs and lecture me for my personalities, or chide me for using the only sort of argument that will penetrate your thick head and rhinoceros hide; and lastly, Sanny McGlaister, thou compound of the graces aforementioned, I warn you that if you touch me again with your dirty fingers, or bring your unsavoury carcase within smelling distance, I will visit your vanity with the most terrible crusher it has ever got – viz., completely ignore and boycott you from this time, henceforth, and for evermore, amen. – I am, yours &c,

John Smith, Broxburn

West Lothian Courier –
OCTOBER 1, 1887

THE BROXBURN DISPUTE

Sir, – As I've been workin' again for the last fortnicht, an' my hauns are gey stiff wi' haudin' the pick, I thocht tae gie the pen a rest for a wee, but in decidin' on that I had nae idea I wis tae come under John Smith's lash. Man, he's a scorcher! In readin' his last letter I began tae shake, for it lookit as if I wis in for a broken heid at least, but och, och! it turned oot hes only gaun tae boycott me. Ye ken, that's aboot the best compliment I could wish frae ane o' John Smith's kin'. But its a peety tae, tae see sich a prominent Tory in oor toon adoptin' the Parnellite's creed. He micht at least hae manufactured a new word for hissel' – he has plenty at command. Then he pays me anither compliment in classin' me alang wi' 'Observer', an' the rest o' the teetotalers! &c, &c. Man, I'm rither prood o' that; bit is he no' a wee inconsistent in talkin' o' a bottle holder tae teetotallers? Hooever. tae get on. Let the 'Bathgate Pup' be whatever kin' o' paper it likes, its issue o' July 30th had a pretty full report o' the speeches made by Mr John McGeogh and Mr John Wilson at the miners' meetin' held at Bathgate, an' nane o' the twa o' them has yet denied that it wisna correct. As for the meanin' o' the words used, they're ower plain tae be mista'en, an' nane o' the twa o' them's a Gladstone tae turn aff a sentence wi' half-a-dizzen o' different meanin's. Even John Smith, wi' a' his great abilities, is no' able for that – an' possibly he's regrettin' it.

As for the rest o' his squirilous harrangue, puir as I am, I've mair pride an' self-respeck than lower mysel' tae his level. Its a peety tae see hoo low education has fa'en here, an' it micht be worth the Schule Board's while – seein' they'll be kinna slack the noo onyway – tae consider whether they couldna fa' on some ways an' means o' elevatin' the standard tastes o' the masses an' classes, an' teachers tae, of course, when they're at it. Hooever, that's by the way.

In layin' doon John Smith let me say, sir, seein' he has noo incloodit me in his coterie, that if he canna keep tae the ordinar' style o' argument or comes awa' wi' ony mair o' his newly adoptit Biggar an' Tanner specimens, I may be temptit tae imitate the action o' the Speaker wi' ane o' his new freens lately – pounce upon, aye an' even name the honourable an' gallant gentleman. In my last letter I expressed the hope that we were approachin' a settlement through the mediation of Mr Haldane, but that's a' tae the win's noo, an' little thanks he got for his trouble. On his last visit he had tae submit tae be lectured by McGeogh an' Wilson wi' their impident 'kid-gloved gentry' phrases, an' a' the rest o't, so he's no liking tae bother them in a hurry again. Then we're tae hae Mr Cunninghame Graham some o' thir days, but maybe we're as weel withoot him, for its weel kent there's nae peace or settlements in his programme whaurever he gangs. Hooever, we've a' gotten startit again, except the Broxburn men, an' it'll tak' some gey tall talkin' tae bring us oot in a hurry again. An' efter a' the blether an' bounce we've had, tae creep in at the haill break! Eleven weeks' idle set for naething – an' less than naething, for its thrown mony an honest man intae debt, that he'll no get the better o' for a lang time tae come. An' mair than a' that, jist let me try my haun at a calculation for Mr Wilson's diversion. I'm supposin' that a' this staun's been tae try an' get back the half o' the reduction, or tippence a ton. Weel, allowin' a man tae pit oot three ton a day, or we'll say twa ton tae please the weeds, that wid mean four pence a day, or twa shillin's a week we've been fechtin' for, against that pit doon whit we've lost in the fecht. Twa ton at twenty pence is three an' four pence a day, or a pound a week, an' as we're idle eleven weeks that makes eleven pounds. Supposin' we had gained oor point, an' started on the half reduction only, it wid jist hae taen twa years an' six weeks o' tippences tae male up oor loss, but noo we'll never mak' it up for we've lost it completely, an' left oorsel's waur than ever. Maybe oor executive hae anither way o' coontin', bit it's worth thinkin' aboot onyway. I may hae something mair tae say on that an' ither pairts o' the executive's programme o' proceedin's efter my hauns get soopled up a bit. Meantime I'm aye

Sanny McGiaister

West Lothian Courier –
JANUARY 10, 1887

BROXBURN EXCURSION
(THE CATHOLIC BANNER)

Sir,– Will you allow me to occupy a little of your valuable space with a few remarks on the annual excursion from the town on Friday 15th inst. It is what is called the Catholic trip, but it is supported by all creeds and classes. Well, sir, the day was fine, and the turn-out was large; not less than 500, young and old, journeyed to Musselburgh, and there spent a very pleasant day. They were headed by the Bathgate Brass Band, who deserve the greatest praise from Scotch friends and Irish admirers. The crowd that turned out to see them go away was enormous. Now, sir, the cause of this extra crowd was to see the National Banner of Broxburn, which is reckoned the best in Scotland. This banner was got up in 1882-83, and hoisted for the first time in 1884 despite a heavy down-pour of rain and a strong westerly wind. The first eight men carried it close on four miles, which told well for both their knowledge and pluck, when we consider the storm they had to contend with. We know that the poles were in bad order, but there has been £3.16s expended on the poles since, so the banner as it stands cost £30, and yet they cannot carry it. They tried it in 1885 and failed; tried it in 1886 and failed. So, lo and behold! our dismay on Friday last when we saw no banner; it was left at home. Now, sir, I am not a Catholic, but I paid 5s to help the fund, and some Scotchmen in this town paid £1 and some 15s, and yet they never saw it. This whole state of things was brought about by some twenty Catholics who paid nothing to it; yet they must rule it as they like. I received this statement from one who knows. I am open for contradiction on this point. Sir, I will expose in my next letter some of the dark deeds against labour in this town.

Yours, &c.,
A Lover Of Liberty.
(John Wilson)

WEST LOTHIAN COURIER – APRIL 12, 1922

DEATH OF MR JOHN WILSON,
MINER'S AGENT
A STRIKING PERSONALITY

Although not unexpected, in view of his long continued illness, the announcement of the death of Mr John Wilson, miners' agent, which occurred at his residence, Argyle Place, Portobello, on Monday night, cast a gloom over the whole of the Scottish shale fields, and particularly among the miners in Broxburn and district where his name has been a household word for the past quarter of a century. In the summer of last year, Mr Wilson contracted a chill which threatened to have serious consequences and he found it necessary to take up residence at West Linton, in the hope that the invigorating air would effect a cure. For some time hopes were entertained of a complete recovery, but he suffered from a relapse towards the end of the year and was removed to his home in Portobello. He never regained strength and for some weeks previous to his death, his recovery was regretfully regarded as practically hopeless. By his death the miners of Scotland have lost the services of one who for twenty-five years has been closely identified with their affairs and a prominent figure in the industrial struggles between Labour and Capital, as represented by the miners and the mineworkers, which have marked the period covered by his career. If not actually born in Broxburn, Mr Wilson is claimed as a native of this centre of the shale fields. As a young lad, he was a shale miner in the employment of Broxburn. Oil Company, and up till the age of 23 was actively employed 'at the face'. 'Sufficient for the day is the evil thereo:', but without desiring to rekindle the dying embers of past controversies, in which many of our readers still representing the respective interests of the masters and men were engaged, it may be permissible to recall the circumstances leading up to Mr Wilson's appointment as a miner's agent as showing how great issues in the life of an individual often originate in what are at the time looked upon as comparatively insignificant incidents.

MR WILSON'S EARLY CAREER

As a young man Mr Wilson was of a deeply religious temperament so much so that he commenced to study with a view to entering the ministry. Full of evangelical fervour, he took a zealous interest in church affairs and religious work generally. Along with Mr Alexander Kerr, another employee of the Oil Company, who fought shoulder to shoulder with the deceased for many years, Mr Wilson was passing through the Sports Park on his way to a prayer meeting, in the month of April 1886, when their attention was attracted by a miners meeting being held there. Speaking to his companion, he said 'Let us go over to this meeting'. As they approached, the miners were appointing delegates to interview the manager of Broxburn Oil Company, regarding a certain grievance. Having taken in the situation with that readiness which has characterised all his work as an agent, Mr Wilson suggested to the meeting that they would be far better not to send such a large deputation, because it would mean that some of the members of it would be under the bann (sic) of the oversmen. It was that trivial incident that led to Mr Wilson's appointment as a miner's agent. On the morning following that meeting, he was curtly informed that he would not be allowed to proceed down the mine, thus being the very first to suffer under that victimisation against which he had warned the miners to be on their guard. Only a few days were allowed to elapse before the miners appointed him as their agent. At that time he was residing with his mother in one of the Company's houses in Holygate. Carrying their resentment of Mr Wilson's action to extremes, the Company's representative informed his mother that she would have to clear out of the house if her son continued to stay with her. Rather than see his mother disturbed, Mr Wilson took lodgings at Niddry, where he remained until he was married.

THE TWENTY-TWO WEEKS' STRIKE

Up till the end of 1886 Mr Wilson devoted his time as agent, to placing the newly-formed Miners' Association on a thoroughly sound footing, the sympathy for him aroused among the men by what they considered the Company's high-handed action being distinctly favourable to success. Extending the scope of his activity, Mr Wilson organised Branches of the Union all over the shale fields, with the result that when the miners became involved in a strike over the question of hours in the beginning of 1887 they were able to present a united front. At the end of a fortnight the

men returned to work, having won the day, and they have since been working a nine hours' day. This only proved to be a preliminary skirmish,..and in the month of July of the same year, another strike, which lasted for twenty-two weeks, was declared, as a protest against the action of the Oil Companies. in deciding to reduce the wages by one shilling per day in view of the poor state of the industry at that time. Through all those weeks of acute privation and suffering among the miners, Mr Wilson was the central figure in the crisis – 'the villain of the play', as Mr Robert Smellie has been designated during the recent coal miners' strike. While carrying on negotiations with the Companies, Mr Wilson travelled up and down the country stating the case for the miners with that persuasive eloquence and power of reasoning which always characterised his speeches. It is not the time nor the place to enter into all the gruesome details of a strike, which is still only too well remembered by many of the shale miners – suffice to say that practically without a Union as we know it to-day and without funds, the men held out for twenty-two weeks and at the end of that time a compromise was effected, whereby the men got the sixpence over the proposed reduction in a few weeks after returning to work and at the end of a year were receiving the wage which had been ruling prior to the strike. In addition to that they gained recognition of their leaders, for before the strike commenced, the Companies had stoutly refused to recognise Mr Wilson, but the struggle had not long continued when he carried through the negotiations with the Directors on behalf of the men.

A COAL MINERS' AGENT

In the year 1891, Mr Wilson's sphere of activity was widened considerably by his appointment as agent of the West Lothian coal miners, and in his dual capacity as agent for both the coal and the shale miners he has ever since, been the moving spirit on the men's side in the industrial affairs of the county, while his outstanding abilities as a speaker on social and political questions were at the service of the workers all over the country. To facilitate his work and make it easier to deal with the directors of the Companies who had their offices in Glasgow, Mr Wilson removed to the second city in 1898 and there he carried on his work until he came to reside at Portobello a few years ago.

For some years, Mr Wilson was a member of Uphall School Board where he always took up a strong position on any question affecting the workers. As an indication of his popularity among the men it is interesting to remember that on his first attempt to enter the School Board, he was returned at the top of the poll. He was among the first of the candidates nominated by the Labour Party in Scotland and in that capacity he contested Central Edinburgh unsuccessfully. An eloquent advocate of total abstinence, he was one of the oldest members of the Broxburn Tent of Rechabites. He was also a pronounced Socialist, and the Broxburn branch of the Independent Labour party numbered him among its members. While in Glasgow he stood as a Labour Candidate for the Town Council but was unsuccessful.

MR WILSON'S PERSONALITY

Bearing a remarkable resemblance to the word pictures we have of Napoleon in his sturdy build and strong features, he had also a fair share of Bonaparte's dogged tenacity. Having once made up his mind on any question and assured himself that his position was reasonable, Mr Wilson always held his ground pugnaciously, and would seldom submit to compromise. As a miners' leader he had more than his fair share of criticism – reasonable and unreasonable – but once given an opportunity of meeting the men face to face, his magnetic personality and argumentative ability, seldom failed to bring them round to his way of thinking. Whether agreeing with his position or not, no one could doubt Mr Wilson's sincerity and earnestness on behalf of the cause he so ably espoused. If the men at times showed an inclination to kick over the traces, the employers with whom Mr Wilson had to deal, never forgot that the men's position was in the hands of one who knew the ropes and could manipulate them skilfully. At the close of an arbitration case, conducted on the men's side by Mr Wilson, Sheriff Jamieson, while deciding in favour of the employers, paid a deservedly high tribute to his reasoned advocacy of the men's claims. His death causes a gap in the ranks of the miners' leaders which will be exceedingly difficult to fill.

Mr Wilson was twice married, both his first wife – Miss Maggie Watson – and his second – Miss Jeanie Scott – being infant Mistress, of Broxburn School before they were married. He is survived by a widow and two daughters of the first marriage. Mr Wilson's mother is still living and resides in Kirkhill Road, Broxburn

Mr Wilson was 50 years of age. It is not too much to say that the last twenty-five years of his strenuous life have been sacrificed to the cause of the toilers, and however much or however little justification there may be for the abuse which is the unhappy lot of all miners' leaders, no one will venture to suggest that Mr Wilson's motives were anything but the highest.

THE FUNERAL

Amid manifestations of sincere regret on the part of all sections of the community, the mortal remains of Mr Wilson were laid to rest in the family burial ground in Uphall Cemetery yesterday afternoon. The arrival of the hearse from Edinburgh was awaited by hundreds of the deceased's admirers and as it passed along Main Street, the window blinds were drawn and many business premises were closed. A halt was called at the Public Hall where a funeral service was held. There was a large and representative gathering, including delegates from the various branches of the Miners' Union all over the county oversmen, contractors, colliery officials and personal friends from far and near. Headed by Broxburn Public Band playing the Dead March with heads uncovered as the cortege passed, the crowds of men, women and children paid their respects to the memory of one who had been a familiar figure in the district Those attending the funeral, numbered between two and three hundred by the time the cemetery was reached. The brief but impressive ceremony at the grave was conducted by the Rev. Mr Mitchell and the Rev. Mr White. Included among the beautiful wreaths laid on the grave, was one from the colliery managers in the district covered by Mr Wilson's activities.

The 'aristocracy of labour' is a useful descriptive term because it starts from the assumption that the working class is divided in many ways historically – by trade, religion, gender and so on. John Foster, a historian of the Scottish working-class[14], has used it effectively to describe how, from about the middle of last century, skilled sections of the working-class were allowed, indeed encouraged, by their employers to become relatively privileged and to assume positions of authority and supervision over the unskilled. In sectarian times in Scotland, this inevitably meant the Protestant Ascendancy overseeing the catholic community in general, and the unskilled and immigrant catholic Irish in particular. While sectarianism is better documented in relation to Glasgow[15], Edinburgh[16] and Lanarkshire[17], it has also been stated quite openly in relation to employment practices in the shale industry in West Lothian:

> Both the Past Grand Master and the Past Grand Depute Master [of the Masonic Order in Scotland] believed that historically freemasonry and anti-Catholicism had been linked because most Scots, and consequently most masons, shared the intense prejudices against Catholics and Irish, and that much contemporary anti-Catholicism in masonry today is a relic of those sentiments. The Past Depute Grand Master, a retired doctor who had worked with the oil industry, gave an impressive example of what he believed to have been the active discrimination suffered by Catholics in Scotland, and he explained the beliefs which were used to justify this blatant prejudice. He revealed that: 'I was born and brought up in a Scottish Oils area. I was in practice there. Scottish Oils and BP, up to – not too many years ago – never promoted a Catholic up to the rank of foreman or above. Didn't matter how good his qualifications were! He never became a foreman.' When asked how the policy operated, he replied:

> 'It was unspoken policy; absolutely unspoken policy – but it happened. It doesn't happen now, but it happened then. Any BP person of the older age group, of my age group, will tell you that. It was just unspoken policy. It just didn't happen. A man would be asked what his religion was before he was appointed to any job. And it was a definite bias. But it had nothing to do with masons. It was just to do with the fact that Scottish Oils and BP were controlled by old Presbyterian stock; and that was it! Just strong men as Protestants, who wouldn't allow these Irish Immigrants and Catholics to go into any position where they could have advanced their friends. But in masonry that's never been a problem.'

> Though there is no reason to doubt the statement that masonry itself played no part in this particular example of anti-Catholic discrimination, the oil companies did give considerable assistance to masonic lodges in oil-producing countries, which were primarily for their employees when abroad. Strong Protestants would no doubt wish to encourage an organisation seen to be fundamentally supportive of Scottish Protestantism and unsympathetic to Catholics. The association between the two may have led some to believe, erroneously, that masonic influence was at work here just as it played ball with Rangers at Ibrox Park... the actual prejudice does not lie within masonry; it is embedded within the particular culture, and the closer that masonry is bound to that culture, the more will masonry express the prejudices of that community.[18]

Tom Gallagher is here arguing that masonry reflected the strong Presbyterianism that existed generally in Scottish civil society and so it was not, as such, a 'conspiracy' against Catholicism. Of course, this was not how the Catholic Church chose to view masonry, as Stephen Knight's hostile study of The Brotherhood states: By the 1880s eight Popes had already condemned Freemasonry... Leo XIII classed Freemasonry as a grouping of secret societies in the 'kingdom of Satan'... He qualified Masonry as subversive of Church and state, condemned it for its rejection of Christian revelation, and for its religious indifferentism – the idea that all religions are equally valid'.[19] In these terms, masonry would not really have needed to proscribe Catholics because individuals wishing to join the organisation would have faced excommunication from their own faith as a consequence.

Are you a Catholic?

James: drawer, born 1903, Broxburn

'No, oh no, we're Orange – are you a Catholic?

       'No, it's just I've seen so many stories about the Irish

               coming over and the Irish being Catholic.

'Aye, there are an awful lot of
Catholics in the Broxburn area,
oh terrible. They came across here
to work in the oil works at the end
of the last century.'

A Century of Shale

Scotland's Forgotten Industry

Raymond Ross

The Irish Invasion

The industry attracted a huge immigrant Irish population whose main roots stretch back to the first oil-boom of the 1860s. In his singularly outstanding, pioneering research into The Social History of the Scottish Shale Oil Industry, 1850–1914, (an unpublished PhD Thesis) J.H. McKay, former Lord Provost of Edinburgh and an ex-shale worker himself, notes that the 'non-indigenous population... grew from 8,384 in 1851 to 28,238 in 1911, an increase of 336 per cent... much of it from Ireland'. Like many before him, my own grandfather came to howk shale from County Mayo. He too had worked at Tarbrax, a village reduced now to a cluster of houses. Internal migration was very much a feature of the shale districts with some mines being exhausted even in periods as short as five or 10 years.

The immigrant Irish population is now pretty well integrated. Only a surname (or perhaps the school you went to or even the team you support!) reveals the Irish lineage. But it wasn't always so. At one time, according to Cadell's 'The People of West Lothian', 'There were so many Irish in the Broxburn-Uphall area that it seems they had little to do with the local people at all.'

Irish immigration was a common enough feature of 19th century Scottish life. But it may be that the huge influx into West Lothian, in particular, was facilitated by the newness of the shale industry. It must have been easier to seek work in the West Lothian oil boom of the 1860s when the infant industry was crying out for labour than to try to get a start in a more established mining area – like the Lanarkshire coal-fields.

Jock Wardrope, though, gives the reverse side of the coin: 'The management went across to Ireland and brought them over by the shipload, to cut doon the wages. That was the purpose. You could pay the poor buggers anything at all'.

Two interesting figures in this connection were Patrick Gallagher ('Paddy the Cope') and John ('Jack') Mulherne.

Born on Christmas Day 1873, Gallagher was to receive his nickname as the founder of the Templecrone Co-operative Society in his native Donegal. Inspired by his dealings with the Pumpherston Co-operative Store, a branch of the West Calder Co-operative Society, Gallagher became 'an organiser of strong determination', as Berresford Ellis describes him, in the fight against Gombeenism, the despotic usury of traders in rural Ireland. He is sometimes – wrongly – citied as the founder of the Co-operative Movement in Ireland. As Berresford Ellis says of William Thompson of Clonkeen, County Cork (1775–1833) 'Thompson rather than [Robert] Owen' was 'in the forefront of the Co-operative movement' as early as 1830.

Gallagher's first job in the shale districts was labouring in the building of new retorts. Later he became a retort man and, then, a miner, working in Glendevin, Tarbrax, the Holmes mines and Portnuck pit. He wrote his autobiography 'My life' (1939) at the behest of A.E. (George Russell) and it is, as Peader O'Donnell describes it, 'a human document alive with infectious gaiety and hope'.

It is also, in part, a fascinating first hand account of life in the Broxburn shale area from his first refusal to get a start in a local oil works ('that gas would kill me') and the primitive sanitary conditions in the miners' rows to his experiences as a retort man:

'It was very warm work taking the burned shell [sic] from the retorts. The shell was dropped red hot into hutches. Every two men with a hutch, one in front, the other behind, drawing and pushing them out of the gullets to the endless chain which took them to the top. There were three spells for work, from six to nine, 10 to one, and from two to five o'clock. We got four shillings a day and seven days in the week. It was a good wage, 28 shillings a week, but the work was very warm. Each of us used to drink at least half a gallon of water each spell, but it ran out of us in sweat as fast as we drank it. We wore a light pair of trousers, a small navy-blue simit with no sleeves, we had a belt or cord round our waist and cords round our legs under our knees to help keep up our trousers. When we young fellows would be going to our lodgings, if we saw any women coming along the road we would face the hedge, as the sweat would be running out of our trousers and we feared that the women would think we had wet them. We soon got accustomed to it and did not care who saw us'.

He reports that on rising to get his breakfast 'the night-shift men slipped into our beds as soon as we got out'. This was a common occurrence, certainly among the Irish. A ban on such lodgers in company houses was one cause of a strike in Addiewell in 1870. Even in Jock Wardrope's day 'The beds were three shifted, backshift, dayshift and nightshift. The beds were never cauld. Men were going in as others were tumblin' out'.

The oil works that Gallagher refused a start in he calls 'Jack Mulhern's Oil Works'. Born in Cleendra in County Donegal, Mulherne, in fact, was a publican in Broxburn and he seems to have acted as a kind of unofficial Irish recruiting officer for the local shale industry. He was often the first port of call for those new off the boat. Dr Joe Scott (b. 1907) of Broxburn recalls:

'... everybody knew John. He was rather a gaunt chap, with a bit of a stoop, white hair and a very red face... an awfully nice soul... He used to recruit Irishmen from the west of Ireland – Galway, Mayo and so on. And the story is told that, on one occasion, a coachload of Irishmen came down to Broxburn from the old Drumshoreland station, and asked where 'Mr Mulherne's oil works' was. He was a very powerful man in the community.

Footnotes:

1   George Garson No Idle Bread (1986) p.13.

2   H.R.J. Conacher 'History of the Scottish Shale Oil Industry' The Oil Shales of the Lothian (HMSO 1927) p.264.

3   J.H. McKay The Social History of the Scottish Shale Oil Industry 1850-1914, PhD Thesis, unpub., Open University (1984) p.216.

4   P. Cadell The People of West Lothian (1984) p.6.

5   Garson op.cit. p.13.

6   Peter Berresford Ellis A History of the Irish Working Class (1985, 1st pub 1972) pp.172, 90.

7   Patrick Gallagher My Life by 'Paddy the Cope' (1939). Introduction by Peader O'Donnell p.9.

8   Ibid pp.61–62, 58.

9   Garson op.cit. p.13.

10 Ibid p.42.

Where Do You Come From?
James: drawe, born 1900, West Calder

'Irish?
Don't talk to me about the Irish.
They came across here in the 1920s.
All these came across and we asked them,
'Where do you come from?'
          – 'Shotts.'

I asked another one,
'Where do you come from?'
          – 'Shotts.'

They all came from Shotts.
They had just landed over here with the one big boat.

Oh no, there were about eight or nine of them came over.
And my god, strong looking men.

Oh, big looking men.
One of them couldn't sit down on that carpet
without some of his backside being out at each side.
Oh dear, but for all them being big and strong looking,
they'd no knack about them.
Clumsy.
They came in for me many a time, many's a time,
to lift a hutch on, come down in the cuddy,
and the hutch would stoat off that end. They'd say,

'You couldn't lift that hutch?'

And it was the easiest thing in the world
to stop it from happening, you know.
Oh, they were stupid men!
Oh aye.
There were a good lot of them.
A good lot of them stayed on, you know.
And they were quite good workers.
But eh,
they were never any bother or anything.'

A fuller understanding of local community history, and cultural history, certainly in Central Scotland, is just not possible therefore,
without an appreciation of the existence of that level of division.
Some of the voices in this study give occasional reports of such lega-
cies, although there is still a dearth of detail. How were the Catholic
Irish settled in places like Addiewell, for example, built cheek-by-
jowl beside the strongly Protestant West Calder? There are hints and
suggestions of Catholic Irish 'streets', 'quarters' or even 'villages' in
other places too – such as Niddry in relation to Winchburgh.

In his autobiography, *Paddy the Cope*, Patrick Gallagher refers to
newly arrived Irishmen looking for 'Paddy Mulherne's Oilworks'
(the name of a foreman) at Uphall in the 1890s, and Gallagher himself lodged at Niddry.[20] Various comments in the oral histories also
imply that the immigrant Irish tended to work in the oil works and
on the surface, tipping the blaes onto the bings, as indeed did Paddy
Gallagher. This would have been relatively unskilled work, mining
last century tending to be inter-generational, with sons often starting
off working with, and for, their fathers or other family members, and
by this means inducted into the craft.

Shale oil workers, Winchburgh, pre-Great War

My father's family had strong Masonic/Presbyterian connections yet he joined the Labour Party at a time when it was considered by wide sections of the Protestant community to be a vehicle for Catholic advancement.[21] His obituary in October 1978 reads:

> One issue which caused tremendous controversy and passion through-out Bob's editorship was educational segregation. He chose to ignore the strong feelings and resentments engendered in his determination to heal a society divided against itself. He was not particularly interested in any other aspect of religion; the Masonic Lodge and the Orange Order were also condemned on occasions as equally divisive.[22]

Perhaps it should be made clear that we are talking here against the background of a district where memories still persisted that Manny Shinwell lost (by 642 votes) the 1924 General Election in Linlithgow in a head-on contest with the Conservatives (when no Liberal stood) because (or so it was said) Catholics would not vote for a Red Clydesider;and where, 40 years later, the local MP's marriage to a Catholic, albeit a relative of John Wheatley, was viewed with deep suspicion, as was Tam Dalyell himself – an ex-Tory, Old Etonian and local Laird. Tom Gallagher informs us that until the 1960s, very few RCs were returned in Scottish Labour seats and that, in 1959, Coatbridge and Airdrie – which border West Lothian – nearly fell to the Conservatives after Labour nominated an RC candidate. My father's public support for 'Tam' was perhaps symbolic – confirma-tion that religion was no longer the predictable indicator of voting behaviour it had once been in the district or country as a whole.

David McCrone has pointed out some of the reasons why many

Protestants voted Conservative and why that party performed far better electorally in Scotland up to their high point in 1955 – when they were the largest single party – than social factors would have predicted. In other words, why a large section of the Scottish working class did not routinely vote Labour, the avowed party of the Scottish working class:

> Religion has always mattered in Scottish politics, and it dominated 19th century cleavages to a remarkable extent. These influences were carried into this century in potent form. While direct and systematic evidence on the middle years of this century is hard to come by, survey data from the 1950s and 1960s suggest that strong religious connotations were present in Scottish politics. National and local surveys show that 'one important influence – religion – does seem to carry a different and stronger weight among Scottish electors when they are compared to English electors' (Budge & Urwin 1966). Bochel and Denver, on the basis of a survey carried out in Dundee in 1968, found, if anything, a closer tie between religion and voting. Of Church of Scotland manual workers, 39.5 per cent voted Conservative compared with only six per cent of Roman Catholic manual workers.
>
> These surveys were carried out in the 1960s when many of the social mechanisms underlying Catholic-Labour and Conservative-Protestant voting associations were losing their force, but they do testify to the power of Unionism to mobilise an older – essentially Protestant – sense of what it meant to be Scottish. As Callum Brown has pointed out, even as late as 1986, 45 per cent of Kirk members claimed to vote Tory (and only 17 per cent Labour) [Brown 1990]. This identity consisted of a complex of inter-related elements of Protestantism and Unionism welded together by a strong sense of British and Imperial identity, and symbolised by the Union Jack (still the emblem of Glasgow Rangers football club). This version of Scottishness was not at odds with Conservative rhetoric about British national and imperial identity, given the powerful strand of militarism that ran through Scottish society in the late 19th and early 20th centuries. The mobilisation of men for war during the later imperial period and on through two World Wars helped fit together Scottish and British identities. The connection was reinforced by the religious factor, which in turn received emotional resonance and respectability from the national and imperial elements of the complex.[24]

It is by no means unlikely, therefore, that my father's grandfather, his father and his Uncle John would have voted between them Liberal, Conservative or Conservative Unionist during the Elections of the 1920s, to oppose Manny Shinwell becoming MP for Linlithgowshire. Shinwell became West Lothian's first Labour MP in 1922 with 46 per cent of the vote, against 33 per cent for the Conservative Unionist, James Kidd, a local lawyer. The Courier blatantly backed Kidd, the sitting MP, who got twice the coverage of

Shinwell inside the paper while his election address was printed on the first page. Wm. Cuthbertson, Broxburn Lodge, is given as one of Kidd's 'assenters'. My father's Uncle John acted as presiding officer at Winchburgh.

Balanced *Courier* reporting of the 'Socialist Menace', August, 1922

A Great Opportunity
Friend of the Worker:
'Why not let us have peace in industry, and then you can get this?'
Labour Leader (to the man with the flag):
'Will you go away? You'll give the game away with your shouting!'

West Lothian Courier
FRIDAY NOVEMBER 10, 1923
MR SHINWELL'S CANDIDATURE
AT LONGRIDGE

On Tuesday evening Mr Shinwell addressed the electors in Longridge Public School. Mr David Johnston presided over a packed hall.

Mr Shinwell said that in this contest Labour was in a unique position. It was the only united Party and he was the only candidate in West Lothian who did not require

to withdraw anything he had said at the election in 1918. (Applause.) He came across the other morning a leaflet issued by the Tory candidate at last election, and he would consider that leaflet that night. In that leaflet they were asked to vote for Kidd and punish the Kaiser. In a newspaper of a few days ago he observed the Kaiser was about to be married. Whether that was a form of punishment was a matter for married men to answer. (Laughter.) When in 1918 they were asking to vote to punish the Kaiser they spoke with their tongue in their cheek. Then in this leaflet they were to vote so that Germany would be made to pay. Well, Germany had, in the form of goods, paid £54,000,000 but our Army of Occupation on the Rhine cost £56,000,000, so that Britain lost £2,000,000 on that transaction. Was that a business transaction? Nay, it was preposterous. But that was not all. The payments were made in goods. We got 250 ships in part payment, and the result of that was to reduce employment in our shipbuilding yards, and hundreds of workers had to be provided with unemployment doles. Another of the payments was in the form of coal. The result – dislocation of the coal industries and miners thrown out of work. Yet the men who did this had the impudence to come to the country and ask for the people's support again. Justice was to be done by the ex-Service men. Had justice been done to the men who fought and won the war? Could it be justice that forced such large numbers of these men to go week after week for the unemployment dole? If that was justice then he said they would be better without justice. Ex-Service men did not ask for justice of that description, they asked for work. What did Mr Kidd do? Oh, he helped ex-Service men for, in August, 1919, he voted for £585,000 being given to 19 ex-Service men, all Generals of the British Army. (Laugher.) That was the kind of justice the Coalition – Tories and Liberals – believed in. Mr Bonar Law, who had as his henchmen the Tory candidate for West Lothian, had told the country that the Ministry of Pensions would be abolished if he and his party were returned to power. That, in his opinion, was the prelude to reducing pensions to the minimum if not, altogether, to the ex-soldiers among the working class. In reply to the 'Glasgow Herald' Mr Law said that the ex-Service men who had pensions would not be affected, but the people were entitled to be sceptical. They were told in 1918 that the rents of the people would not be touched but in March, 1919, the Government changed their tune and on that date Mr Kidd supported the Government in making possible a 10 per cent increase on house rents. (Applause.) The Labour Party fought that the increase be retained to five per cent. But the Tory candidate in August 1919, voted that cer-

tain Cabinet Ministers who had £2,000 per annum as salaries should be each increased to £5,000 per annum. Yet he and those of his party said they were out for economy. Yes, economy so far as the worker was concerned but not for their own section. (Hear, hear.) Again on 23 June 1920 Mr Kidd voted in favour of spending £35,000,000 in order to secure and keep for Britain Mesopotamia, for which thousands of our men had fought for and died for. Yes, but he never voted for a 1d being given to help the shale industry of West Lothian which had been ruined because of the oil wells in Mesopotamia. That was how Mr Kidd voted in the interest of his West Lothian constituents. Wages to-day, in comparison with cost of living and taxes, were never lower in living memory. Obviously if the workers were to get relief, taxes must be reduced. Well in June 1921, in the House of Commons, the question of the duty on tea was raised. Mr Neil McLean, Govan, moved that the tax be repealed. Mr Kidd voted against any reduction being made. In July, 1921, Mr Kidd also voted against a reduction in the tax for sugar, and the result was that users of sugar paid in taxation £15,000,000 per annum. But on the question of the tax on sparkling wines, such as champagne, Mr Kidd voted for a large reduction being made. In regard to unemployment, Mr Kidd in June, 1921, voted that the rate of unemployment benefit be reduced from 20s to 15s in the case of men, from 15s to 12s in the case of women. He also voted that a married woman get 5s per week and each child 1s per week. Was that man fitted to represent the workers? He thought not. (Applause.) He had neglected the interests of the largest body of the voters – the workers – but had ever supported the calls of the rich and those in high authority. (Hear, hear.) Let them consider carefully what the Tories and the Liberals had done, let them study the Labour programme and what reforms they proposed. If they did that he was sure that they would vote for Labour and so secure justice. (Applause.)

MR KIDD AT AN ORANGE GATHERING

On Friday night a social gathering was held in the Public Hall, Broxburn, under the auspices of Hearts of Oak LOL, No 44. The chair was occupied by Bro. James

Phillips. The chairman intimated that a few of the speakers expected had been called elsewhere on election duties.

The gathering was so large that tea had been served in relays. The Broxburn Cooperative Society had great credit in their purveying. After tea an address was delivered by Miss John, Hon secy. of the Eastern Lodge of the Workers League. After speaking of the aims and objects of the League she said that in Bonar Law they had got an absolutely straight, clean, honest Scotsman as their Prime Minister. They could trust him. He never made great promises, but he had pledged himself to the security of Northern Ireland. (Loud applause.) They would all work hard to return Mr Kidd as Member for West Lothian. (Renewed applause.).

Ex-Provost Gordon Bathgate, said he had never been at an Orange social in Broxburn before, but he was there that night for the purpose of congratulating them on the purity of their Lodge and the purity of their Order. At this stage Mr Kidd entered the meeting and received a great ovation. Continuing, Mr Gordon said he had only acted as stop gap till the Chief of the Clan appeared. (Cheers.)

Mr Kidd said the faith of some might falter, and the loyalty of some might fail, but it was his experience that in every contest in which he had been engaged he could trust implicity to the perfect loyalty and faith of the great Orange Order. (Cheers.) In the 1910 contest his greatest support and his finest encouragement came from their ranks. In 1913 again it was their support that had led him so near to victory. In the great fight of 1918 when they and he were working to oppose all the forces of disloyalty and disorder his experience of them was again the same. They were engaged in a fight no less strenuous today, in a fight of no less moment, and he knew that in that fight no men and no women would rally to his standard with greater zest than those he saw around the tables before him. They and he stood together in a support of a common liberty and a common freedom, and so far as Ulster was concerned they would never depart a jot or a tittle from the common flag. (Great applause.) Let them not presume upon his large majority in 1918 that he was perfectly safe. On this occasion the vote be split, and although his Liberal opponent could have no earthly hope of success his presence in the field would endanger his (Mr Kidd's) cause. If everyone of their own supporters went to the poll he (Mr Kidd) would not only win but would add enormously to his majority. (Applause.) He wanted to kill Socialism once and for all in this county. (Renewed applause.) Socialism was hindering beyond words the development of trade; it represented broken time and distressingly low wages. In conclusion he asked them for the sake of Ulster to see to it that this county was pledged not only by the word of its member but by the overwhelming majority of his constituents to support their countrymen in the liberties for which they were prepared to fight and die. Let them never forget Bonar Law's guarantee – Ulster will never suffer wrong. (Loud and prolonged cheering.)

As his family believed in 'respectability', so my father believed in the dignity of labour and meritocracy, a battle still being slugged out, toe to toe, in the Depression years. Jock Wardrope, president of the Shale workers Union at Seafield and a local Labour councillor, has provides vivid testimony regarding the political struggle being fought out between the Wars. Jock and his ilk faced head-on the conservatism of his fellow miners: 'I had a lot of enemies then, and was fighting in the streets tae... pulled the hair oot o' ye'.[24]

The slogans from earlier times would spring unbidden from my father's lips even in the late 1960s/early 1970s, arguing politics with his several sons. According to him a Liberal was – 'a Tory wi' a sair heid'. He described this as meaning – 'a Tory with a conscience' but, in reading Jock Wardrope's account of Tory miners, it seems clear that 'a sair heid' often meant exactly that. Also according to my father, a Communist was – 'somebody wi' nothing who wants tae share it wi' everybody.' In my radical youth, I once suggested that everybody, including the unemployed, should be paid the same. He looked at me as though I'd gone completely daft and asked why anyone would want to 'strip a stent of shale' for someone else to 'piss it against a wall?' Such phrases, were no doubt gems of oratory once heard on the hustings and stuck in the gin-trap of his fabulous memory. Another such, as I recall, he pulled out when Margo MacDonald won a Hamilton By-Electrion for the SNP in the late 60s/early 70s. I asked him what he thought of her as we watched her being interviewed on a flickering black and white TV screen: 'a formidable opponent in a stairheid row', he said, only half smiling.

The days of the big political gatherings, a good means of countering a hostile press while providing entertainment, is inscribed on one of his stories. A Tory candidate is addressing a meeting, and getting heckled by some miners. Finally, he is driven to say – 'I'll have you know that my ancestors fought for this land.' Whereupon, a big miner (it was always a big miner at the back who speaks up in my father's stories) shouts out:

'Well, come doon here and I'll fight ye for it.'

Fifty years earlier, Orange miners had heckled Keir Hardie.

My father and, more particularly, his family may have been strong Protestants but they certainly were not Orange, a phenomenon brought to Scotland in the early 19th century by Irish immigrants, primarily from Ulster. The rapid industrial expansion of Lanarkshire through coalmining and iron manufacture in the middle decades of that century not only led to a concentration of the Orange Order there, as well as in Ayrshire, but in the wake of continuing Irish immigration the Order was able to exploit the fears and prejudices held by many native Scottish Protestants towards the Irish Catholics. As industrial expansion continued beyond Lanarkshire, so too did the Order expand particularly into mining areas, and in the 1870s District Lodge No 26 was established in the Armadale/Whitburn coalfield, to be followed soon after by District Lodge No 48 at Broxburn, situated in the heart of the shale field.

The riot and disorder which then attended the Order – and which led to a ban on all public Orange processions in West Central Scotland from 1857 to 1867 – would not have appealed to the respectable Presbyterians who composed my father's family – either in social or religious terms – as a recent study of Orangeism in Scotland helps make clear:

> Orangemen enjoy the religious trappings which surround the Order but they are less interested in the responsibilities which flow from them. It could be said of most Orangemen, then and now, that they were Bible loving if not Bible reading. It is instructive that, in comparison with Ireland, the Order in Scotland had only brief flirtations with both temperance and Sabbatarianism, finding no real or lasting support amongst the membership of either.[25]

In the same study, William Marshall usefully places the Orange Order within the wider cultural developments which were shaping an industrial proletariat in late Victorian/Edwardian society, albeit a section with a negative and reactionary ideology, but which nevertheless mirrored some traditional working class values and aspirations centred round brotherhood, mutual aid and communal solidarity:

> Entire communities had evolved on the basis of an ethic of communal solidarity and mutual aid. Most adult males were literate and many of them were enfranchised. Membership of a trade union was now legal. Leisure time too gradually became more available to the masses with visits to the music halls and attendance at football matches becoming very popular forms of entertainment. ....Orangemen were not immune from these wider societal developments and Orangeism, viewed as a cultural and social phenomenon offering its own unique world view within this more universal milieu, came to represent a somewhat perverse manifestation of working class society's central tenets: mutual aid and solidarity.[26]

West Lothian Oil Company, 1883–1892, no date, c. 1890
photo: William Marjoriebanks

Gradually, the zealots on both sides of the sectarian divide began to lose their ability to 'deliver' either the 'Orange vote' to Unionist candidates or the 'Irish vote' against Catholic-but-Red Socialists (such as John Wheatley) as the inter-war generations began increasingly to vote for their collective 'class' interests, despite often blatant appeals to sectarian emotions and loyalties:

> Whilst the majority of Orangemen probably continued to vote Unionist during the inter-war period, it was apparent that there were already an indeterminate number who were prepared to vote for the Labour Party or the ILP. This was despite the protestations and dire warnings of Orange leaders. By the 1930s it was quite clear that Labour was committed to social democracy and not Marxist revolution. Whatever else Ramsay MacDonald and the other Labour leaders were, they most certainly were not Bolsheviks. The Labour Party was obviously constitutionalist in character and many Orangemen have taken the view that a vote for it was not an act of betrayal. Of course, other Orangemen who voted Labour quite probably did not even bother to think too much about these considerations. If their behaviour was contradictory then too bad. They were prepared to live with that.[27]

My father thrived on argument, of course, and his stories often reflected his amused dismissal of 'eejits' of whatever description – Left, Right or Deeply Bigoted. He laughed at the local Orangeman who sent his laddie back out to the ice-cream van to return a bottle of Limeade (because it was Green) and he told the story of the ventriloquist appearing at Harthill Miners Welfare (which reputedly rang two bells at 'closing time' to allow those not prepared to 'stand for the Queen' to leave after the first bell, or risk being 'claimed' after the second bell if they did not indeed stand for the national anthem). So this ventriloquist is on stage at Harthill Miners Welfare, arguing with his dummy, who is saying he wants to sing and the ventriloquist keeps saying he can't sing until, eventually, from the back of the hall, a big miner shouts:

'if the wee fella wants tae sing, effingwell let him sing!'

Such stories, told to me in the 1960s, indicate not only the presence of sectarianism but its decline. In the face of an increasingly secularised proletariat, bigots and bigotry did not so much retreat as were left standing on ground no one but themselves wished to defend.

The photograph below – an end cottage in the 'Old Rows' in Winchburgh, painted Rangers Blue, and just up from the Masonic Lodge – would have amused my father almost as much as Harthill Miners Welfare did, and for much the same reason: both, to his mind, totems of a bygone age. In his day, he might have said, no one would have bothered painting the outside of their house Blue or Green for the neighbours knew anyway which foot you kicked with – even those who didn't give a damn. And those, it seems, were gradually on the increase.

The lone ranger: popular protestant culture? Winchburgh, 1996
(the end cottage is painted Rangers blue)

*   *   *   *   *

Out of History

Alistair Findlay

The American tourist looked at me from across the
restaurant table and asked if I was a Lowland Scot
and did I still feel enmity towards the Highlander.
I said my ancestors came from Shetland, Mull, the
Black Isles, Berwickshire and the West, from Glasgow
and quite possibly Ireland, to the Lothians two hundred
years ago, where we worked in pits and some of us married
Catholics. I said I nearly signed for Aberdeen FC when
Eddie Turnbull was the manager, and I bear no grudges.

Eejits and bloody eejits

One explores an inheritance to free oneself and others

John Montague

Last century my father's family was part of the strong Protestant community of West Calder. His great grandfather, Thomas, was born there in 1808, a coal miner and fiddle player of some repute, the possessor of a 'black' fiddle which had apparently been handed down to him. Like his father James before him, he was the kirk precentor and so some musical talent may have run in the family. His oldest son, Thomas, was also known in the area as a singer. Robert, my father's grandfather, was born in West Calder in 1854, the year that old Thomas died, and it was he, the youngest son, who was to become renowned in the locality as an amateur dramatics player.[1]

The West Lothian Courier –

19th April, 1890

Dramatic Entertainment – The members of the West Calder Dramatic Club made their last appearance on the stage this season on Tuesday evening last before a good audience. The piece selected for the occasion was Allan Ramsay's famous pastoral comedy entitled 'The Gentle Shepherd'. The club has given a representation of this piece on a previous occasion, but it nevertheless seldom fails to draw a good audience in country districts. The piece was carried out with strictly local talent, no professional aid being called in. Mr William Bryce as Sir William Worthy showed great improvement on his last appearance, and gives promise of being one of the most capable members of the club. Mr James McLean deserves great praise for his excellent portrayal of 'Patie, the Gentle Shepherd', while Mr W. Watson, though practically a new member, gave an able and efficient impersonation of Roger. Mr R. Robb as Symon, and Mr Anderson as Gland, both gave a natural and neat execution of their respective parts. The acting of Mr R. Findlay as Bauldy was well nigh perfect; he invested the character with all the necessary humour, and in several scenes he drew forth well-merited applause from the audience. Mr W. Rankine and Mr R. Davidson gave sprightly and skillful representation of Peggy and Jenny, while the other parts of Elspa and Madge were also competently filled by Mr Tweedie and Mr Clarkson. The club have reason to look back upon the season which has just terminated with pride, as it has probably been the most successful both financially and in the improvement of the individual members that they have yet had, and we look forward with high expectations to the programme they will bring before the public for next season.

At the turn of the century, local dramatics could easily attract several hundred people – gatherings that were both 'appreciative and respectable'. Reviews of such in the People's Hall, West Calder, cite audiences of 1,000 with no hint of this being particularly remarkable. Subtlety may sometimes have been lacking, of course: one production of *Rob Roy* is described as hitting on the idea of casting the Highlanders and the Redcoats from people who were none too friendly in private life. This was to give realism to the stage battle which took place between the two forces, and it worked so well that at times the battling groups had to be separated when the battle became too serious.[2]

The Halls, West Calder, c. 1910, where my great grandfather tread the boards

My great grandfather's forte seems to have been 'realism', particularly in the role of Rob Roy:

West Lothian Courier –
Saturday, March 20, 1886

WEST CALDER DRAMATIC ASSOCIATION

WEST CALDER DRAMATIC ASSOCIATION

Last Friday and Saturday evenings, the members of the above club gave a public rehearsal of this popular play in the People's Hall. On Friday evening, the attendance was good; but on Saturday night, it had fallen off by a few hundreds. It is a pity that the public did not turn out better as they missed an excellent treat. The proceeds were for a divisional benefit between the hall organ and the dramatic fund. The get-up of the pieces was par excellence, and the dresses and costumes displayed were astonishing. The scenery which was painted by Mr Cowan, a number of the company, was surprisingly good. Mr R. Findlay acted the part of 'Rob Roy' in a style which left nothing to be desired. His muscular development, giant strength and fine physique made his imitation of the 'Highland Chief' as nearly real as possible.

Such was his acclaim in the role that exponents of 'Rob Roy' had to suffer comparisons being made even some 30 years later:

> Where all did so well it seems unnecessary to go into detailed reference. We were particularly pleased with Mr Jas. Boyd's impersonation of 'Rob Roy', nothing finer has been done since the days when Mr Findlay made this character his masterpiece. It was an extremely clever presentation of a character which is always difficult to present.[3]

But hardly the stuff of working class legend this, my great grandfather, the old shale inspector, tramping the boards of the People's Hall, West Calder, a Highland Chief, 'Rob Roy' MacGregor no less, a local dramatic star a century and more ago. And surely more 'gothic' than 'realist', the romanticism of re-cycled Scott meeting the horror of the 'penny-dreadfuls' then being serialised in the popular press – each in their own way feeding the need for an imaginative escape from the reality of everyday life. Fifty years later, the off-spring of these same audiences would be flocking to the cinema, and for much the same reasons. The photograph of my great grandfather, in his gear, has about it an air of parody I find hard to resist – like one of his aphorisms – the utterance, it seems to me, of some kind of secular Calvinist:

> the world is full of eejits and bloody eejits:
> eejits have opinions, bloody eejits have nane

My great grandfather, Robert, acting like an eejit c. 1880/90s

He was praised in the local press for a variety of other performances as well:

**West Lothian Courier –
MARCH 26, 1887**

The Scotch romantic drama, in two acts, entitled, 'Gilderoy'... It is full of the best humour. In this piece Mr Jas. McLean assumes the leading character, 'Gilderoy', which he does very ably, but at times seems a little timid. Mr Cowan, as Walter Logan, would make a splendid character were he to change his voice slightly from the tone of a stern disciplinarian to that of the old Scotch farmer. Mr R. Findlay, who takes the part of Jock Mair, does his part in an excellent way, and is certainly by far the best character.

**West Lothian Courier –
DECEMBER 11, 1886**

He is reported as sustaining 'a certain amount of liveliness throughout' in the role of 'Cassidy' in 'the far-famed and highly interesting historical drama, in three acts, entitled, 'Jessie Brown or The Relief of Lucknow'.' Other characters included 'Nana Sahib, Rajah of Bithoor' plus 'Hakeen sepoy traitors' forby 'Miss Effie Goodwin', who appears as Jessie Brown, a Scotch girl, [who] imparts to the character with which she is invested the vivacity, sprightliness and loveliness necessary to its success, and is worthy of the love of both Sweeney and Cassidy. Her rendering of the different Scotch songs during the acts was highly commendable.

A review of Scotland's cultural history notes that during this period, the established theatres in the cities catered mostly for middle-class audiences – with an almost unvaried diet of what happened to be fashionable on the London stage, and the theatrical fare of the working classes in the towns and countryside usually plays and entertainments in their own language and accents, using Scottish music, songs and dances. There was some crossover, but generally speaking, Scottish plays [i.e. adaptations of Scott's novels like 'Rob Roy' and John Home's 'Douglas'] – which at the start of the century were the apotheosis of national theatrical pride and were presented on the most prestigious stages in the country – ended the century on the margins of society seen only as fodder for social inferiors.[4]

The same review goes on:

> The rise of the music halls and later the variety theatres in Scotland was the most significant development in late 19th century Scottish theatre, as these paved the way for the parallel traditions of Scottish pantomime and variety which have now become one of the most interesting features of Scottish theatre. It has, however, taken most of this century to stop apologising and feeling ashamed of this. In many ways the typical contemporary Scottish play, if such a thing exists, will ramble, be based round sketches, and direct audience address and owe more to the national dramas of the early 19th century than to Chekhov, Brecht or Pinter. This tradition also allowed working-class playwrights in the 20th century to develop a unique and distinctive style, unencumbered by any notion of the well-made play which was to be such a burden for James Bridie in his attempts to please the West End.[5]

Written in 1927, my great grandfather's obituary states that in his younger days he took a great interest in curling and football and was a prominent member of the West Calder Dramatic Club. His internment at West Calder Cemetery was attended by a large number of the general public, twenty or so years after he had left the area, a testament perhaps to his local renown.[6]

A scene by scene description of *Rob Roy* as performed by the juvenile choir of the United Free Church in Winchburgh, my grandfather's church, was printed in the Courier in 1922, and it would no doubt have been closely scrutinised, and possibly even attended by 'Rob Roy' himself, the old Crawpicker, and his grandson, my father, who was then eleven years old:

West Lothian Courier
FRIDAY MAY 12 1922
WINCHBURGH

Rob Roy Kinderspiel – Under the auspices of the UF Church the children of the juvenile choir gave a splendid performance of the musical play Rob Roy in the Mission Hall on Thursday and Friday last. Despite the fact that no tickets were on sale and a silver collection only was taken, the hall was filled on both occasions and a substantial sum was cleared.

The first scene, A Border Village, opened with a chorus by the villagers, 'All on a summer's day', and songs were tastefully rendered by Francis and Diana. Scene 2, Glasgow Bridge, introduced the 'Watchman's Chorus' and a song by Mattie which was greeted with applause. The next scene, Cell in the Tolbooth, gave us the chorus, 'O sleep that folds the wearied sight', followed by the College Gardens scene, in which the students sang well.

Scene five, The Clachan of Aberfoyle, showed clearly how well the children had been trained. It included songs by Jean and Major Galbraith, a chorus, 'The Land of Bracken', a duet by Jenny and Duncan, a Highland dance, a 'Military March', and concluded with the favourite chorus, 'Now tramp o'er moss and fell'. In the next scene, Pass of Lochard, we had a duet by Alan and Ewan, songs by Helen MacGregor, a song by Dougal, and the chorus, 'Hail to the Chief', followed by a Highland dance. The final scene, Clachan of Aberfoyle, introduced the chorus, 'They bound him wi' a hempen cord', a song by Francis, a duet by Diana and Francis, and the final chorus, 'Then let us strive to help our friends'.... Rev. Mr Balfour in a few words congratulated the children and those who had helped to make the entertainment a success. He asked for votes of thanks to Miss Balfour and to Mr and Mrs Robertson and Mrs Reid for assistance given.

My father's uncles – George and John – were, like their father, members of amateur dramatic clubs, and it would have been strange if he had not been exposed to something of the music-hall and variety while growing up in such a household. Faint echoes may even have reached down to my own childhood, for I can remember as a youngster badgering my father to sing some of my favourite verses – which he did with much gusto, and the buoyant rhythms of what I might now recognise as pantomime:

> O, run away doon for Geordie Broon,
> and tell him tae hurry alang,
> the biler's burst, the lum's oan fire,

and everything's gang wrang,
whatever it is that gangs amiss,
they aye adopt this plan,
they send for me because ye see,
I'm a richt guid handy man.

My father's repertoire of New Year songs, following 'Mary Morrison',
would include 'Goodbye Booze', which sounds like a popular ditty
about the Boer War, and which he might well have picked up from his
grandfather who, unlike his Uncle John, was no Rechabite:

I'll tell you a good old story
you've never heard before,
how we fought for death and glory
in the good old Zulu War,
how we fought with backs together
to keep the foe at bay,
when a fella next to me,
got a bullet in his e'e,
and I heard the poor bloke say –

O goodbye booze, for ever more,
my boozing days, will soon be o'er,
and when I die, don't bury me at all,
just pickle my bones, in alcohol.

The first time I remember my father speaking to me about his grandfather directly was in my fifth year at school after I had returned
from the County sports with a medal for the shot-putt. He looked at
me as though I was a thorough-bred, and announced that his grandfather had been one of the few men in the county able to lift some
huge stone up at West Calder. At least that was how I remembered
it, and so I was pleased to come upon his comments regarding an old
news item he had unearthed (in the *Courier* of 1906) on the subject
of 'bulleteers':

The editor of the day advised a correspondent that 'bulleting' was ille-
gal, several persons having been fined at Falkirk for indulging in it.
What was bulleting? Older readers will know that it was nothing to do
with guns. It was in fact a sport consisting of throwing a round stone
or bullet along the road between two towns or villages, the competitor
who got his bullet over the finishing line in the lowest number of
throws being the winner. It seems to have been something like golf
without clubs. I believe the sport was sometimes called 'hainching'
because of the method of throwing the bullet underarm off the hip or
'hainch'. My grandfather, the late Mr Robert Findlay, who was a well-
known West Calder worthy in his day, and reputed the strongest man
in the parish, used to boast to me about his prowess as a 'bulleteer' and

claimed that he was the unbeaten champion of the district at throwing a stone a series of throws all the way from West Calder to Forth. The sport was very popular among miners.[7]

When I shared this last piece of family legend with my younger brother, he said: 'West Calder to Forth? And uphill all the way?' Orwell stood in more awe of the physical prowess of miners than this, as well he might. The physical demands of what was essentially a pick and shovel operation is no doubt unimaginable to later generations. My father would talk of drawers competing for fun to see how high they might lift – and I remember the phrase – 'a twelve stone man standing on the tip of a shovel'.

There are several references to my father's grandfather winning the shott-putt at West Calder sports days during the 1880s. It is reported in the *Courier* that on 7 August 1880, he threw a 16lb iron ball a distance of 36ft. 3ins; W. Goodwood threw 35ft. 3ins and A. Prentice 30ft. 5ins. Anyone wishing to examine this more closely might consider getting a seven kilo bag of potatoes from their local super-market but, before hurling it anywhere, try carrying it to the carpark without the aid of a trolley.

Over the years we sometimes caught a glimpse of the power such work had endowed my father, even 20 years after he had left the pits. On one occasion, my brother needed a piano moved downstairs and so he called in my young brother and my father, who was then pushing 60. My father was nominated 'anchor-man' at the top of the stairs and he had a rope, one end of which was tied round the piano, and the other end loped around his neck and back. My two brothers took up position beneath the piano, an old upright, to support and guide it round the bend at the bottom of the stair, but it was so tight at one point that neither of them could get any grip on it at all, and so they both stood back, keeping it off the wall-paper, while the piano swung gently to and fro from a rope slung around their old man's neck: he didn't seem to notice.

Yet my brother's scepticism is not out of place. The heroic narratives of mining and masculinity are not untrue – just endlessly repeated – while perhaps more remarkable feats – of the imagination – go unsaid: a shale inspector becomes a Highland Chief and the People's Hall, West Calder, the Clachan of Aberfoyle.

As a youth heading for university rather than the pits, there was little reason for me to talk to my father either about his grandfather or the shale industry. We spoke about football, politics or the books I was reading. I asked him once why my English teacher, a brilliant Oxford scholar (and a high Tory), didn't write books. 'A teacher is a man among boys, and a boy among men', he opined: thus spake the Old

Man. About that time [1966], we talked about a Scottish novel I was reading for this English teacher – *Sunset Song*, by Lewis Grassic Gibbon. He said that he had never heard of it, and what did I like about it. I told him of Gibbon's description of a local policeman whose feet had 'a good grip of Scotland'. That was an old one, he thought. I asked him if any Scottish writers had written about mining, and he told me about Joe Corrie. What I mean by this is that he spoke the following poem to me like it was a love song from Robert Burns:

The image o god

Joe Corrie

Crawlin' aboot like a snail in the mud,
Covered wi' clammy blae,
Me, made after the image o' God –
Jings! but it's laughable tae.

Howkin' awa' 'neath a mountain o' stane,
Gaspin' for want o' air,
The sweat makin' streams doon my bare back-
bane
And my knees a' hackit and sair.

Strainin' and cursin' the hale shift through,
Half-starved, half-blin', half-mad;
And the gaffer he says, 'Less dirt in that coal
Or ye go up the pit, my lad!'

So I gi'e my life to the Nimmo squad
For eicht and fower a day;
Me, made after the image o' God –
Jings! but it's laughable tae.

Grim laughter this:

> The human situation was comical even when it was tragic. The dialect poets see clearly how people are made foolish – by pride, by love, by poverty, by old age, even by death itself – and they can laugh about it. The best dialect poets assert the dignity of man, even when he is undignified by circumstance. They assert the quality of man, even when he is humiliated by his betters.[8]

A mordant wit and the refusal to bow, mentally, before the aegis of your betters was about as much as there was keeping self-respect intact: eejits at least had opinions; bloody eejits had nane. In an ill-divided world, your status as a human being, let alone as an individual, often came down to its assertion, and in the face of most evidence to the contrary.

A community exists in its anecdotes

The basics of shale – shale, miner, hutch, muscle, humour

> they all met at the end house
> they maybe played pontoon
> they talked
> some great characters
> Old Jock Murray
> there's no corners to hear them at now
> know what I mean?
>
> *James: extract from 'No Corners'*

A strong inter-generational sense of 'community' is evident in the oral histories as well as my father's stories and writings regarding not only football, but mining life and 'locality' in general. When I first read the following passage – a description of the small Shetland island community of Whalsay – it struck me how easily it could have been written by my father about any shale mining village in West Lothian between 1900–50, and with the full agreement of the inhabitants:

[There is] is a powerful sense of historical continuity in which the past and present are curiously merged. The past is ever-present, in yarns about characters of old, in the minutiae of place names; in the historical association of families with their crofts and parts of the isle... Conversation thus spans and concertinas the centuries. In this and in the extensive knowledge of geneology and kinship history there is a pervasive sense of rootedness, of belonging, as if people were as immovably and inherently part of the island as the very features of its landscape.[1]

Substitute in the above 'crofts and parts of the isle' for 'rows' or mines, oil-works, 'gaffers', football teams, local 'characters' and so on, and you will probably have the shale villages. Finding less deadly ways of relating, of ignoring or laughing at the chronic political and religious differences too easily found in these workplaces and localities, and by channelling them into competitive, contested and sometimes aggressive sports and past-times, may help explain some of the following, if that is, it needs any explanation at all.

Mining communities were, like other small communities, bounded by a humour in which people could recognise themselves and each other. My father often wrote about or quoted local characters who were in many respects unofficial public figures – such as 'Old Jock Murray' from Winchburgh – who was several times mentioned in the oral histories taken. It was to him that my father attributed the phrase – 'ye'll laugh, but ye'll no pu' gress' (quoted in my transcribed poem 'Niddry') – allegedly said by a youngster who had just soiled his breeks, rebuking his pals for not taking his plight more seriously. The grim poverty of the period probably made such incidents not uncommon, and the grim humour that accompanied them just as inevitable. The paler versions of such stories my father would sometimes smuggle into print, such as the article, 'Humour in the Shale Mines', written in 1951, which begins with some reflections on the nature and source of local humour as arising from the working and social conditions of miners. Its opening implies attitudes towards 'study' and the acquisition of general knowledge which are suggestive of both the Scottish Enlightenment and what has recently come to be called the 'democratic intellect':

Folk unacquainted with the mining fraternity often express surprise at the high standards of intelligence and knowledge exhibited by miners. It is not really surprising because mental relaxation is the natural antidote to hard physical labour. That is why so many miners study a variety of subjects entirely divorced from their own everyday job of work. Study is a hobby with many of them and as they are not compelled to specialise, they gain a wide knowledge of many subjects. The student miner will hold his own in any company because, in addition to his studies, he has an unrivalled opportunity to examine human nature in everyday experience. The miner is always something of a philosopher and fatalist, and humour must thrive in these circumstances.

Every mining community has its wags, men whose comments upon everyday incidents at work or in the world at large are eagerly listened to and retold with relish by their workmates. Such a one was the late Jock Murray who enjoyed much local fame as a natural humorist at Winchburgh. Jock was a true Scot, a hardy, independent, quick moving man of medium height with always a twinkle in his eye. His wit was as natural as it was flashing and had that sardonic, dry tang to it that stimulates and is so peculiarly Scots. Jock had something to say on whatever happened and some of his sayings became classics in the village... On one occasion the local sewing teacher, who owned a Baby Austen car, was involved in a collision with a bus. The car was badly damaged and got locked on to the front of the bus. Fortunately, the driver was uninjured. Jock and some of his pals had been sitting at a nearby corner and came to render assistance. Some of them got round the miniature car and lifted it bodily away from the bus. As they stood thus, Jock turned to the teacher and asked – 'Whaur will we hing it?'

...Best known of the Broxburn wags was the late Andrew Sibbald. Stories about him are legion and one of the best is about the time he was on strike and was feeling very dry the next morning. He was also broke. He called to see the local bank manager and delivered himself thus – 'Noo, ye may say that ye're no gaun tae gie me it, but ye canna say ye hinni goat it. Could ye lend me five bob?'[2]

Many of my father's best stories were reserved for the pub rather than print and some of these provide better insights into the culture than those just quoted. They also provide an insiders account of the mining community in contrast to George Orwell, for example, who wrote some memorable passages describing miners working underground in the 1930s, and what it was like going down a coalmine:

Usually it is bad going underfoot – thick dust or jagged chunks of shale, and in some mines where there is water it is as mucky as a farm-yard. Also there is the track for the coal tubs, like a miniature railway track with sleepers a foot or two apart, which is tiresome to walk on. Everything is grey with shale dust; there is a dusty fiery smell which seems to be the same in all mines. You see mysterious machines of which you never learn the purpose, and bundles of tools slung together on wires, and sometimes mice darting away from the beam of the lamps. They are surprisingly common, especially in mines where there are or have been horses. It would be interesting to know how they got there in the first place; possibly by falling down the shaft – for they say a mouse can fall any distance uninjured, owing to its surface area being so large relative to its weight. You press yourself against the wall to make way for lines of tubs jolting slowly towards the shaft, drawn by an endless steel cable operated from the surface. You creep through sacking curtains and thick wooden doors which, when they are opened, let out fierce blasts of air. These doors are an important part of the ventilation system. The exhausted air is sucked out of one shaft by means

> of fans, and the fresh air enters the other of its own accord. But if left
> to itself the air will take the shortest way round, leaving the deeper
> workings unventilated; so all the short cuts have to be partitioned off.
> At the start, to walk stooping is rather a joke, but it is a joke that soon
> wears off.[3]

All of this is very well expressed, of course, and one is left wondering what Orwell would have made of the discussion in 'no rats' about how mice find their way down mines. He would have enjoyed the story about a long walk to 'the face' which my father attributed to Jock Murray's brother when he went to work in a Fife coalmine at the start of the First World War. Accordingly, on his first day down the mine, the said Murray eventually got to the face after a great many detours, only to be met by the gaffer who gave him a great speech about them being at War and how it was everybody's duty to produce, for King and Country, as much as he could in order to defeat the Germans. To which Jock Murray's brother replied, still blowing from the effort it had taken him to reach there: 'Nae wonder they're fighting us. We're stealing their bloody coal'.

For all the accuracy of Orwell's descriptions, they remain the observations of an outsider. The difficulty in trying to tell the story of these story-tellers, however, is getting beyond the stories themselves. It may be that the stories are all that remain or are all that ought to matter. At any rate, my father behaved as though his stories just spoke for themselves, 'stories' in the proper sense – not just 'jokes' – but parables and homilies shot through with the times, and the culture of the times. He would sometimes unleash a stream of anecdote and folklore until he, the listener and the 'characters' he was describing, all seemed to meet on the same plain of time and history, and then he would walk away. And the culture he was describing was a bit like that as well: if you didn't get the point, then the point would probably end up getting you.

A couple of examples may serve to illustrate this better than a couple of thousand words of mine. The first story concerns a miner (who else?) and his wife who were having trouble with their two laddies' 'swearing':

> Miner and wife are in bed and the wife says –
> 'you'll need to do something about they laddies.
> They're swearing something terrible. They wont
> listen to me.' 'Right', says the father, 'we'll see
> about that the morn.' Next morning, the mother
> is making breakfast and the father is sitting at the
> table, reading his paper. The first laddie comes in
> and the mother says – 'What would you like for

your breakfast Willie?' And Willie says – 'An effing biled egg.' The father reaches out from behind
his paper and biffs Willie and, as the lad is sliding
down the wall, the father calmly turns the next
page of his paper. The mother turns to the next
laddie, who has been watching all this, and says –
'And what would you like, Hughie?'

And Hughie says – 'No an effing biled egg.'

The story conveys all the significant aspects of working class life
during the period: the father as authority figure, able and willing to
assert himself physically if required; the mother is in the kitchen,
ignored by, and ineffectual against, the willpower of her male off-
spring; the underlying dilemma – the 'threat' which 'swearing' represents in that community, namely the loss of working-class
'respectability'; the sting in the tale – the revelation that traditional
authority, even when it says and does what traditional authority has
always said and done, cannot guarantee the compliance of 'the
young' – which was the problem facing all those attempting to maintain 'control' [not only of 'the young' but of other forces] against a
background of general class conflict.

It is a story about culture and class, language being a central part of
the process. Just as my father's article on 'humour in the shalemines'
opened with a disclaimer – that manual labour need not be equated
with ignorance or inferior knowledge – many of his stories presume
an intelligent and educated working-class existing within their own
traditions and forms of 'speech', despite a social order which has
done its best to excluded them.

One story deals directly with 'Scots', the language of the streets, and
generally admitted into classrooms only in the truncated form of the
[carefully selected] poetry and songs of Burns. A visiting American
Professor is seeking the English equivalent of the word 'thrawn' and he
is told that, although there is none, a story might help explain it. The
tale involves a miner and his 'laddie' who is beginning to exhibit the
rebelliousness associated with youth. The lad has a stomach-ache but
is refusing to take the medicine his mother has offered. The father
decides on direct action, and a furious physical struggle ensues which
lasts until the son is eventually trapped in a hammer-lock. The son,
with tears in his eyes, grudgingly concedes – 'Aw right, faither, I'll take
it, but,' he adds, 'I'll no swallow it.' 'And that's 'thrawn'?', the
Professor asks. 'No', he is told, 'that's just 'determined'. So another
desperate struggle ensues, worse than before, until the lad finally calls
out – 'Aw right, faither, I'll take it,' before adding, 'but I'll no keech.'

And that, the Professor is told, is 'thrawn'.

These stories seem to me symbolic of the community as a whole: personal memories interwoven with collective memory and group identity – not standing outside history or society – but part of it. My father's weekly newspaper column, 'Bathgate Brevities', was perhaps the written equivalent of Jock Murray and his cronies standing on 'corners' in every mining village in Scotland – trading observations with the like minded, certainly – but acting also as a transmission belt for collective knowledge and identity. In 1959, a dozen years after he had left the mines, my father could still be found passing on the sayings of one Wull Kerr – an emigre from Bathgate to Australia, itself a sort of transcontinental 'Scotch-Corner'. Anything remotely interesting was sure to be passed along:

> Wull Kerr has sent me a note concerning blaeberries. Referring to himself as one of my stravaiging friends, Wull says the blaeberry crop promises to be a record one. Berries apparently are big and plentiful and although the old Blaeberry Mair was burnt off two years ago, a visit to Cairnpapple should prove worthwhile. Wull's note concludes: 'I admit the blaeberry is 'fiky tae poo'.[4]

You can almost hear Jock Murray nodding.

Jock Murray: Winchburgh's native wit – Obituary

Jock Murray, 'Mount Hooley Jock', to distinguish him from other 'Murrays', died aged 80 years at Winchburgh in November 1950. He lived most of his life in and around Winchburgh and Philpstoun. A soldier in his youth, he saw service at home and abroad with the Royal Scots. He was an active member of the British Legion and was laid to rest with a Union Jack draped over his coffin. When he left the army, he became a shaleminer and remained so until his retirement. A keen admirer of Burns, he gave many recitations at Lea Rigg Burns Club functions. He was regarded with great affection by the whole community as a wit and raconteur and such was his art that no offence ever seems to have been taken by the victims of his humorous sallies, mostly his workmates and 'gaffers' – who were his most prized targets. My father thus concludes the obituary which appeared in the *West Lothian Courier*, 1 December 1950:

> A favourite spot of his was the seat at the Steel Bridge [Winchburgh] where, on fine days, he held court and great were the quips and reminiscences.

No Corners

James: oilworker, born 1910, Winchburgh

'Was there much rivalry between villages?'

'Heavens, aye.
Niddry and Winchburgh.
You know Niddry up there,
they would fight and die for each other,
at that time.
They were a great community up there.
There was in Niddry some characters.
They used to think that us in Winchburgh were snobbish.
But they had works up there, you see,
and just where the tips start,
the work was opposite the first tip, you ken,
the left hand side by the garage,
the row started right hand side,
just at the foot of the wee hill,
and it went right along the site in front of that tip,
right along,
a single row,
and then they went right down to the farm at the far end,
same again on the left hand side of the brae,
Niddry Brae,
there was a back row.
It was a right community.
It was great.
In fact,
when we were at school,
we were afraid to go round – 'we are the Niddry Boys!'
And there was a team called,
Niddry Celtic and Winchburgh Albion.
In fact Winchburgh Albion,
the juvenile team the now,
who celebrated their Golden Jubilee about three or four
years ago,
never been down.
And they were called the –
just Winchburgh laddies.
They're still not all Winchburgh play for it now,

maybe ten from each side.
Used to be great rivalry.
And where the bottom of where Millgate is,
there now,
that was Niddry's football field.
Now see when they met,
there was skin and hair flying.
They got pulled apart, oh aye,
oh dear.
I remember one time,
Winchburgh Albion,
they were playing,
Willie Thornton was playing for them at that time.
He played for Rangers for years after that.
His father was under manager in the mine.
He played with them,
and was pretty local at the time.
They went through to Eastfield at Cambuslang.
They drew 5-5 in the Scottish Cup,
so they came here the following Saturday,
big crowd,
only one local policeman when it started.
It finished up with five policemen, two doctors,
and an ambulance.
It was in the Post headlines the next day.
A fight started between some of the Winchburgh boys,
and some Eastfield boys,
and if anyone got hurt,
they were just taken across to this house,
where the doctor looked at them.
One boy got taken away in an ambulance,
a Glasgow boy.
They thought he'd a broken leg.
Took him up to Bangour.
He nipped out at night and got home.
Aye, there was skin and hair flying that day!
The local rivalry was great,
but it was never bad,
it never lasted.
It was rivalry, not hatred.

There were characters in those days.
As I said to one boy,
'there are no characters now',
he says,
'John, but there are no corners now.'
See what we call corners,
up at the Tally Ho there,
well the men used to meet there at nights,
after the backshift,
anything from 6 o'clock onwards,
and there was always some humorist there.
Talk about comedians!
The same at Niddry.
At the end of Niddry at the top of the brae,
they all met at the end house.
They maybe played pontoon,
they talked,
some great characters,
Old Jock Murray,
there's no corners to hear them at now,
know what I mean?'

Willie Thornton: local hero

(left to right) Willie Thornton, Sammy Cox (Glasgow Rangers) and
Bobby Evans (Celtic) preparing for a Scottish International, July 1949
photo: Hulton Getty Collection

Willie Thornton was born in Winchburgh on 3 March 1920, into a
shale mining family. He was spotted by Bill Struth, manager of
Glasgow Rangers, as a 16 year old goal scoring prodigy with
Winchburgh Albion. Willie was a village son who took over as centre-
forward with the Albion from another village son, my father, when
he gave up playing to become the club's secretary. Despite his subsequent fame and fortune, Willie remained a regular visitor to the
village to see family and friends and to present medals and trophies
at Albion 'socials'. My mother can remember Willie standing with
the men at weekends at the corner of Main Street in Winchburgh,
just along from where we lived. My father used to take him running
along the canal bank to improve his 'pace'. She can also remember
going with my father, Willie's brother Jim and various locals on the
train through to Glasgow to see Willie play in several cup finals in
the late 1940s. Willie remembered my mother too, and her flaming
red hair, when a family friend visited Ibrox in the 1980s. He also
remembered my father and, in a typically generous statement, said
that my father had taught him all he knew about football when he
was a youngster. Well, my father taught me everything he knew
about football when I was a youngster, and it didn't get me a game
for Rangers!

Willie signed for Rangers in March 1936, becoming a professional player a year later. He started off playing on the wing, a skilful and stylish player. He won the first of his four League Championship medals in 1939 at the age of 19 years. He also won three Scottish Cup medals, two League Cups and seven Scotland caps (plus two unofficial). The War intervened, of course, during which he was awarded the Military Medal in the Italian campaign with the Duke of Atholl's Highlanders.

He formed a formidable goal-scoring partnership, and later a managerial partnership, with Willie Waddell, a prodigiously powerful outside right whose crosses to Thornton's head became legendary in the Rangers successes of the late 1940s and early 1950s. Thornton headed 'hat-tricks' against East Fife in the 1949 Scottish Cup semi-final and the 1950s Scottish Cup final. A high proportion of his 188 goals in 303 games for the club were in fact headers. His reputation and popularity amongst fans was based on quality play, exceptional talent in the air and goal scoring ability. He also became a by-word for sportsmanship during a period when a high level of physical contact and endurance was tolerated, indeed expected, from those who played and watched the sport. His personal courtesy and conscientiousness was noted early on by Bill Struth, a disciplinarian of the old school before the days of the 'track-suit' manager, who praised him as a youngster for the polish he got on his boots and his diligence at training. If memory serves, I believe Mr Struth was even moved to give Willie a couple of shillings for the shine on those boots, and one suspects there could have been no greater praise.

Willie Thornton was Scotland's Player of the Year in 1952. He retired from playing in June 1954 to become manager of Dundee FC and then Partick Thistle FC. I believe he was also a journalist for a time. He later became assistant manager at Ibrox to Willie Waddell and wrote 'Blue Heaven', a guide to the Ibrox Trophy Room, to which he would act as host to visitors to the Stadium. The Thornton Suite at Ibrox has the fitting inscription – 'One who wore the Light Blue to the honour of himself and the club he served'. It seems to me that in his personal reserve and grace combined with skill and grit, he was the product of the shale community as much as, if not more than, the Ibrox community. Willie Thornton died on 26 August 1991, after a short illness at Gartnavel Hospital, Glasgow, aged 71 years.

Fitba' Cliché

(The Ba's No For Eatin)

Alistair Findlay

I remember being told by Big MacIntyre
tae take mair time oan the ba'. Listen son, he says,
yir playing like the gress wis oan fire.
Yir blindin us a' wi the stour.

This is a gemm fur men,
no boays, or weans, or jessies.
If yir good enough, yir big enough, they say, but
never listen or play tae the crowd,
an forget a' yir faither's advice,
and yir great uncle Tam's an a',
wha' played wi Champfleurie Violet's Cup Winning Team.
They days are a' gaun, like snaw aff
a Geordie Young clearance.

Then
it wis the people's gemm,
a' aboot the ba' an beatin yir men,
this way then that, then swingin it ower frae the wing,
an up like a bird tae heid it awa' and intae the net.
The goalie, auld as yir faither an dressed like yir grannie,
stuck in the mud like a big stranded whale – Goal!
And a hundred thousand voices sang in Hampden Park.
Ye couldnae see the sun fur bunnets.

Romantic?
Ay, and a' for the glory o'it.
Well, that's a' shite noo son,
the ba's no for eatin oanie mair.

Time was
when ye could tell a prospect
by the way he shed his hair,
or jouked bye his relations in the scullery,
but we still believed in Empire then,
ken,
when The Wee Blue Devils buried themsels at the England end
and half o' Europe, for a glory that wisnae worth haen,
oor ain, singin an deein like cattle,
brought hame not one lullabye in gaelic.

> In the room the punters come and go
> Talking of De Stephano

On the terraces,
beneath the stand,
a poet speaks for a nation:

> the ref's a baam.

Hunting the leather

Football was a ruling passion as far as my father and most of his generation were concerned and a central part of their identity and culture, indeed, a metaphor for 'life' itself – an arena for skill, courage and character to be played out. His description of 'Winchburgh Win Scottish Juvenile Cup' (1953) is of a community celebrating its own values – solidarity, continuity, and sacrifice: the social individual not bourgeois individualism is the basis of that society and culture, and you can almost touch it:

> I marched behind the Band pretty near in tears. It seems funny, but it's true. I thought back on the early days of the local boys who formed the Club, of our triumphs and our defeats and of the great legion of fine boys who have worn the black and white and helped us to build our great reputation and tradition which was crowned today. I thought of Moleskin Murray, of Matt Stewart and other former Albion lads who gave their lives for their country with the same cheerfulness and determination as they had played football. I felt that their spirits marched with us, sharing the triumph. It seemed to me that it had been given to us, a humble football club, to achieve something for our village; that we have been directing the energies of youth in the proper direction, for football is but life in miniature, and if you play it in the proper spirit then generally you will play the game of life the same way, and I felt very humble.[1]

West Lothian Albion (1908): joined the Senior League 1906

WEST LOTHIAN COURIER – 12 JANUARY 1945

WINCHBURGH CLUBS

Prompted by our report of the revival of Winchburgh Albion FC a reader has given us a copy of the minute of another meeting held in the village to form a football club 52 years ago. The minute was contained in a notebook belonging to an official of Young's Oil Co., Ltd., now probably deceased, which has come into the possession of our reader, but who the owner of the book was he does not know.

It is headed, 'Winchburgh Football Club', and states: 'Committee, Messrs Fullarton, Stevenson, Wilson, Brown and Hardie. Treasurer, R. Gemmell, Secretary, R. Lindsay. A public meeting held in Winchburgh Public School on 18 March 1892. The Rev. Charles Fullarton in the chair, met to consider the formation of a football club.

MINISTER AS OFFICE BEARER

The chairman said that he had seen Mr Somervail, who was willing to grant the use of one of his fields for football purposes, for a sum not exceeding £5 per annum.

The meeting considered this satisfactory. It was settled that an entrance of 2s be paid be each member and a sum of 1s per month thereafter for the maintenance of the club.

Many readers will spot one slip by the writer of this minute. The minister referred to was not the Rev. Charles, but the Rev. George Fullarton, a much loved minister of Winchburgh Parish Church, who died a comparatively young man and to whose memory a plaque can be seen on the wall of the church. We are told that he was a man of sporting tastes and played with the club he helped to raise. His name is still closely linked with the village since our County Councillor, Walter George Fullarton Scott, is named after him.

The treasurer, R. Gemmell, preceded Mr Scott's father as manager of Glendevon mine, while the secretary, R. Lindsay, was a pipe maker at Winchburgh Brickworks. The committee member was probably Mr Daniel Wilson, Meadowpark, who died some months ago and was always a great football enthusiast. The Brown referred to was probably Mr Andrew Brown, who lived until his death years ago at Duntarvie View, Main Street, but so far we have been unable to find out who Hardie was but some older reader may be able to inform us. The same applies to Stevenson.

WHICH WAS THE FIRST FOOTBALL CLUB?

Like the reader who gave us the copy of the minute, we were of the opinion that this was probably Winchburgh's first football club, but on enquiry, we discovered that opinions differ on this point. All of the old Winchburgh men we have spoken to about the matter remember the club, and it did actually play in Mr Somerville's, then tenant of Glendevon Farm, field, the second field past Black's property on the north side of the Linlithgow Road, but some say that even before then a Winchburgh club played on the ground behind Castle Road cottages between there and the 'Greenshale'. Mr David Brown, who played with the club to which the minute refers, says that he previously played with the Castle Road club and that was before there were any houses there. Mr Wm. Wilson shares his opinion. He remembers both clubs and came to Winchburgh when very young 60 years ago. Mr Frank Lacey, who is 78, and was born at Broomhouse, says that the Linlithgow Road club was first and several other agree with him. Since we have no way of settling the argument, being 'too young at the time!', we must leave them to settle it themselves.

One point on which they are all agreed however, is that a club, Broomhouse Violet, played at Broomhouse before either of the Winchburgh clubs, and Mr D. Brown played with all three clubs already mentioned. Broomhouse Violet might have been a Niddry club since even then when there was no oilwork at Winchburgh, Niddry work was going strong. The club lost its ground at Broomhouse and moved to Niddry where they played on a pitch on the ground on which the old Niddry tip now stands.

In those days football had not reached its full peak as a national sport and was something of a new craze with the workers. Consequently the competitive side of it had yet to be developed. There were some cup competitions but no leagues and the clubs played friendly games mostly.

NIDDRY VIOILET

There was a club, Niddry Violet, who were probably the first tenants of Niddry Sports Park round about the beginning of the century, whom old-timers still consider were the best juvenile club ever in this district.

They were defeated in the semi-final of the Scottish Juvenile Cup at Easter Road, and it is still thought that they should have won the trophy that year, Mr B. Gorman played with this club and other players were Mr Frank Donnolly, goalkeeper; the late Mr F. Finnegan, whose wife and family are still in Winchburgh and no doubt there still remain other members of the team in the district. Their most famous player was the famous Dan Gordon, Broxburn, Scottish International and Celtic back. Following Niddry Violet there arose round about 1906 a West Lothian Albion of which Mr Gorman was secretary. At that time almost every village had its senior club and the Albion were a strong going club and produced many good players. Even yet we hear of the great days when Leith Athletic and other famous clubs visited the village.

This club played at Niddry Sports Park and as the shale oil industry came to Winchburgh itself, Recreation Park, Winchburgh, was opened. This pitch was used first of all by a succession of Juvenile Clubs notably Winchburgh Thistle, but it was the great junior club, Winchburgh Violet which really put the village name in the forefront.

WINCHBURGH VIOLET

During the last war and the years immediately after, the Violet simply walked through all opposition in the East of Scotland. Even yet local enthusiasts swear that never was there a Junior team like them. Eventually Winchburgh Thistle again rose under the Junior banner to challenge the Violet and we had two Junior clubs in the village. The Thistle got nearly all of its players locally, the famous Willie Harper kept goal for them and the brothers Willie, Tom and Colin White also played as did the McLean brothers, David and Robert. Following this we again had a succession of Juvenile clubs, Winchburgh Juveniles, Winchburgh Rose and then the present Winchburgh Albion which is 15 years old and has probably a longer history than any local club. They also reached the Scottish Club semi-final to fall very tamely to a club they should have beaten out of sight, Renfrew Waverly, at Armadale in 1938.

Junior Football came back to the village a few years before the war with the formation of Winchburgh Juniors FC. This club somehow never seemed to make the most of its opportunities but did reach the semi-final of the Scottish Junior Cup failing to Armadale Thistle first at Easter Road, and later in a protested replay at Falkirk.

That, briefly, is a summary of local football history. Football has been a part of the village life for many years and the game enthusiastically supported. There is no evidence that enthusiasm has diminished any and it is our belief that the village would welcome and support when times are more opportune than these a good-going Junior team. With our football history, it seems only but fit that we should have one.

MORE MEMORIES OF FORTY YEARS AGO

Last week's article about the football clubs of Winchburgh and Niddry has brought a contribution from an Edinburgh correspondent who was in touch with the game in the district about forty years ago. He writes:

I was interested in the article last week describing the formation of the first football club in Winchburgh in 1892. My recollections do not go as far back as than, but from about 1900 up to the outbreak of the last war i knew the football personalities in the district with some degree of intimacy. It struck me in reading the article that Winchburgh was lucky to have a parish minister like the Rev. George Fullarton, who was broadminded enough to be one of the founders of the first football club's in the village. It would be well if more ministers took an interest in the sports of the masses.

FLOURISHING NIDDRY VIOLET

About 1900 Niddry Violet were the flourishing team of the village. They played on the Sports Park, Niddry and made their mark in Scottish and East of Scotland Junior Cup competitions in which they had strong local rivals in Broxburn Athletic, Vale of Grange and Bo'ness, 'Our Boys'. Sports Park is now the site of a housing scheme. As a football park, it had its peculiarities, being level for about three quarters of its surface, and sloping sharply at the south end, where many fine feats of goalkeeping were done against forwards whose pace was quickened by the gradient. Old timer will recall that kicking the ball into the canal in the nearby cutting could be a very annoying time-wasting expedient.

But despite these drawbacks, Niddry Violet gained a reputation for clean and clever play and many of the players were lads who did a hard day's darg in the mines before taking part in the match on the Saturday afternoon.

DAN GORDON'S COACH

Dan Gordon was mentioned as one of their most famous players, but I do not think it is correct to say that Dan became a Celtic player and an internationalist. His name does not appear in the international records. My recollection is that Dan went from Niddry to Broxburn when the senior club played on Crow's Nest Park. He had a pair of legs that looked as if they were made for football. His speed was above the average for a full-back and he had a ready kick.

I think he learned a lot in position play and in tactics generally through playing alongside Peter Meechan in the Broxburn team. Peter had had experience in England and it was he who coached young Dan in the art of sizing up an oncoming forward and getting in an effective tackle. Dan went from Broxburn to Everton and saw service also with Southampton, St Mirren and Falkirk and Middlesborough. He returned to Scotland with a back injury that ended his football career.

Niddry Violet lost so many players to the seniors that the club had to close down in 1905 after a long and distinguished career. It was, no doubt, with the object of getting some of these players back to Sports Park that a senior club with the name of West Lothian Albion was formed in the spring of 1906. Among those who returned were Dan Clark, Peter Finnigan, Charlie Devine, W White, and Peter Law.

WHEN ALBION TOOK THE FIELD

The Albion's first match was against Broxburn Athletic at Albion Park on the opening night of season 1906–07, when they drew 0–0. I remember the new team wore dark blue jerseys with white shorts and dark blue stockings with white rings, and a very favourable impression they created.

Their left wing, Devine and Waugh, earned something of a reputation in the season that followed. Charlie Devine was a football artist, quiet and unassuming, and able to put the ball where Waugh, all speed and fire, could dash ahead and score. Danny Clark had, I think, already given his best to Broxburn. He was big and strongly built and at home on any position on the field, not excluding goal.

FOUR GAMES TO DECIDE THE WINNER

The Albion were able to give all their neighbours a shake at the most times. On one occasion it took four games to dispose of Broxburn Shamrock in an East of Scotland qualifying cup tie. All four games ended in favour of the Albion, but in three the Shamrock successfully protested on the ground of professional irregularities. In the fourth game, extra time was required, so that the tie entailed 390 minutes' play – a prodigious but tiresome cup-tie.

CLASHES WITH LEITH

In the Scottish Qualifying Cup competition the Albion had two exciting encounters with Leith, then in their hay-day as a Second Division League Club. On both occasions, Leith won by the odd goal. I have no doubt many Winchburgh folks will still recall the stir created by the influx of Leith supporters.

Among officials who served the club well I recall Bernard Gorman and Andrew Nicol, both of whom were players of some account before taking on secretarial duties. It is obvious that the village still is potentially rich in football skill and in the post-war years may produce more Gordons, Harpers, and Thorntons. It can hardly be otherwise where the team sprit is so actively cultivated as among the miners and oil-workers of Winchburgh.

West Lothian Courier –
JUNE 12, 1954

'Winchburgh Win Scottish Juvenile Cup Civic Reception and Scenes of Great Enthusiasm'

Saturday 7 June, proved to be a red-letter day in the annals of Winchburgh Albion FC, and the village of Winchburgh. Fresh from their emphatic and fighting victory over Bayview youth club in the final at Easter Road Park, the team and players arrived home in triumph with Captain Willie Pryde proudly bearing the handsome trophy, bedecked in black and white ribbons.

They are nothing if not confident in Winchburgh. Defeat was never thought of. Everything was arranged as if it were a certainty that the Scottish Cup would arrive home with the team. Winchburgh Public Band has their orders and Queensferry District Council had a civic reception all laid on. Councils, of course are not so impulsive as football clubs and the District Council, assuming rightly that it was a great feat for a village club even to reach the final of this mammoth competition, which has a yearly entry of nearly 500 clubs, intended giving the reception win or loose. It was a sensible arrangement but it needed the Cup to really round off the occasion.

There is only one way of describing the scenes. Winchburgh went daft. When the team and officials arrived by bus with the Cup, every man, woman and child in the village and surrounding district seemed to turn out to greet them. The Band waited at Castle Road, the whole team clambered onto the roof of the bus – most of them had been there nearly all the way from Edinburgh in any case, and the triumphal procession began. It was hard to believe that so many people could be living in Winchburgh. The cheers rolled loud and long. The crowd cheered the Cup, they cheered the team and they cheered the Hon. Presidents Willie Thornton (Rangers FC) and John Johnston (Motherwell FC), and their wives, who had been the Club's guests at the game and came back to Winchburgh with them to share in the celebrations. Even the Band seemed to surpass themselves, and never had music sounder sweeter. Behind the Band marched the Catholic Youth Club. Real enthusiasts they are, and organised. Most of the boys wore frock coats and tall hats decorated with the black and white of Albion and drawings of Cups and footballs in white paint all over them, and with the Youth Club, marched the youth of the village, united in acclaiming the local team. The Albion Committee, as always, were in the background, but with their chests well out. For them, this was a realisation of a 23 year dream. They had dreamed of such a triumph and had seen their hopes dashed with it in sight on many occasions. Now that it was here, the feeling was pretty overpowering. One of them described it thus: I marched behind the Band pretty much in tears. It seems funny, but its true. I thought back on the early days of the local boys who formed the Club, of our triumphs and our defeats and of the great legion of fine boys who have worn the black and white and helped us to build our great reputation and tradition which was crowned today. I through of 'Moleskin' Murray, of Matt Stewart and other former Albion lads who gave their lives for their country with the same cheerfulness and determination as they had played football. I felt that their spirits marched with us, sharing the triumph. It seemed to me that it has been

given to us, a humble football club, to achieve something for our village, that we have been directing the energies of youth in the proper direction, for football is but life in miniature, and if you play it in the proper spirit then generally you will play the game of life the same way, and I felt very humble.

PROCESSION CHEERED

This was the first National Trophy ever to reach Winchburgh and the reception the villagers gave it was worthy of the occasion. Along Main Street, down Niddry Road, and up through the Millgate back to the Tally Ho Square went the procession to cheers and counter cheers from the crowds lining the way.

In the Square, the team and the Cup took farewell of the Band, who had blown lustily and long on the grand tour, and retired to the Lea Rig Hall where the District Council and a civic reception awaited them. There was one discordant note. Centre-forward Bruce Cowan; one of the heroes of the day, had met with injury during the course of the game. Bruce typified the spirit and determination of the team by struggling on, obviously in great pain, until within five minutes of the end only when victory was inevitable did he retire, and the stands rising to him as he did so. After the removal to Edinburgh Royal Infirmary, his trouble was diagnosed as a split kidney. And he had played with it for 80 minutes! Bruce thus missed the great celebrations to which with everybody else, he had looked forward so very much.

The District Council were there in force to welcome the Club, headed by their chairman, Councillor James Todd, Kirkliston. The Cup was given the place of honour in front of the Chairman, and an excellent high tea was served by Broxburn Co-operative Society, Ltd. The excitement and exertions of the day made it certain that all did justice to the meal. How sweet is victory! Never has there been a more amiable or proud gathering in the village. The Council deserve the credit for their enterprise in giving this famous occasion public recognition. The ratepayers, we feel sure, would vote the money well spent. Cities and Burghs honour their heroes, so why not the villages!

Councillor Todd, in his remarks, paid high tribute to Albion FC and their achievement. They had a very illustrious record and had been prominent in football for many years and in winning the Scottish

Cup had brought honour not only to themselves and Winchburgh , but to the whole of West Lothian. He paid high tribute to the officials and Committee. While others devoted their time to watching Hearts, Hibs, Rangers and other famous Senior Clubs, it said a lot for their enthusiasm and public spirit that they were prepared to spend their time organising small village clubs, thus providing the facilities for youth to play organised games and at the same time nurturing the community spirit, which is so very important. Winchburgh Albion FC had shown a great example in this respect and thoroughly deserved this triumph in bringing the Scottish Secondary Juvenile Cup to West Lothian for the third time. Previous winners had been Easton Rovers and Armadale United.

WILLIE THORNTON'S COUNCIL

Willie Thornton also spoke, and expressed his happiness at the great triumph won that day by his first club and native village. He had been invited before the game to give the lads some advice, but had felt that on such an occasion it would be presumptuous for him to attempt it. He had merely said, I have heard you are a good team. The fact that you are in this final proves that you are a good team. Go out to this game in the same spirit as you have gone out to all the others. Chase every ball, never give up trying, will yourselves to win and come back with a victory'. Everybody who had witnessed the match would confirm that the team had done just that. They had secured a glorious and fully deserved win. Willie also congratulated the Committee. It was no mere coincidence that those now running the team were still largely the same men as he had played with at the Club. This was the triumph these men had been working for and he was very proud to have been there to see it. It would be left to the Committee to decide what form that bonus would take. Willie concluded by saying, 'Despite the fact that this has been a very dear' day to me, I here and now make the same offer for next season if Albion can retain the Scottish Cup'. (Loud Cheers).

Councillor George Glass, in a short speech, pointed out while cities and burghs had a common interest in honouring outstanding achievements by individuals and organisations, a District Council is different. It represents a wide and scattered area and he wished to thank on behalf of the people of Winchburgh, the members from outside areas who had been unanimous in supporting the proposal to give the Albion FC a civic welcome, win or lose. This was a historic occasion. It was the first authentic civic welcome given by any District Council in the Landward Area of West Lothian, and possibly the first in the country. Councillor Glass also paid tribute to the work done by the football committee and the example it has shown to the village generally. There seemed to be heredity in it. Certain families, the McLeans in this instance, seemed to take the lead in some branch of public effort. No community can exist without such enthusiasts. The Club has been a source of inspiration to the youth of the village and has won unstinted support from the youth of all denominations in it. Such healthy enthusiasm was commendable and if cultivated went a long way towards solving the problem of juvenile delinquency which is troubling the authorities to-day.

MORE CONGRATULATIONS

Councillor James Buchanan also spoke and added his congratulations. He was proud to be associated with the public recognition of the football club's activities. The function of the District Council and the bodies which preceded it used to be mainly paying out parish relief to the unfortunates. It surely indicated some progress when the Council were now able to arrange public recognition of a great feat accomplished by a local club.

Mr Robt. Findlay, Secretary of the West Lothian Secondary Juvenile FA who was accompanied by the Treasurer and Delegate to the National Council of the Scottish Secondary Juvenile FA, Mr Geo. Bertram (Bridgend Rovers) brought congratulations from the County FA. The SSJFA is a large and very efficient organisation catering for the recreation of the youth of Scotland. There are three units, first, the individual Clubs, next, the County Associations, and lastly the National Council. He felt that West Lothian FA could share in the reflected glory of the Winchburgh achievement, which was thoroughly merited and for which they have striven so long. It would give a boost to the game in the county and would inspire others to follow the Winchburgh example.

Mr Andrew Thomson, Vice-President, and Mr T. Stirling replied on behalf of the Club and expressed thanks to the District Council for the magnificent reception given the Club.

Shortly before he died, my father wrote an article about the founding of his local football club, Winchburgh Albion, supplying a photograph of the original team in 1930, with himself at centre-forward, bulging out of a jersey which he said 'you could have spat peas through'. His purpose was, he said, 'to set the record straight' – verifying that Willie Mclean of Winchburgh Albion had been the first West Lothian holder of the office of President of the Scottish Secondary Juvenile Association. Such things were known in, and thought to matter by, the communities that my father wrote for, and about.

Winchburgh Albion Vintage '30

West Lothian Courier
FRIDAY DECEMBER 16, 1977

WINCHBURGH ALBION –
VINTAGE '30

The name of Albion was the Roman one for Britain, meaning 'White Land', chosen because when they gazed across the Channel from France they saw the White Cliffs of Dover. Later, enemies of ours added 'perfidious' to the title, but they were all jealous!

Winchburgh Albion did not take the name from the Romans but from the first football team in the village about 1900 when Winchburgh became a shale mining centre.

That club was West Lothian Albion, which had Senior status and played in an East of Scotland League along with Leith Athletic and others.

The Albion team pictured here was practically the first to represent the club in a bogus tourney at Broxburn, bogus in that it was not under the auspices of any national association.

The line-up was Jimmy Donaldson, Willie Robertson (father of Alistair of West Brom), Adam 'Cookie' Crooks, John Robertson, Andrew Taylor, Willie Law, Willie 'Dougs' Davidson, Tommy 'Fish' Stirling, Bob Findlay, Willie Moleskin's Murray and Bobby Sinclair, (Hearts, Falkirk and Chesterfield).

Willie Murray was to lose his life during the war when he went down in a troopship, sunk by the Japs.

Only Willie Robertson and Willie Low did not take part in the Broxburn tourney. They joined the following year from Newton Rangers when Albion joined the West Lothian Secondary Juvenile FA and League.

The year was 1930. The picture was taken at Mauchline on a trip there to play the local Green Lea in a friendly.

The real founder of the club was the goalkeeper, Adam 'Cookie' Crooks, who bought the first strip from local draper Mrs W. Hogg for a couple of quid. The colours were black and gold and you could have spat peas through the jerseys.

Albion are thus the oldest club in membership of the County FA and have been amongst the trophies nearly all of their history. They have won every trophy open to them including the Scottish Secondary Juvenile Cup, which they won in 1954, and the Lady Darling Scottish Consolation Cup.

Actually, Winchburgh saw the advent of Secondary Juvenile football in the county. Willie McLean was a founder member of that body.

And to set the record straight, the present holder of the office of President of the Scottish Secondary Juvenile FA, Dick McGregor, of Whitburn is not the first West Lothian holder of that office. Willie McLean beat him to it in the 1930s, over 40 years ago.

Willie resigned the secretaryship of the County FA to take that post. He was the real father of Secondary Juvenile football in the county and played a leading part in amalgamating the Broxburn and Bathgate Leagues to form the West Lothian Association.

Both of those Leagues had a membership of at least 16 clubs. Broxburn and Bathgate each had at least four clubs.

The articles describing the history of Winchburgh Clubs contain the rich detail of oral testimony supplied to my father by the village's older residents, no doubt including his own father, a supporter of Broxburn Juniors. His grandfather was also, in his younger days, keen on football and would have been able to read in the *West Lothian Courier* of controversial matches such as that played in 1885 between Bo'ness and Durhamtown Rangers – a testament to the rivalry and passion which the game could arouse at local level. Below, a correspondent (a Bo'ness supporter, it must be said) claimed that his team was so harshly dealt with the week before by the Rangers, in a 'friendly', that they had to send a 'scratch' side to play against Broxburn Shamrock the following week.

West Lothian Courier
SATURDAY JUNE 27, 1885
'FOOTBALL
BO'NESS V. DURHAMTOWN
RANGERS'

The Rangers visited Bo'ness on Saturday last, for the purpose of playing a friendly game. McPhee for the Rangers won the spin up, and elected to take advantage of the strong wind. Bo'ness set the ball in motion, but the Rangers soon got possession of it and brought it into Bo'ness goal, when J. Kelly sent in a good shot which would have made No. 1 for the Rangers had Grant (back for Bo'ness) not prevented it by putting up his hand in the mouth of the goal and throwing it out. Little more, however, occurred on either side until within two minutes of half time, when the Rangers sent in a shot which escaped both hands and feet of Grant, and also the goal-keeper, thus making No. 1 for the Rangers. After ends being changed it appeared that the Rangers settled into their usual style of play by bringing the ball against the wind twice in succession into the Bo'ness territory. On the ball being brought up the third time, Grant, capt. of Bo'ness team, perceiving the danger to which his goal was then exposed, allowed the ball to pass him, and, to the great surprise of the players and spectators, gave Murnin, left wing of the Rangers, a deliberate kick, which left him prostrate on the ground, at the same time saying 'You know what that is for'. At this point, the capt. of the Rangers took his men off the field, which think was a very wise and proper action. On the Rangers seeing the anxiety of the spectators to have the game played out, offered to do so on condition that Grant be put off the field. To this, however, the Bo'ness team did not seem to concede then the Rangers left the ground. It may also be stated that the Rangers received several promises from the secretary of Bo'ness that they would get half the gate money. It would appear that this was one important part of the game which they kept to themselves.

This version of events is contradicted by a Bo'ness supporter who even manages to bring the after-match purvey into the account:

West Lothian Courier

LETTERS TO THE EDITOR
'BO'NESS V. DURHAMTOWN
RANGERS'

Sir, my attention has been drawn to a paragraph in last Saturday's Courier, regarding the above match which contains many false statements, and which give to the conduct of the Rangers a roseate hue; but I will state the facts as they occurred, and leave your readers to judge for themselves which team is to blame. In the first place it stated that Grant, one of Bo'ness backs, prevented the Rangers from scoring by putting up his hand and throwing the ball out, which is untrue, as had Grant done so a foul would have been claimed which was not done. It is next stated that the first goal was got within two minutes of half time. Now, Sir, when half time was up. I tried to draw the attention of the Rangers umpire to the fact, but was unsuccessful, and the Rangers first goal was scored one minute and a half after time should have been called and which I could get proved by a hundred spectators. The paragraph then states that after ends being changed, and while the Rangers were pressing the Bo'ness goal, Grant, captain of the Bo'ness team deliberately turned and kicked Murnin, left wing of the Rangers. Now the true facts are, that while Grant was dribbling the ball before him, Murnin was following him, and seeing that Grant was likely to save the goal, he (Murnin) jumped up behind and planted his heels on Grant's hip, and in the heat of passion, after being treated so cowardly, Grant turned and let kick at Murnin, using the expression reported. Of course Grant should not have done as he did, but his foot scarcely touched Murnin, and as to laying him prostrate on the field is rather drawing it too far. Further, I went to Grant's house after leaving the field and saw where Murnin had kicked him leaving a very nasty mark which can be seen still. It is next stated that the Rangers were to get half the gate. I admit they were, and if they had finished the game, they certainly would, but did the Rangers ever hear of a club getting half the drawings after refusing to finish a game? The Rangers also forgot to mention that they were entertained to a splendid tea by the Bo'ness team, but of course it was not policy on their part to make that fact known. To show more plainly how the Rangers play a friendly match, may I state that two of our players were unable to work for a week after owing to the severe kicking and charging they had received, and on the Saturday following, as the men were still unable to play, we had to send a scratch team to Broxburn to play a charity match with the Shamrock, on behalf of some of their players who had fared rather badly with the Rangers a week or two previous, an arm being broken, besides other injuries. – I am, & c.,

D Thompson, Umpire
Kinglassie Terrace, Bo'ness

The local rivalry was great, but it was never bad.
It never lasted. It was rivalry, not hatred.

James, 'No Corners'

Examining the origins of local football clubs from the end of the last century may tell us more about the cultural identities of the shale communities than most standard histories of the period. There was

Durhamtown Rangers, for example, which, rather confusingly, played in blue but were all Irish Catholics. And there was also Broxburn Shamrock – less confusion here perhaps.

Durhamtown Rangers came from Bathgate and their park was situated near James Young's Chemical Works at Birniehill – which was built in the 1950s across the road from Durhamtown. The park was on the road up to Standhill at the foot of a 'black bing' and a railway signal box – both now gone, like Durhamtown itself. The club was formed in 1883 and as a report of one of its concerts held in 1885 makes clear, the Irish connection was still proudly borne. In the 19th century, Durhamtown was known locally as 'Kelly Flats' because of the preponderance of Irish there. The chairman that particular evening was Dr Kirk, a local personality with profound philanthropic credentials, sporting enthusiasms and masonic tendencies. His reception was good humoured and the main speaker, Mr Gilbertson, was applauded when he referred to himself during his speech as 'a Scotchman amongst Irishmen'. He was given more applause when he said that he hoped to see a good spirit of rivalry kept up between the Rangers and the other local club, the Volunteers, and that there would be a good feeling on both sides.

Dr Kirk suggested that he had been invited along for what he shared with those present, namely, a love of football. The concert proceedings are described in some detail below, giving too an insight into the musical tastes of the day.

West Lothian Courier – DECEMBER 5, 1885

THE RANGERS CONCERT AND ASSEMBLY

An amateur concert followed by an assembly, under the suspices of the Durhaintown Rangers Football Club, took place in the Corn Exchange, Bathgate, on Monday night. There was a good house and the affair passed off in a highly successful manner, which augurs well for the success of future entertainments of a similar character. Dr Kirk occupied the chair and beside him on the platform were the Rev. Thos. O'Carroll, Mr Wm. Roberts, auctioneer and Mr L. Gilbertson, publisher. In the centre of the platform table, under a suitable glass shade, stood the Edinburgh Association Consolation Cup, which was brought to Bathgate for the first time by the Rangers last winter.

The Chairman in opening the proceedings said it struck him that possibly there had been quite enough of speeches delivered from the same platform during the last two or three weeks (Applause) and that the audience had come rather to hear the sweet warbling of some of our local singers than to hear remarks from him. He supposed it was because he was an old football player that they had asked him to preside on the present occasion. (Applause) He then proceeded to speak of the merits of football, which he designated as the best game out, requiring good wind, good legs, and above all, good temper in very trying circumstances. (Applause). He hoped to see a good spirit if rivalry kept up between Rangers and the other local club, the Volunteers, and that there would be good feeling on both sides. (Applause)

Between the parts of the musical programme Mr Gilbertson was called upon to make a few remarks. He said at the outset that few positions were more unfortunate for a public speaker than to be sandwiched

as it were between parts of a musical programme, and it was a question in such circumstances whether the audience or the
speaker were more to be pitied. His
remarks however might have the effect of a
tonic and steady their nerves after so much
fine music and rollicking fun and humour
as they had been enjoying. (Laugher and
applause.) One important point in his
favour was having a good subject, and he
believed it was one in which they would all
be interested, the career of the Durhamtown Rangers. (Applause) The club had
been formed in 1883 and in the many
matches which they played in their first season they sustained only three defeats. One
of the three was unfortunately in the first
round of the Shield ties; another was in the
first round of the Consolation Cup ties; and
the third was an honourable one, the result
of a friendly match with the Hibernians,
acknowledged to be one of the best clubs in
Scotland. (Applause) In the second season
(last winter) they were more successful,
especially in Association ties, running to
the 5th round for the shield,and they were
only prevented by a small score made by
the University, a crack Edinburgh club,
from entering the semi-final. In this competition they had the honour of meeting such
clubs as Mossend Swifts, whom they beat
after a draw of 3 goals each by 7 to 3; and
Bo'ness, one of the best clubs in the
County, whom they beat by 3 to 0. As the
Bo'ness club were the first winners of the
Consolation Cup, the Rangers showed in
beating them in this encounter that they
had brought the cup honourably to
Bathgate. (Applause)

In the Consolation Cup tie last season
their success was complete, not stopping
short even at the final which they won by 5
to 0, thus bringing for the first time such a
cup to Bathgate, where it has its resting
place at least for one season – let us hope
for longer – at least Bathgate would give it
up only on one condition that they bring
the Shield itself instead. (Applause) In this
competition they met the following clubs –
West Calder, who scratched to them;
Mossend Swifts whom they beat by 2 to 1;
aster 3 to 1; Glencairn 2 to 1, after a drawn
game of one goal each; and Sarafield, the
final, 5 to 0 – the last of all Edinburgh clubs
of good standing. Their record last season
1884-85 – was one of the best in the
Calendar of Edinburgh Association they

having played 21 matches, of which they
won 15, lost three, and drew three – won
60 goals and lost five. (Applause) This season had already seen them in the fourth
round of the Shield ties, having played off
Oakbank Thistle by 6 to 1; Pumpherston
15 to 0; Norton Park one of the best in
Edinburgh by 5 to 2. During this short season they had won 27 goals and lost three.
(Applause) They were also in the second
round of Linlithgowshire Cup ties having
beaten Uphall Bluebell by the very decent
score of 16 to 0. (Applause)

They were now pitted against the
Ballstane Birds, and no doubt would polish
them off too. (Applause) Their score in
both Association competitions was goals,
won 42, lost three. In friendly fixtures they
had also been very successful. This season
they had played 10 games of which they
had won eight and lost two. They won 33
goals and lost seven; making the total number of goals for this season, won 75, lost
10. (Applause) The 2nd Eleven had only
sustained two defeats during their whole
career. They entered for the 2nd Eleven
Trophy last season and were successful in
the first round, but were unfortunate
enough to incur the displeasure of the
Association and were disqualified. This
season they were in the second round and
intended to give a good account of themselves. These were all the facts and figures
he meant to trouble them with, but he was
sure they all wished the Rangers continued
success, and if a Scotchman might offer an
advice to Irishmen, he would say to the
Rangers, Adopt as your motto the motto of
that gallant regiment the Royal Scots Greys
– 'Second to none.' (Applause)

The musical programme included an
exceptionally fine variety of sentimental
and comic songs, which were most cred-
itably performed. Miss Donnelly exhibited
the fine quality of her voice to good
account in 'Jessie's Dream' and the 'Bells of
Shandon;' and Mrs McGuire's rendering of
'Killarney' met that appreciation which this
emerald gem never fails to evoke. Mr
Colston gave a finished rendering of the
'Death of Nelson,' and was deservedly
encored for his 'Village Blacksmith,' also
favouring the company in the absence of
Mr Dunlop with an effective rendering of
'The Battle of Stirling.' Mr D. Roberts
received a well merited encore for 'Gae
bring to me,' and also gave an enjoyable

rendering of 'The dear little Shamrock,' instead of Mr Dunlop. Mr H. Gordon sang 'Scots wha hae,' in good style, and in his rendering of 'The Good Rhine Wine,' which was encored, he showed the fine quality of his voice to no mean advantage. Messrs Binnie and Paterson varied the programme with a number of duets, and the Irish comic role was taken to perfection by Messrs Bingham and Bennet encores being quite irresistible on each appearance of these gentlemen. Miss Bryson presided with great ability at the piano.

The usual vote of thanks concluded the proceeding, and Mr Roberts, in moving the vote to the singers caused no little amusement by thanking specially Captain Flynn (Mr Bingham) for having reminded him who gave them the Irish Land Act. He hoped they would keep it in mind the next day at the poll accordingly.

The audience was thoroughly sympathetic throughout, and seemed thoroughly well pleased with the evening's enjoyment.

The assembly which followed was well attended.

There is also a report of a cup-final played two years later, in 1887, when Durhamtown Rangers were beaten two goals to nil by their great rivals, Armadale – then a strongly Protestant community. It took three games to decide the winner, the first game being halted after a break-in by the crowd at Broxburn. A 'lament' for the defeated team states that it is to be sung by 'Baker' (Thomas Brown, the Rangers' captain).

There is an ironic suggestion in it of 'Love' being in the Armadale team, but surely in name only. 'Baker's' football history is given too, one of a series of 'pen-sketches' of famous players of the time – commonly called 'leather hunters' – and a more descriptive term by which to convey how 'Baker' and his team mates went about their weekly business is difficult, if not impossible, to imagine.

West Lothian Courier
SATURDAY JANUARY 18, 1890
IV – PEN SKETCHES
THOS. BROWN, ARMADALE

For fourteen years, Thomas Brown has followed the leather and has indeed proved himself to be the 'Grand Old Man' of the district. His football started in the village of Arden, a little above the Plains, in the year 1876, when he was among those who started this club, and he remained in the ranks till it was broken up in two seasons after, after having had anything but a brilliant career. Thomas Brown never until this club started had anything to do with the game, but with it began his love for the leather hunting, which has always been the case ever since, and he is without a doubt the oldest football player in the district. From Arden, Thomas shifted his camp to West Benhar,

which had only a cricket club at that time, but very soon our hero managed to get football introduced into West Benhar – the second club he was among the forerunners in. The fame of the old Benhar is well known up and down the whole country, it was indeed the model of a country-club. 'Bakers' success followed in the train of the team, and the back division was just to perfection. With this team he played the final of the Lanarkshire Association, as in 1883, he played for them against Renfrewshire. During the whole period which the Benhar period lived, it being nipped in the bud also by players being drawn away &c., Thomas Brown was always to be found in his place and a dangerous opponent to any team. But the Benhar lads succumbed to bitter fate in the year 1886, and the players were earnestly looked after. The Durhamtown Rangers were greatly in need of a back at the time, and the bait was flung out to 'Baker' who, with all the fire of youth in the game, accepted it, and appeared in the semi-final of the Shield competition at Bathgate against the University – a very memorable tie, one at which the students cried out pretty sore, and had a great reason to do so. This was the year after the Rangers won the Consolation Cup, when McPhee was playing with them, and the two, although they looked bulky, they were a strong tower in the defence of the team, indeed without a doubt, their superiors were not to be found in the county. After Hugh McPhee left, Thomas was put on as captain of the eleven, a most unsettled team, a team that was never on the ground from one match to the other. What may be remembered well was the repeated Armadale and the Rangers, meetings that were anything but of a friendly nature, the bitterest of feelings being kept up between the two. In these games, the 'Baker' played his part and was always a thorn in the side of Armadale. But the Rangers (or Rovers as they were called in later days) have also

passed over to the majority, and now we find that the old feeling of hatred between Armadale and Bathgate has died away and the 'grand old man' has cast in his lot with them. In the county he has played one representative match, the first the Association played against Stirlingshire, and was also selected to oppose the ESFA last Saturday but unluckily missed the train. Throughout all these years he has played a grand game which may not be without faults, but he has always been a man for his team, and true to the district in which he plays in. Many have been his great games, but yet I fancy that the most stubborn bit of work performed by him was on the splendid ground of Hawkhill in that memorable Shield semi-final with the Athletic. He is getting a little the worse of the wear, but yet we would not like to miss him; but when his time comes to retire from active service, I am sure that he will carry the best wishes of all country footballers, for he is indeed really the 'grand old man' of east country football.

Did I say that 19th century footballers gloried in the name 'leather hunters?'.

West Lothian Courier
SATURDAY APRIL 30, 1887
'LINLITHGOW CUP FINAL TIE
ARMADALE 2: RANGERS 0

These two teams met on Saturday for the third time this season to decide the resting place of the cup. Great interest was taken in the event until their second meeting at Bo'ness, where the front rank of the Rangers was seriously maimed for at least the remainder of the season, in the consequence of W. Murnin getting his leg broken in the contest. It will be remembered that their first meeting in Broxburn, where the spectators broke in shortly after half-time when the score stood 3 to 1 in favour of Armadale. Their second meeting was at Bo'ness where the accident which we have already mentioned, made the resting place of the trophy almost certain. This game ended in a draw of 2 goals each. The association ordered them to play their tie on the ground of the Champfieurie, which, owing

to the heavy rain, which fell during the latter part of last week and continued during a good portion of the game, was in a very heavy condition and was a great disadvantage to both sides. The front rank of the Rangers had to be re-arranged, Boose filling the place of Murnin, and G. Byrne played centre. Armadale played the same team as did work for them at Bo'ness.

McPhee won the 'spin' and elected to defend the eastern goal, with a slight wind in his favour. Johnstone kicked off with a pass to the right and the Armadale were in a moment round the Ranger's goal, where they pressed for a time; a bye kick, however, gave relief and a splendid run by Cox and Byrne transferred play to the other end, where the backs displayed very credible form. The Rangers kept up the pressure, but bad shooting and good defence lost all chances. A bye gave Armadale temporary relief, but a run up the Durharntown left brought them in close quarters, a good pass by 'Ginger' being badly taken by Cox right in the goal mouth. A corner was the result, but by clever play in the half-back line, the leather was transferred to the other end. Armadale kept well intact and Norton saved some hard shots. After a deal of hard work the Rangers returned the ball to mid-field, but the half-backs of Armadale had little trouble in returning it, and after a hard struggle, Sneddon sent in a shot which beat Norton. Half-time was now nearly up and the Rangers did not forget they had the wind in their favour. Byrne kicked off with a strong drive, which Armadale returned, but again the ball was sent into Armadale ground, but Cowie lost a good chance. Play was soon returned to mid-field, and as no further scoring took place, half-time found the score standing one goal to nil in favour of Armadale. Byrne started with a pass to 'Ginger' who passed to Cox who centred too weak, and thus Stewart stopped the rush. Armadale got well into the Rangers' territory, where McPhee and Brown did good work. The 'blues' kept up the pressure, and after about 15 minutes of restarting a rather soft shot went through, Norton thinking it was going bye drew back his hand and the ball, striking the upright, bounded through. Armadale kept the Rangers well hemmed in; they only getting a few runs, until about 20 minutes from time, when the Rangers began to get determined and broke away, taking the ball close to Armadale goal, where Cowie sent in a good screw which Love cleared. The Rangers kept well into the Armadale territory until the whistle sounded, when they had to retire, beaten by two goals to nil.

'The Lament of the Durhamtown Rangers'

(to be sung by 'Baker')

Paddy Flynn

Where's now our county 'pot?'
    Far, far away,
(Gone wid yez dirty lot,
    Far, far away.
Gone where the 'Loyal Green'
    Fair-play have never seen,
From Armadale it should have been
    Far, far away.
Where now are all our hopes?
    Far, far away.
What though we watched our stops,   [full-backs]
    Far, far away.
Durhamtown were badly used,
By one and all they've been abused.
Their protests always were refused,
    Far, far away.
From Mr McCombie's yet the 'pot' will be
    Far, far away.
And Rankine's bounce all up a tree,
    Far, far away.
Shure little room they've got to crow
While poor 'Brasseys' lying low,

To the Calton Jail they ought to go,
    Far, far away.
Soon we hope the 'blues' will be
    Far, far away.
Their faces all we wish to see,
    Far, far away.
They boast of Love within their ranks,   [a player]
'Well, if its 'love' to break wan's shanks
From us we wish such loving pranks'
    Far, far away.

The Late Bernard Battles

Durhamtown Rangers flourished until the season 1890–91, when it amalgamated with the senior club, Bathgate Volunteers, to become first Bathgate Rovers, and then Bathgate FC. Among the Durhamtown Rangers players who transferred to Bathgate Volunteers was Barney Battles, who had formed a formidable full-back partnership with the aforementioned 'Baker Brown'. Battles went on to play for Hearts, Celtic, Liverpool and Kilmarnock and was also capped for Scotland in 1901 against England, Wales and Ireland. He is reported to have stood 5ft. 10 in tall and weighed (wade?) in at 14 stones. He died suddenly from a viral infection in 1905 at the age of 29 years, while still a player for Kilmarnock FC.

He was accorded a massive funeral in Glasgow, watched by 40,000, the mourners assembling at Celtic Park. A procession of a thousand, led by Celtic, Kilmarnock and Rangers players, directors and officials of the day, marched to the house of the deceased to pay their respects. His son, also called Barney, and later a footballer with Hearts, attended a Durhamtown Rangers 'social' as a guest of the club in 1931. This was a few seasons after the club had reformed into a Secondary Juvenile club, reaching the final of the Scottish Cup that year, only to be beaten by Edinburgh Milton. A report of the evening is included. It contains references to important players and episodes earlier in the club's history, a story which could be told for any number of clubs throughout the district during the same period.

West Lothian Courier
SEPTEMBER 11, 1931
DURHAMTOWN RANGERS F.C.
County & Kelso Cups Presented
BARNEY BATTLES' VISIT

On Friday evening, in the Co-operative Hall, Bathgate, under the auspices of the Durharntown Rangers FC, a social and dance were held. There was a large gathering presided over by Rev. Father McGrail.

The platform party included Rev. Father Campbell, Mr Barney Battles, of Hearts FC., son of Barney Battles who commenced his football career in the old Durharntown Rangers FC, which later became Bathgate Rovers, finally Bathgate FC., which continues today as an amateur organisation, Messrs William Kelly, and William Murnin, two playing members of the original Durharntown Ranger FC., E. Toban, president of the recently set up Durhamtown FC. Mr McNeil, Livingston president of the West Lothian Secondary Juvenile Association and Mr George Burt, Heart of Midlothian FC.

After tea, Rev. Father McGrail said that the Durhamtown Rangers FC, though a recently formed organisation really was an old club name resuscitated. There was a Durhamtown Rangers FC. existing in the year 1882. At least it was formed in that year. In season 1883–1884 they were members of the Edinburgh Football Association. The club continued to flourish until the season 1890–1891. In this season the committee of the senior club, Bathgate Volunteers and the Committee of Durhamtown Rangers, met and agreed to amalgamate under the name of Bathgate Rovers. Among the players in the new club who had been playing members of the Durhamtown Rangers Club, were Thomas Norton, Hugh McPhee, James Kelly, William Kelly, William Murnin, John McCall, Barney Battles, Michael Tobin, Christopher Connolly and James Tobin. (Applause).

In the season 1891–92 Bathgate Rovers won the County Cup and the King Cup. They reached the sixth round of the Scottish Cup but were then defeated by Greens Park. The Bathgate Rovers ultimately became Bathgate FC which is the name of the present club.

The present Durhamtown Rangers FC had been set up only a few seasons ago and the players last season, 1930–31 had excelled themselves. They had won the County Secondary Juvenile Cup, and the Kelso Cup. They also reached the final of the Scottish Secondary Juvenile Cup, and were defeated by Edinburgh Milton. It was a fine achievement and officials and players were to be heartily congratulated. (Applause). They wished officials and players all good wishes for the future. (Applause).

They had with them that night, Mr Barney Battles of the Hearts, a fine player himself, the son of Barney Battles, who started his playing career with Durhamtown Rangers of over 40 years ago and became one of the foremost players of his day and generation and whose name was world wide. (Applause). This was Mr Barney Battles's first visit to Bathgate, but he could assure him he was among his ain folk for to many present his father was known and loved and for the sire's sake the son was carrying on in the football world the best traditions of his father (Applause).

He then called upon Mr Battles to present the two cups to the captain, Mr Hugh Sharkie and County Cup badge, Kelso Cup badge and Scottish Cup finalists badge to each of the following: John Hunter, Hugh Foy, William Hunter, Hugh Sharkie, William Watson, Frank Dowds, James Welsh, Joseph Pearson, Charles O'Raw, Patrick McCall, and Patrick Dougan, the recognised regular team and Edward McPhilips, Robert Simmonds, Michael O'Raw and Hugh Pollock, who had died, the medals were handed over to his father and sympathetic reference was made to the passing of such a fine playing member as was Hugh Pollock.

Mr Battles said that he felt it a great honour to be asked to come that night and hand over the Trophies and badges. The players had done splendidly and players and members of committee deserved every congratulation because the results had been secured by all working harmoniously together (Applause). Had the Hearts in one season secured as many trophies as had Durhamtown Rangers they would have got a civic reception. (Laughter and applause). That night it was pleasant to hear of the early exploits of his father. Because of his being the son of an honoured father they had given him a great reception. He never experienced such a reception in all his life and for that reception, which he felt was given most whole heartedly, he thanked them most sincerely. (Applause). This was his first visit to Bathgate, but he hoped to be again with them under as happy auspices. (Applause).

An excellent variety programme was

then submitted. Miss Ferguson rendered 'Doun the Burn' and 'Kirkconnell Lea' with graceful charm; Mrs McLean maintained her fine reputation as a vocalist with first class renditions of 'Killarney' and 'Passing'; Mr James Boyle, another favourite, delighted with 'Bonnie Wee Thing' and Mairie, My Girl'; Mr Peter Rankine, Armadale, as Society Entertainer, had great receptions in the 'Goal Keeper's Ghost,' and 'A Presentation of Prizes.' Miss Bessie Sharp was an excellent pianist.

After the social a dance was held, which was a great success. Messrs C. Connolly and H. Sharkie were MCs and the music was provided by Reilly's Band.

The interlacing of the public-political personalities of the shale oil industry and the local cultures which sustained them is perhaps well emphasised in the case of Walter Nellies, who became general secretary of the National Union of Shale Miners and Oil Workers in 1924, and whose obituary features earlier in this book. As a young man, he played football for Douglas Water FC, Lanarkshire, and gained National honours as a Junior, playing for Scotland against England in season 1902–3. He signed for Motherwell FC after this game, in Motherwell's first season in First League football. He retired from football soon after to pursue a public service career, being elected as a county councillor in Lanarkshire, by which route he eventually became leader of the shale workers' Union, a councillor and JP in Bathgate, and a director of the Cooperative Society, as well as receiving an OBE in 1937.

The all-pervading nature of football within local popular culture is thus well founded, and captured, in the following short story.

Spug's Transfer
(A shale childhood: 1949)

Alan Findlay

Alan was the Winchburgh Albion hamper boy, him and Spug Getty. The Albion were the best Secondary Juvenile team in Scotland, even though they had never won the Scottish Cup. When they did, Willie Thornton, centre-forward for Glasgow Rangers, was going to give every player in the team a Parker pen. Willie stayed in Glasgow now but he came through every year to the Albion's Social to present the medals to the players who had won the cups the season before. Alan's father, who had been the Albion centre-forward for years, became the Secretary when Willie arrived, and he had been the Secretary ever since.

Alan, his big brother Bobby, their wee brother Jimmy, and their mother and father stopped in the Old Rows, in the Gaffers Row, from the time when their father's grandfather had been the Crawpicker at Duddingston mine. All the men in the Old Rows were shale miners, like their father, or else worked in the Oilworks, or had retired. If they left the Company, like Roy Mason's father, they were put out of their house. The New Rows and Duntarvie View were the same. The Millgate and the Steelhouses belonged to the Council.

Greenshale Rangers was the Old Rows laddies team, but Alan only got his game when the bigger lads didn't turn up. His big brother Bobby, Pidgy and Rubbie Rutherford, and Spug Getty were sitting on Rutherford's front step, when Alan landed on them. Pidgy was doing the talking, as usual, and it sounded like Spug was getting transferred to Duntarvie View Violet.

'A hunner, Spug, and that's it.' said Pidgy. 'I cannae go ony less. Away up to Duntarvie and tell Brandy Scott.'

'A hunner!' said Spug. 'That's too much. They've no long started collectin. Seventy. At the maist.'

'Naw Spug.' said Pidgy. 'You're worth mair than that. Greenshale Rangers wid be the laughin stock o' Scottish fitba' if we let ye go for ony less.'

Spug's face fell. Pidgy paused. Alan held his breath. 'Seventy then. And nae doublers.' said Pidgy.

'Nae doublers!' said Spug. 'There's naebody in Winchburgh wi' seventy fitba cairds, no countin doublers.'

'Seventy.' said Pidgy. 'But nae torn or dirty yins. And nae Billy Steeles. I've four o' him already.'

'This is no right, me organisin ma ain transfer.' said Spug. 'Could ye no send him?' pointing at Alan.

'I'm warning you!' said Pidgy, but Spug was already on his way.

Pidgy was player-manager of Greenshale Rangers. He knew things Miss Tripney would never read about in books. Pidgy was 14 and aged to get in at the Institute billiards. Bobby and Rubbie were 12, Spug was 11, and Alan was ten and a bit. It was only on Sundays, when the Institute was closed, that Pidgy took much to do with them now.

'Are we really transferrin Spug to Duntarvie, Pidgy?' asked Alan.

'Shut-up you!' said Bobby, before Pidgy could answer.

Bobby and Spug were best pals and he was peeved that Spug was getting transferred to another team, but feart to say so. Bobby dunted Alan in the ribs and nearly couped him off the step.

'Your mother's lookin for you. Better get hame!' said Bobby.

Alan bit his lip, but sat his ground. It was hard lines Bobby wasn't getting transferred, but who'd take him?

'Leave him alane!' said Pidgy. 'Aye, Spug's up for transfer. It's that time o' the year. SFA rules say transfers must be completed the day. Said so in the *Sunday Post* last week.'

'When Spug goes, I'll be gettin his place. I'm first reserve. Ye said so yersel!' said Alan.

'I've no made up ma mind yet.' said Pidgy.

'But Pidgy, there's naebody else tae pick frae. Jist me!'

'Oh, is that so?' said Pidgy. 'Whit aboot Nan Clark?'

'Nan Clark! Ye widnae play a lassie, Pidgy? Wid ye?'

'Nothin in the rules against it.' said Pidgy. 'Onyway, somebody was sayin she beat ye at long-shootie. Is that right?'

Alan looked at Bobby smirking and resolved to tell their mother when he got home that it was him that had made the hole in the blanket bigger.

'But Pidgy, it was jist a kickaboot. And she was keepin the score. And, onyway, I beat her right efter at heiders.'

'Spug will be a hard man to replace.' said Pidgy. 'We'll jist have tae see at the trials next week.'

Spug came back as Pidgy was writing out his transfer-papers on a page torn out of Rubbie's school jotter, but he was having bother sticking down Billy Steele at the place they were to sign their names across.

'Could only get 47 cairds, Pidgy, two penny carmels, and a whussle.' said Spug.

'That'll dae fine.' said Pidgy.

The rest of them looked at each other and groaned. Pidgy would have done anything, even shown his bum to the lassies, for a whistle. Without even bothering to count the cards, Pidgy dived into the lobby and reappeared in a flash with an old red table-cloth round his shoulders. It was – The Scarlet Horseman!

The legend of the Old West cleared the steps with one bound and galloped away across the prairie towards the Greenshale. Just before he reached the planting and disappeared from view, he gave a shrill blast on the whistle. The rest of them staggered to their feet and trotted after it, left arms across their faces, just below eye-level, skelping their bums with their right hands.

The Scarlet Horseman was a rich, crippled rancher who was confined to a wheelchair until the next set of baddies got as bad as the last lot, and then he would away and put on his scarlet cloak and redde them up. And all that was heard was the sound of his whistle.

They had about as much chance of catching Pidgy as Stirling Albion had of beating Rangers in the league, but they had to follow the sound of the whistle wherever it took them. Spug must have been desperate to play for Duntarvie View Violet, thought Alan, as his trusty steed reared and then plunged, and they galloped off headlong into the gloaming of the Greenshale.

Births deaths and marriages

John Benson's social history of the 19th century British coalminer shows the extent to which pit-life intruded into home-life. It wasn't just the miner who was roused from bed in the early hours but the wives and daughters who fed and washed the backs of their husbands, fathers, brothers and working sons along with the dirty clothes they constantly brought back from the pit, nursed broken bones, bruised limbs and sickness in homes in which every cough was heard and usually caught. The domestic intruded onto the miner too, and as far back as 1843, if we can believe this one:

> Of a' the plagues a poor man meets,
> Alang life's weary way,
> There's nyen amang them a' that beats
> A rainy weshin' day.
> And let that day come when it may,
> It a'ways is maw [my] care,
> Before aw [I] break maw fast, te pray
> It may be fine and fair.
> For it's thump! thump! souse! souse!
> Scrub! scrub away!
> There's nowt but glumpin' [sulking] i' the hoose,
> Upon a weshin' day.[1]

Lack of physical space, or peace, in the house had various pre-dictable social consequences. Children played outside for a start, and made their own amusements:

> All over the country they played marbles; made slides in winter; built boats; played schools; played hand-ball and whip and top; fought with 'slings' (balls of rolled up paper at the end of three or four yards of string); played 'tip cat' (hitting a piece of wood into the air with sticks) and so on. Popular too were games based on death, death which they saw so often when a baby sickened or when a miner was injured in the pit.[2]

Schooling was rudimentary for the many, usually in large classes, and strict and boring for children who knew they were going down the pit or into domestic service. Children above toddling age were viewed as small adults, childhood was a preparation for work and communal existence:

> Girls were encouraged to make themselves useful around the house. 'Mother wasn't keen on reading 'trash'. All books were 'trash'. She thought one's time was better spent on mending, darning, knitting.' Boys too were expected to do odd jobs like digging the allotment and bringing in the house coal from where it had been dumped.[3]

By the turn of the century, Benson concludes:

> With the single exception of drink it was sport and religion which had the most profound impact on the ways in which mining communities used their time and money.[4]

Interestingly, he sees a new working class culture based round the chapel and the church emerging in many places as the only real alternative to the pub. Women and children in particular obtained a new focus for their social and cultural life through penny readings, temperance classes, choir practices, Bands of Hope and Boys Brigades:

> Religion and studying were never so popular as drinking and fighting and it would be absurd to pretend otherwise. Yet all too often attention has been focused on the hard-drinking, hard-fisted miner to the complete exclusion of his opposite number, the serious, ambitious men hurrying from the pit to the reading room or the public lecture hall. Neither was typical but neither should be forgotten.[5]

All this would have been familiar enough to those whose stories were tape recorded by Sara Randall. She interviewed a few women on their own or in pairs but mainly it was married couples, the normal pattern being for the husband to talk initially about his working life and then gradually the discussion took in 'home' aspects. Of course, people would tell stories as these occurred, and in their own way, but the order in which these came up reflect very much the values that were present in the culture itself: work and wages given first priority and everything else relegated to that end – men in the outside world of work and politics and women at home, looking after the children.

It is important to note that when these people were born and growing up in the early part of this century, women did not yet have the vote. This is not to imply that women saw themselves as inferior but that the social order regarded men as the bread-winner while women were viewed as wives, mothers and home-makers: a social fact. Iron times, however, could produce iron women as well as iron men. My mother tells of the time she first met my father and a neighbour telling her he was 'idle about the house', even allowing his grandmother (who was in her 80s) to split sticks for the fire. On taking him up on this, my father complained that his grandmother would not allow him to do anything in the house and, furthermore, he 'could not get up early enough for her' – and he rose about 4.30am. His grandmother just got up before him and did everything. No one, clearly, was going to tell her what to do in her own house – even if it was owned by 'The Company'.

My mother's mother was an Old Tory, a former lady's maid for the toffs, well-spoken and rather dignified, a champion conversationalist who, despite being bed-ridden when she and my grandfather came to live with us in Winchburgh in the late 1940s, had a regular train of visitors to her room: neighbours, children, doctors, ministers,

book-makers and my father – who eventually persuaded her to vote
Labour. Apart from formidable personalities, such as Sarah Moore,
a Labour pioneer and local councillor, the lives and interests of
women were, in general, restricted to the home – supporting and
bolstering their menfolk and bringing up the children.

1940s: my mother, Isa Moffat, whose father's grandfather was a mole-catcher
in the Borders, and her mother, Sarah MacKinnon, whose grandfather was a
gamekeeper from Ardchattan, Loch Etive

My grandmother placed a daily '3-Cross-Irish' bet on the sport of
kings. She also once won a consolation prize for her entry in a 'John
Bull' magazine competition for 'the best way to get your own back'
– 'pissing against the wind', she replied – which they regretted they
could not print. Both she and my mother were more interested in
fashion than drudgery, having had their fair share of that.

My mother came from the Borders, the village of Ayton. She was
'in service' in Edinburgh and met my father at a dance in
Winchburgh: 'I thought his name was Ralph and he was a grocer,
then I discovered it was Rab and he was a miner', she said. They
married in 1939. She left school aged 13 when her mother became
crippled with rheumatoid arthritis. In 1949, when I was born into
the miners rows in Winchburgh, my grandparents were in one bedroom, my three brothers in the other, and my parents in the set-in
bed and me in a cot in the living room.

My mother's rural background and domestic service prepared her
for the kind of life most miner's wives were born into. As an incomer,
she provides insights into the community she had come to, and the
one she had left: 'I didn't know what a catholic was until I came to
Winchburgh'. My father would not let her join the Eastern Star, the
women's wing of the masons, which she thought of as simply a
women's club. She joined 'the rural' – Womens Rural Institute – to
play cards and beetle drives, and went to the church or the pictures
in Broxburn. She was surprised that the back-doors of houses were
always open and 'neebors' just chapped and walked in, but she was
horrified to find women strolling up and down the rows with bairns
wrapped in shawls round their backs – 'just like tinkers'.

Joining mining communities was a typical 19th century experience
for those migrating from rural to industrial locations. My father's
grandmother, Elizabeth Jamieson, came from Walls, Shetland, married the old Shale Inspector, Robert Findlay, in 1885 and lived in
West Calder until they moved to Winchburgh in 1905. Her family
links were still strong some 30 years on, my grandfather being
stranded in Shetland for six months when the First World War broke
out. Her mother-in-law, Jane Russell, the old Shale Inspector's mother,
took the reverse journey, from city to country. She was born in
Glasgow in 1818 and in 1839 she married Thomas Findlay, the Shale
Inspector's father, a coal miner who was born in West Calder in 1808
(the family coming from the Black Isles the previous century). Jane
was widowed in 1863 at the age of 45, and worked as a field labourer.
She had seven children and never re-married. And who could blame
her?

In the kind of communities being described, Jane Russell, Elizabeth
Jamieson, Sarah McKinnon and Isa Moffat would have been expected
to be, and probably were, much the same kind of wives and mothers.
And all of them, with varying degrees of ruefulness, would have been
intrigued to hear Alex. Laing Esq.'s pronouncements on 'marriage'
which he delivered in a popular lecture in the Public Hall, Broxburn,
on 17 April 1886, reported in the *West Lothian Courier*, 'The Pathway
to Matrimony or Councils to the Single':

> [marriage] is a serious and solemn matter, and should never be entered
> on without seeking counsel from above... Amongst the qualities to be
> looked for in those who want to marry – equality of age, social posi-
> tion, tempers opposite generally agree best, cultivation of mind, reli-
> gious principles, the man having the power to select, the woman the
> right to reject; the countenance and sanction of parents (if still alive),
> the domestic qualifications needful in a woman to fit her to take the
> management of a home, the right use of a woman's power to give the
> home domestic attractions; the necessity of sitting down in a house free
> of debt, with all the furniture paid for before the wife is brought home;

not to begin in too high a style, 'better to begin with brose and end with chuckie' than the reverse; never to have secrets from one another, nor let a third know your differences; never to feign sickness to gain your end; the party who makes peace, should there be any difference, is always the victor, because it is God like.

God-like or not, there certainly were an almighty number sitting round Findlay hearths, and similar hearths, during the period, converging on West Lothian, following their kin and looking for work. Jane Russell's grandfather, James Russell, was born in 1774 in Old Monklands, Lanarkshire. Thomas Findlay's grandfather, James Hope, was a journeyman tailor, born in Selkirk in the same year. They and their wives, Catherine McCasslan from Glasgow, and Grace Sommerville from Carnwath, are buried in the family grave at West Calder. Census records for West Calder in 1851/61 show Jane and her brood living cheek by jowl with these and other extended family members. Inter-generational households prevail, grandsons and nieces living with grandparents, aunts, uncles and lodgers – one such being Ann Paterson (43 years), a sewing teacher, born in Leith. Those who were too old to work were unceremoniously written down in official documents as 'paupers'. These now lie in the same grave, an array of names linked by kinship, marriage and long obscured relation.

They were not unknown to the Kirk Session, though. The marriage of Thomas's parents (James Findlay and Mary Hope) was deemed 'irregular' in 1801 at West Calder – meaning it had not been performed by a minister (which cost money). This was not untypical. The Statistical Account for 1796 states, for example, that nearly all marriages in Whitburn were 'irregular'. Pre-marital pregnancy and illegitimacy ratios rose too as the 19th century progressed, and the Kirk had views on that as well. The following Kirk Session entries concern my father's grandather's father, Thomas Findlay, and his father, James Findlay, and their families last century:

27 November 1801, Kirk Session minutes, West Calder

After prayers said, the Rev Mr MacKenzie, James Leggie, John Gowans and Hugh Morton, Elder – appeared James Findlay and Mary Hope and produced lines of marriage dated 1st September 1801, and being interrogated they both declare that they are married persons. The Session agree to rebuke them for the sin and absolve them from the scandal, which was done accordingly. Concluded with prayers.

14 February 1830

having understood that James Findlay the Gravedigger has charged three shillings for digging Janet Boag's grave they having allowed ten shillings as the price of her coffin, are of the opinion that he ought to charge nothing for digging the Graves of the Poor until he have the authority of the Heritors and Session for that purpose as he receives two pounds yearly salary from the Heritors.

22 May 1835

Confessed Thomas Findlay and acknowledged the impropriety of his past conduct, in as much as he had used intoxicating liquors to excess. Having expressed penitence and promised amendment, he was admonished and absolved.

19 June 1835

The Moderator reported that Thomas Findlay, who had been engaged as Kirk Officer, had written him a letter saying that he did not intend any longer to attend church. The Session therefore resolve to deprive him of the Office and to appoint as church officer in his place James Wallace, one of the Elders having stated that he believed that he had reason to believe that Wallace would accept of the situation.

3 August 1836

Ann Findlay (Thomas's sister) admitted she was with child to Robert Black. James Wallace resigned as Kirk Officer and James Dunlop took it.

3 March 1839

Thomas Findlay and Jane Russell admitted antenuptial fornication and were rebuked and restored to the bosom of the church.

The Session also records some of Jane and Thomas's children being baptised in the 1860s, when they were adults. This could have been to save money or because Thomas had broken with the church (Jane later returning to it), or both.

And that, perhaps, is where we should leave them be.

* * *

Sex and sexual relations did not enter Sara Randall's questioning explicitly nor, unsurprisingly, did such matters arise unbidden during interviews. We know from Sybil Cavanagh's article that in 1931 West Lothian had the highest overall fertility in Britain and the eighth highest marital fertility – which suggests that sex was certainly taking place. The currency of the phrase 'one every divided' suggests that contraception as a popular practice was either absent or botched regularly. I asked my mother in later years about birth-control methods when she was young and she indicated that 'coitus interruptus' was the main option, a finding confirmed by more conventional research.

She did not express it in these terms, of course, being my mother, but called it 'jumping off at Haymarket' – which is the railway station just before Waverley, the main railway terminus in Edinburgh.

Sex education was a thing unheard of even during my school days up to the late 1960s, never mind for the generations considered here. Sex was certainly never discussed in our house with my parents when I was growing up. The nearest thing to a 'man to man' talk I ever got from my father was when I was about to go out to 'the Palais' for the first time, shortly before my sixteenth birthday. I looked rather older than my years, it must be said. I was combing my hair in the bedroom when I heard my father's heavy tread on the stair, and his characteristic cough as he approached the door. I deduced that my mother would have told him of my impending 'debut'. He entered the room and stood, arms akimbo, as if waiting to throw something onto a hutch, and looked rather to the ceiling and to the side than directly at me.

'You're goin' to the dancin?', he said. 'Ay, Da', I said. 'Well, don't get mixed up wi' ony tarts', he said. Naw, Da', I said, parting my 'shed', as he clumped back down the stairs for his tea.

*　*　*

For most of the period, then, in Winchburgh at least, a woman's place was in the home along with other women and children, just visible on the edges of public life, serving haggis and howking tatties. In the 1940s my mother, Mrs Wright and Mrs McPhee would sometimes earn a mention in my father's reports of Learigg Burns Suppers which were printed in the Courier, along with a dozen similar events. Every year they would wait on him and his Uncle John, 'the principal table' – and were no doubt happy to do so. In 1949, when the main speaker at the Learigg was Douglas Young, a distinguished Scottish Nationalist writer and academic, my mother was not present, being about to give birth to me a few days later. It is a fairly safe bet, though, that the haggis would not have been dished up in her absence either by my father or my father's Uncle John.

WEST LOTHIAN COURIER – JANUARY 28, 1949

PROMINENT SCOT AT WINCHBURGH

Douglas Young and Burns

Rightly considered one of the most important Burns Suppers in West Lothian and indeed the East of Scotland, Winchburgh Lea Rig Burns Club's annual tribute to the National Bard last Saturday evening worthily maintained that high tradition. The chief guest this year was famous Scot, Mr Douglas Young, MA Edinburgh, who is recognised as a leading figure in contemporary Scottish literature and is well known for his fervent Nationalism and as a politician, orator and broadcaster.

With such a celebrity on the programme the demand for tickets was keen and a record attendance was obtained. Every available seat was taken when Mr J.B. George, MA hon. President opened the proceedings in the Lea Rig Hall last Saturday evening. Accompanying him at the principal table in addition to Mr Douglas Young were a company of distinguished guests including Mr James Seager, managing editor of *Edinburgh Evening News*, and Mr A.D. Mackie, MA, editor of *Edinburgh Evening Dispatch*, and other well known men in and around West Lothian.

The proceedings opened with the ceremonial entry of the haggis, piped in by Piper George Duncan, Junr., and carried by Mr A. Johnstone, who has carried out that duty at all the annual suppers under the auspices of the club. The 'Address to a Haggis' was then recited in excellent style by Mr George Scott. An excellent supper was then served, following which the chairman rose to introduce the chief guest.

Sometimes famous men whose advent is eagerly awaited do not measure up to what is expected of them when they actually appear in person and an audience keyed-up in anticipation of something unique and memorable are disappointed, Mr. Douglas Young was a very notable exception to this. He more than satisfied his hearers and such was the power of his oratory that one could literally feel the grip he had over his audience. One might have heard the proverbial pin drop as he spoke. There was no gainsaying the might of his intellect and his powerful message was at the same time inspiring and interesting. It sparkled with wit and there was no doubt its sternly Nationalistic sentiments struck the right chord with his audience. It was a great occasion for the Lea Rig Club.

THE IMMORTAL MEMORY

Mr Douglas Young in proposing the Immortal Memory,' said the solid and continuing reasons that induced us year after year to honour Bums were that he was the first poet of modern democracy as we understood it. He lived in an age of political bribery and corruption but Burns looked beyond that to an age of universal liberty, equally and fraternity. He wrote 'A man's a man for a' that' and there was nothing like that in any contemporary poet of any country or in English literature before. Burns went right to the heart of our common humanity and was the reviver of Scottish national literature and of the national spirit in Scotland.

After our ancestors, split up by religious disputes, had tamely submitted to the political and financial manoeuvre which put the Scottish nation under control of the political institutions of the English ruling class in 1707, there was a danger that Scotland would lose her identity and that Scottish character would be lost but there arose a poet who roused the national spirit and stayed that process probably for ever (applause).

Proceeding Mr Young said when this year we proposed the toast of Burns it was fitting to have in mind another great Scotsman whose anniversary came this year. The 26th January was the day on which we commemorated the death of Thomas Muir the Scottish reformer, who was tried and condemned to transportation in the High Court, Edinburgh, 'a place' remarked Mr Young 'with which I am familiar' (Laughter and applause). Muir was the main promoter of that political party to which Burns gave his adherence – the Society of the Friends of the People. He was brought to trial for sedition in August 1793 and Burns prejudice his own safe job as an Exciseman by writing in honour of Muir at that date our national anthem 'Scots wha hae.' He trusted those who were interested in honouring the memory of Bums would do something to help and foster those who ran after not the flesh but the spirit of Bums. (Applause)

For the first time a Government report on education recognised there was a proper place for Scottish literature and traditions in Scottish education. One sign of grace was they were going to set apart a fixed time for the study of these things. If our nation did not have their heritage of Scottish literature we would never become a creatively literary people but simply a nation of newspaper readers and wireless listeners. If we were going to recover our heritage we must recover it in full. Where was it to be found? In text books? The Burns Federation should encourage the production of these in cheap editions. The Scottish language had to be learned as you would learn French. Every Burns club should possess the Scottish National Dictionary. He thought it a national shame that work was still lagging for want of public support. Literature was like a man with one leg, if it went on verse only and not prose. We also wanted a national theatre. Burns wanted that and today we find his idea coming nearer accomplishment through Kemp, McLellan and John Bridie.

We were proud of Robin but he sometimes wondered would Robin be proud of us. Scottish nationality was in a parlous condition under the Anglicising and Americanising influences. The bulk of our press was the instrument of the 'Auld Enemy.' The cinema was the instrument of the high culture of Hollywood. Our bairns were being continually exposed to influences such as these which were destructive to all that was important in our Scottish heritage. He urged them to take an inward resolve to carry on as Burns did the old and glorious traditions of the Scottish people, the Scottish language and Scottish literature. (Applause)

The ovation the speaker received at the conclusion of this address was spontaneous and prolonged, and the company readily echoed the sentiments expressed by the chairman when he rose to propose the toast of the 'Chief Guest.'

OTHER TOASTS

With such a standard set by the principal orator the remaining speakers were set no mean task to maintain it. This they worthily did and there was not a speech that evening but was worthy of the occasion. 'The Commonwealth Forces' was very ably proposed by Rev. W. Mair, M.A. Abercom and just as ably replied to by his Presbyterial colleague, Rev. G.A. Young, MA, Winchburgh. Mr T. Reid, President, proposed the toast to the 'Federated Clubs' and brought forth an inspiring and enthusiastic reply from a man who has devoted a lifetime to the cult of Bums, exProvost T. Russell, Armadale, Mr A.D. Mackie very wittily and with fine sentiments proposed the toast to 'The Lassies' and this was just as competently replied to by Mr James Seager. Dr Thomson, Uphall paid a fine tribute to the Winchburgh club in proposing the toast 'The Lea Rig Burns Club' and in doing so made an offer to the club of an annual prize of £1.1s if the club would sponsor an annual Scottish literature prize for school children. Later in the evening Mr G.C. Irvine, MA, Uphall offered to double this if the competition included Uphall children. The reply to Dr Thomson was made by Mr G.S. Brunten, Linlithgow, in his usual witty style. Mr John Black proposed the toast to 'Our Guests' and Mr Irvine replied. 'The Artistes' proposed by Mr C.H. Ross and 'Chairman' by Mr John Findlay.

Domestic roles and responsibilities are, of course, decided by custom and practice rather than legislation. My father's grandmother protected her right, as she saw it, to split sticks and run her home until old age made it impossible for her to do so. She then went to stay with her daughter in Bradford, my aunty Mary, just before the Second World War. My mother then moved in and set up her own household. My father recalled that his services about the house were as little required under the new regime as under the old. We smirked at that, no doubt, my father's terrible handiwork, from decorating to mending shoes to putting nails in, was the stuff of family legend. Truly, we said, he'd 'learnt all his joinery in the pit', basically putting up roof supports by battering in 'clugs' (logs). My father had a different domestic version of this, of course. He once told me that after their marriage, the first time my mother went to Ayton to visit her parents, he had laboured all week to keep the place shining. When my mother returned, she burst into tears. The house was so tidy he obviously didn't need her! From then on, he said, 'every time your mother came back, you could have steered (stirred) the place wi' a stick' – a matter made abundantly clear in my brother Alan's short story *Painting the Scullery*.

Painting the Scullery

Alan Findlay

They had been at Ayton since Wednesday, and Thursday was Rover day, so their father must have read it by this. Alan could have given Bobby a race for it, but Bobby would just have taken it off him anyway. The bus had halted just at their door on the main street in Winchburgh, the Old Rows, the Gaffer's Row from the time their great grandfather had been the Crawpicker at Duddingston mine, where their father still worked as a shale miner.

They were walking up the path when they heard the racket. Their father was getting it in the neck.

He must have gotten up early and started distempering the scullery. It wouldn't have been so bad if he redde the place up first. But their father was anything but stupid. When they criticised what he had done, he would say you shouldn't show a woman or a daft laddie an unfinished job. Alan looked at the latest.

There were jaups of paint everywhere: the curtains; the dirty dishes; the breid; the chair he was standing on; the bunker; the floor; even his bald patch. Bobby had stood on the wet lid and trailed the stuff all through the house looking for The Rover. You could see where he had tried all the most likely places, even the back-room.

Their mother was bouncing up and down about the mess and how tired she was travelling for hours on the bus, and their father was trying to get in his bit about unfinished jobs. She was just about to tell him about the black man on the bus and had her arm up to point out him who had shamed her in public, when she noticed a daud of paint on the sleeve of her good coat and lost the place.

Bobby had found The Rover but V For Vengeance was missing, back and front, and there was no way of telling if they had managed to assassinate Himmler. He was greeting because it was his favourite. Their father tried to brazen it out but then said it wasn't his fault they had run out of toilet paper. Ay, it was great to be hame.

Jimmy had started raking about the place, tripped over the coal hammer that was lying on the rug in its own dross, and nearly couped the paint tin. Their mother let out a screech but it died in her throat when she noticed the glider, covered in glaur, sitting in the kitchen beside a sack of rotten tatties.

He'd fixed it!

Sneddon's pram was lying in bits behind the big chair.

It was then that Alan noticed his father was wearing the Irish International strip, and it was his turn to get upset. He was captain of the Greenshale Rangers B team, the only laddies team in the whole place that had a strip, four of them, including the short-sleeved Edinburgh Harriers's strip that their father had from his running days.

None of them ever wanted to play in the Irish National strip because it was always covered in paint. He had sat for ages afore their last game picking the jaups off the front, and their father had promised never to wear it again for painting.

Their mother lifted the kettle to make a cup of tea but there was distemper in that as well. Mrs Sneddon came in.

'Ma. I'm starvin', said Alan. 'Can we no get something for eatin? We're gaun tae miss the matinee-bus.'

'You're no gaun wi' me', said Bobby.

'Hey, Da', said Alan. 'Did you get me they autographs?'

'It's nice but, Isa?', their father said.

'You've got back then', said Mrs Sneddon. 'And how's your mother?'

'Pink! For a scullery!', their mother shouted. 'It's bloody awful! And, see, ye've missed a bit!'

'It was the only colour they had left', said their father. 'It'll dae. I'll finish it the morn. I'm away to see Jimmy McPhee down at the Learig.'

'You put one foot out that door and I'm on the next bus back to Ayton!'

'What's a wee pickle paint, man?', said their father. 'I'll redde it up when I get back.'

'Mrs Sneddon, have you ever seen such a – Jimmy!, shrieked their mother. 'Alan! Get Jimmy and take him out the back. And watch his shoes.'

'Look at ma comic, Ma', wailed Bobby.

'You were saying about your mother, Isa', said Mrs Sneddon.

'Bobby, run up to the Store and get half a dozen pies and a plain loaf. Alan, get the pushchair and take Jimmy a hurl.'

'Get!', said their mother, as Bobby began to wail about missing the matinee-bus.

'My God!', said Mrs Sneddon. 'What's happened to my pram?'

* * *

Even when pregnant, my mother would go to the fields to howk tatties during the 1940s. She was amazed that anyone should want to remark on this. She was even more amazed that anyone should want to put it in a book and, more amazing still, that anyone should want to read about it.

Rough and respectable: friends and neighbours

My father's 'best man' was George, 'Pud', Bartley. As young men, they played football together and went (that is, walked) to the local dancing at Linlithgow and roundabout. Pud had the craggy, lop-sided look of Freddie Truman, the Yorkshire and England fast bowler. But beneath the dour exterior Pud, like all my father's close friends, was humorous and affable. It was Pud after all who, reaching the end of their playing days, told wee Tammy Stirling at half-time during a match Winchburgh Albion was losing badly, that a player on the other side had said that Tammy was twenty-six. 'But I stuck up for ye, Tammy', said Pud, 'I telt him ye were twenty-seeven'.

George and Jenny Bartley, at my parents wedding, 1939

Other friends were the Pritchards, Dick and Lizzie. Dick Pritchard left Winchburgh and the shale mines in 1950 to take on an 11 acre small holding at Mannerston, Blackness, a couple of fields along from the Binns. There they kept pigs and grew cereals and tatties. Dick came from a musical family in Bo'ness and was the obvious choice to take over Winchburgh Silver Band from its founder, Robert Wemyss, who owned the Tallyho Hotel. Dick became Bandmaster of the City of Edinburgh Band, one of the top brass bands in Scotland, during the 1950s. He then took over conducting Bathgate Brass Band in 1959. A Winchburgh Silver Band member of the 1930s, John Donoghue, described Dick's qualities as a conductor as con-sisiting in an absolute dedication to everything he did, along with a vast musical knowledge. 'And, besides, he never lost his temper. He was an absolute gentleman'.

When our family left Winchburgh for Bathgate in 1953, the flitting came on Dick Pritchard's lorry. There was an aura about the Pritchard's that had nothing to do with their farm, but was part of the mutual respect and regard that passed between them and my parents. I have less memories than impressions of Dick Pritchard who seemed to me, a youngster growing up in the fifties, a gentle giant of a man. During harvest, our family would decamp to Mannerston to help out. The Pritchard's had four children ages with ourselves – Bobby, John, Dick and Isobel. Bobby became a senior executive with Barclays Bank, John a professional musician and Dick continues to this day the family tradition of playing, along with his two children, in Bathgate Brass Band. As for Isobel, no female members played in Winchburgh or Bathgate bands in those days, and few, if any, anywhere else for that matter.

My memories of Dick Pritchard relate either to Mannerston, usually of him driving a lorry or car about the place, or conducting the band on gala days, a tall imposing figure in a rain coat which almost touched the ground, his hair gleaming, head cocked to one side, a study in concentration, guaging the tempo, establishing the measure. 'Big Dick', as my father called him, had a tremendous timbre in his voice, an instrument itself. He invariably referred to my father as 'Boab', and the word issued forth like a piece of percussion echoing round the Usher Hall. Another image that stays is of the two of them sitting in the front of Dick's small car driving through the back roads of Blackness in the late 1950s. The sun was splitting the trees, yet hardly a ray of it seemed able to squeeze past their joint bulks to those of us in the back, them both deep in conversation and hilarity. And all the while, regular as a metronome, Dick's resonant tones would be booming out, gong-like, my father's name.

Dick Pritchard, 1959, London, finalists, Daily Herald National Brass Band Competition, with three founder members of Winchburgh Silver Band (left to right: Jock Pace, Davy Nicholls, Pat Hannigan)

Everyone knew, of course, that the Pritchard's were a serious musical family. In our house, the only musical instruments were the wireless, the budgie and an old Boy's Brigade bugle. Nobody suspected our father's musical antecedents until the day he was interviewed by Franklin Ingleman when 'Down Your Way' came to visit Bathgate in the early 1960s. The family gathered round the wireless in the kitchen on the Sunday afternoon to hear what record the 'old man' had chosen, because he had refused to say. It was to be a surprise. After he had said his bit about Bathgate, we heard his characteristic cough, which was the signal that he was going to say something he thought important. He told Franklin that he wanted to hear, not the Lonnie Donnigan tune I was hoping for, but 'Furtwangler's air on a fuglehorn' or some such piece he said he used to play on the trombone in the Brass Band. The family collapsed in hysterics. Had the bugle really been a trombone, foreshortened by some furious blowing? Of course, my father's interest in and enthusiasm for brass bands simply reflects their undoubted popularity and cultural importance for most mining communities from the middle of last century to the middle of this one, and from South Wales to Winchburgh, from Ayrshire to Fife.

In general, however, as John Benson's study of the 19th century pitman suggests, the main ways in which mining families used their leisure time and money was on drink, sport and religion. Gambling was likewise 'an abiding interest'. While sociologists, or poets, might try to suggest some connection between gambling your life on a seam and your wages on a horse, my father and his ilk would have had none of that. Rival traditions thus lived cheek by jowl in mining communities as elsewhere.

Self-defined distinctions between the 'rough' and the 'respectable' were rife. My mother touches on some of this when she describes how she would be joshed by my father: 'your father used to say that he neither smoked nor drank until he met me!' He was then 27 years old and an athlete, a sprinter with Edinburgh Harriers. But, unlike the miners Jock Wardrope describes putting a collection for the 1926 Strike on a runner at Newcastle, my father would never bet on anything: horses, runners, football teams, pitch and toss, cards, draughts, dominoes, fights or marbles. Family principle, which meant his family's religious and temperance scruples, effectively prevented him from running for money or from betting on those who did – though he helped train some who did win 'the Powderhall'.

Two big tubs

Thomas: oilworker, born 1904, Pumpherston

At that time, there were dozens of local teams round about here.
Now there's only about half a dozen.
There used to be two junior teams in Queensferry, two in Broxburn,
two in Winchburgh – there's hardly any now.
Well, they had big tubs, you see,
outside the stripping box,
and you know what like they are on the football field,
when it's been raining,
and they had two big tubs, you know,
one for visitors and one for themselves.
And they were only filled with cold water!
It was practically ice that you were washing yourselves with!
It was that blooming cold!
You used to come out and wash yourself.
I even washed myself among the snow in a tub.
Oh, they were tough boys, aye.
And then,
in the local track down there,
– we had an awful lot of good runners in Pumpherston, you know –
during the war – Monteith from Edinburgh, he won the (inaudible),
Jock Bain, and all them were –
oh, they used to come from all over!
I held the watch down there one day for Duffy of Broxburn,
and he broke that half mile record.
Now, wee Benny Grant, wee Benny Grant,
he joined in the same quarter and (inaudible).
He went and broke the half mile record at one of the big games in
Glasgow, and they measured the track after it,
and the track was either a yard or a yard and a half short,
and they didn't get the record.
That was Duffy.
Rodden was his own name,
but it was Duffy that they called him for the running name.
That was his running name.

West Lothian District Library photo: runners training in the 1920s

My father also helped put a few yards on another kind of professional, Willie Thornton, who played for Rangers and Scotland and,
of course, Winchburgh Albion. Willie it was who became centre forward for the Albion when my father retired, becoming the club's secretary. As an organiser and fund raiser for local secondary juvenile
football, my father could have been trusted with the Crown jewels.
My mother tells of him sitting at the table on Saturday evenings in
Winchburgh, counting out the collection and monies from raffles
from the day's match. She would occasionally sneak a silver two-
shilling piece off the table for devilment and watch him count and
recount the piles until he twigged what she had done. He would then
demand the money's return, despite all her pleas about them being
'skint'. At stake, of course, was not some outward show of
'respectability' but the ingrained values of communality and self-
respect. In that community, it was not what you owned or did not
own that counted, but the sort of person you were known to be:
Could you be relied upon? Could you use your head? Could you conduct yourself properly? In the local parlance, were you, or were you
not, a bloody eejit? My father's family were, of course, in the tradition of 'gaffers' and he had inherited the ambition of every gaffer's
son: he wanted to put himself, his family and his community on the
map, and to show the world what they all were made of.

My father could be either 'rough' or 'respectable' as occasion
demanded. The circumstances of his wooing my mother during the
run up to the Second World War may help illustrate this. The lady of
the house to whom my mother was 'in-service' in Edinburgh asked
to meet 'this miner' she was hearing so much about. Was he
respectable? My father's charm proved too effective, however, because
my mother then had to hang around waiting on him and the lady
conversing on books and matters of the day, before they could get
out for a walk together. On one such stroll, they went through the
Grassmarket where a large lout took a shine to my mother then made
the mistake of challenging my father. He was quickly dispatched. My
father was an athlete, certainly, but he was also a drawer in the shale
mines, the most physically demanding job in the pits, to which a long
list of downed centre-halfs would no doubt have borne testimony. A
longstanding jest which he would later use to justify his lack of footballing skill, is redolent also of the good humoured masculinity of his
day: 'I couldn't play much', he would say, pausing meaningfully, 'but
I could stop them that could'.

According to John Donoghue, the Winchburgh crowd appreciated my father's speed and power as a footballer rather than his goal scoring ability: 'We thought he was kinna short-sighted, ken'. A saying apparently developed in the village round his wholehearted approach based on the practice of removing sections of the barrier behind the goals on sports days in order to lengthen the field to allow runners to draw up, a kind of stopping zone after the sprints. Someone in the crowd once wondered aloud why they were removing the fencing behind the goals, and some wag said – 'oh, that's for Boab Findlay' – a reference to his reputation for putting everything over the goal line: goalkeeper, defenders, himself, even the ball, when he saw it.

This chimes with that other well known footballing crowd's expression – 'open the gates' – defined as a vigorous rush up the park that ended when ever the park did. I suspect that the determination and spirit of my father's 'game' might have made him more suited to the 19th than to the 20th century, playing centre-forward for Durhamtown Rangers perhaps? But, by his own admission, my father was more of a runner than a footballer, though he loved both sports. 'The best feeling in the world', he would say, 'is being one hundred percent fit', and I am sure he also included in this the hard labour of drawing in the shale mines. As a young man, there is little doubt that my father would have drawn shale with the same endeavour that he showed playing football or running a race.

My parents' last neighbours in Winchburgh were the Cormies beside whom we lived in Niddry Road between 1951–3. The house was positioned at the half-way line of Winchburgh football park, which suited my father no end because he could walk down to the bottom of the garden and be at an Albion home match. There were major political ructions involved in securing this council house after my father was initially offered a house in Millgate's so-called 'Hell's Kitchen', a collection of what today would be termed 'anti-social families' but who were then considered simply 'daft' or, more precisely, 'bloody eejits'.

The Cormies inhabited the other end of the social scale. Old Jim Cormie was a joiner who had as cheery a disposition as you could wish to meet. Mrs Cormie would help my mother out endlessly too by taking the boys off her hands for a spell, while she tended to my grandmother. The Cormies had a radiogram which my brothers and myself were forever encouraged by Jim to play, and sing along to, his favourite record being – 'A Gordon For Me'.

I also remember regular 'tappings' going on between our front rooms – a poker struck on the back of the fireplace – a kind of 'morse code' between Mrs Cormie and my mother as to whether to send me back for my tea or to come round to render assistance. This despite their back doors being hardly two feet apart. Young Jim Cormie, who became a joiner like his father, and who still lives in the same house, told me years afterwards that while my mother was putting the boys to bed, my father would often come round to their house for some peace, to read a newspaper or a book: 'He never knocked, though, just walked right in. He sometimes never said anything, you know, just as you do in your own family. He would just sit down and read, and then leave'.

What else were neighbours for? Of course, by the same token, the world trailed to our door to visit my grandmother or to see my father about a match, a player, a raffle or something for the paper – either to put it in or, just as likely, to keep it out. But, like gambling, my father never thought much of that idea either.

Alexander Ross: founder and first bandmaster of West Calder Brass and Reed Band; first tenant of Mossend, 1866
photo: John Kelly, District Library

The Five Sisters
(Elegy for Shale)

Alistair Findlay

frae the black isles and the borders
twa centuries ago
they laboured roond the calders
above grund and ablo'
and there was no idle bread

O thir faithers they wir bastards and
ma grandfaithers they say
and ivry man a mason grand
no godless irish they, o no
but I still remember them

mair braw nor a' the Pharoahs
and a' thir chariats hors
and burnished by the burning blaes
but who shall sing for these
the slaves of ancient Egypt?

O ye douchters o' Jerusalem
raise up yir voices sing
men gethered fire in thir airms
t'wrocht cathedrals for thir kings

wherefore,
        let this be thir sepulchre

        till ye hear yir ain skulls crack
        or stare up till the Sisters
        until they stare richt back
        and intil the image o' god

The Five Sisters – West Calder

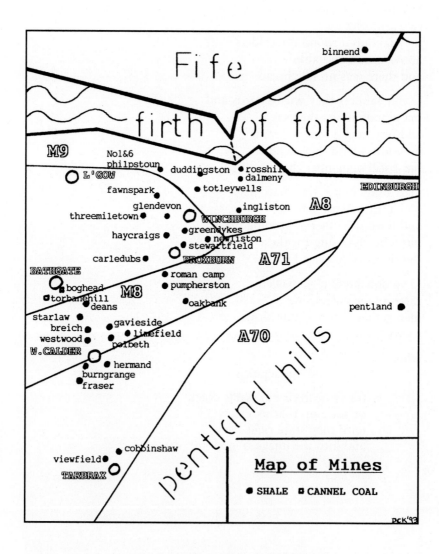

Source: David Kerr, *Shale Oil, Scotland*

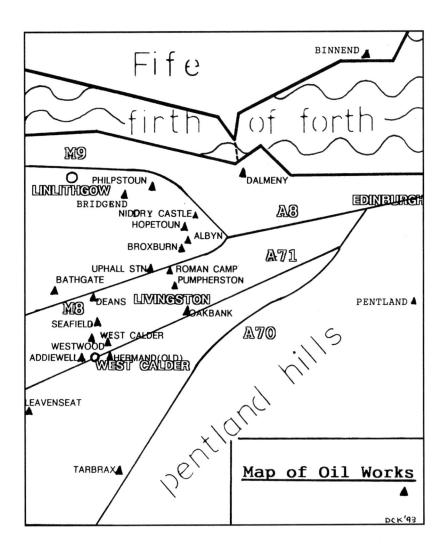

Source: David Kerr, *Shale Oil, Scotland*

What the oil industry owes to Dr James Young

by F.M. Cook

General manager and director,
BP Refinery (Grangemouth) Ltd

Reprinted from *Chemistry and Industry*, 1971

The end of 1970 saw the centenary of the foundation of the Chair of Chemical Technology at the University of Strathclyde. Strictly speaking it would be more correct to say the Chair of Technical Chemistry at Anderson's University, for this is what it was called in the year 1870. It was in that year that a Glasgow cabinet maker's son, Dr James Young, endowed what is now the oldest chair of Applied Chemistry in the United Kingdom, and the forerunner of what later became, in other British colleges and universities, the Chair of Chemical Engineering. The Young Chair has had five occupants since it was inaugurated, the last and present incumbent being Professor P.D. Ritchie.

James Young himself obtained his own technical education at Anderson's University, by taking evening classes, and then, in 1831, was given regular employment as a laboratory assistant in the university. Later he became a lecturer and assistant to Professor Thomas Graham, the first professor of chemistry in the university, whose name is today commemorated by the Thomas Graham Building, which houses the department of pure and applied chemistry.

During this period at Anderson's University, Young formed friendships with four fellow students which were to last all his life. They were David Livingstone, who was studying medicine at that time; Hugh Bartholomew, who became manager of the Glasgow Gas Works; Angus Smith, who became a professor of chemistry and was Young's companion in his later years; and Lyon Playfair who was born in India and who became professor of chemistry in Manchester. It was Lyon Playfair who first aroused Young's interest in oil; in December 1847, at which time they were both working in Manchester. Young was employed by Charles Tenant & Company as manager of their chemical works in Manchester, and Playfair was professor of chemistry in the Royal School-of Mines. Playfair's brother-in-law, Mr Oakes, who had interests in collieries and an iron works, advised him that there was an oil seepage from a coal mine on his estate near Alfreton in Derbyshire. The rate of flow was about 300gal/d. Playfair reported this to his friend, Young, who

Dr James Young

approached his own firm to ascertain if they were interested in processing the oil. They were not; but they had no objection to his doing
so. Perhaps, at this period of time, James Young reminded himself of
the words spoken by Brutus in Shakespeare's Julius Caesar: 'There is
a tide in the affairs of men,/Which taken at the flood leads on to fortune'.

He may or may not have been inspired by these words, but he certainly made up his mind to strike out with the tide and to start in
business for himself – the oil business, in which he ultimately made
his fortune.

In partnership with Messrs Meldrum and Binney, the latter providing the capital, he set up a factory to distil the petroleum for the
production of burning oil and lubricants to be sold to the cotton
mills in Lancashire. Although Playfair drew Young's attention to the
possibilities of wax production following the research work in the
early 1830s by Christison of Edinburgh on Burma oil, wax was not
produced on a commercial basis from the Derbyshire oil. Young was
to do this later.

Because the oil was present in a coal mine, Young formed the idea
that the origin of oil lay in coal; but he was not the first to think this.
The 9th Earl of Dundonald patented a process in 1781 for producing tar, pitch and oil from coal, and works were set up in Fife,
Lanarkshire, and Ayrshire for this purpose. They were crude in
design and construction, the distillation being carried out in masonry
structures, and the condensers consisting of wooden pipes immersed
in water. However, it seems to have been agreed that the real pioneer
of the oil industry was the cabinet maker's son, Dr James Young. It
was he who had the technical skill and business acumen to patent his
process in 1850 for: 'Treating bituminous coal to obtain. paraffine
and oil containing paraffine therefrom' (Patent No 13292 of 17
October 1850).

When the oil seepage in Derbyshire ran out, he returned to
Scotland to set up, in 1851, a works near Bathgate to produce and
refine oil from a rich seam of cannel coal which was being mined on
the nearby Torbanehill Estate. Incidentally, this cannel coal derived
its name from the long, luminous flame it produced when burned –
cannel being the Scots pronunciation for candle – literally 'candle
coal'. Young was already aware that it was good oil-producing material, as he had had a sample sent to him when he was in Manchester
by his friend Hugh Bartholomew, who was at the time the manager
of the Gas Works in Glasgow. The cost of this coal to the new works
at Bathgate was 13s 6d/ton. Ordinary coal was then 4s/ton. The oil
works were welcomed in Bathgate because they provided much needed

employment for the inhabitants of the area, who were mostly hand-loom weavers with earnings barely sufficient to prevent starvation. Young's Bathgate enterprise, therefore, was the start of an industry which since then has provided employment for thousands of people in Scotland and elsewhere.

Eventually the supply of cannel coal became exhausted, and Young turned his attention to producing oil from shale found in the West Calder district. Deposits of oil shale were exploited by others as well as Young; in different parts of the Lothians, in Fife, in North Wales and at Kimmeridge near Dorset. Oil shale is almost black in colour, with a laminated structure, and can be cut with a sharp knife. It does not contain oil, as we know it, but rather organic matter known as 'kerogen', which cannot be removed by an organic solvent. It has to be heated over a range of temperature from 350'c to 500'c to decompose the organic matter to produce oil.

The site chosen by Young for his shale oil works was Addiewell, near West Calder, and in 1865 his friend Dr Livingstone laid the foundation stone. The building of the works meant that Young had also to build houses for his work people as there was insufficient accommodation in West Calder. He erected a brickworks, to manufacture bricks from a bed of clay found on the Addiewell property and was soon constructing houses at the same time as he was building his factory. This brickworks was probably the first to be associated with the oil industry. It was many years later that shale brick manufacture was started in oil works at Pumpherston, near Mid Calder.

At first lubricants and solvents were the main products from Young's works, but there was a demand for burning oil, i.e. paraffin. Young was able to produce a water white paraffin, but he needed the right type of lamp to burn it in. Eventually a type which he saw on the continent gave him an idea for the design and he started the production of the lamps at the Clissold Lamp Works, New Spring Street, Birmingham. One of the original lamps is still in existence with a representation of the Birmingham Works on one side of the globe and the Addiewell Shale Oil Works on the other side (shown on page 235 below).

Another product much in demand at the time was paraffin wax. Young produced this by chilling a waxy distillate and then putting the semi-solid mixture of crystallised wax and oil into strong canvas bags. These were squeezed in hydraulic presses until no more oil would come through the canvas. The oil made an excellent lubricant, but the whole operation was a messy business and the crude wax from the canvas bags needed further treatment and filtration before it attained the 'beautiful lustrous structure' for which Young's wax was famous.

At both Bathgate and Addiewell there was surplus gas from the process, and Bathgate town was supplied with gas from the works. An offer was made to the city of Edinburgh to supply it with gas from Addiewell at the rate of 1s 6d/1,000ft³, but the offer was declined. It was nearly a century later that the city of Edinburgh did take gas from an oil refinery – the one at Grangemouth. A 16in gas main connects the refinery to the Granton Gas Works. Up until 1864, when Young's patent ran out, his competitors in the oil business had a tough time, for he took them to court if their refining processes infringed his patents. Even the Americans had to pay him royalties and he spent three months of 1860 in the States to ensure that he got his cut of two cents/gal. In all he collected £50,000 from the 60 or so American companies operating oil from coal plants at the time, some of them using imported cannel coal from Bathgate. The American oil companies were not all paying him his just dues, and because of this the American Government agreed to extend the life of his patent for seven years from October 1864.

In the year before Young's visit to the States an event of world importance took place. On 29 August 1859 Edwin L. Drake, an American employed by the Seneca Oil Company, sunk the first well for his company and discovered a supply of petroleum. The well, which reached a depth of 69.5ft, was in the state of Pennsylvania in an area where oil seepages were known to occur. More wells were drilled as fast as money and equipment could be found and by the end of the year 2,000 barrels of oil had been produced. Three years later production had risen to over 3m barrels. In the same period the price dropped from $20/barrel to $0.1/barrel. This flood of cheap oil struck the death knell for oil from coal plants in the states. It is interesting to note, however, that now, a century later, we find the Americans again taking an interest in shale oil production because of the vast deposits of rich oil-bearing shale in their country, and because domestic consumption of petroleum has been outstripping the indigenous supply.

The advent of cheap American oil on the British market meant the demise of many of the shale oil works which had sprung up in Scotland about the time that Young started his business at Addiewell. Shale oil products had difficulty in competing in price with similar imported products from petroleum, and the 120 oil works which operated at one time in Scotland were reduced to 30 by 1873 and to six operating companies with 13 plants by 1905 (see Table).

Table

Companies still operating in 1905	Year of registration
The Broxburn Oil Company Ltd	1877
The Dalmeny oil Company Ltd	1871
The Oakbank Oil Company Ltd	1885
The Pumpherston Oil Company Ltd	1883
James Ross and Company Ltd	1883
Young's Paraffin Light and Mineral Oil Company Ltd	1866

Also the yield of oil/ton of shale diminished as the richer seams became worked out. In 1879 the average yield of crude oil, including naphtha, was about 34gal/ton of shale. By 1910 this had dropped to 27gal. The original cannel coal had produced up to 120gal/ton.

West Lothian Oil Company, 1883–1892. Staff photograph, c. 1890
photo: William Marjoriebanks

However, it was in 1910* that the industry had its biggest output – 70m gal of crude shale oil, including naphtha, equal to 273,000 ton of oil from 3,130,280 ton of shale. Big stuff in those days; but a drop in the ocean today when it is considered that the oil terminal at Finnart on Loch Long is handling tankers carrying 200,000 ton of oil, and one of these will only maintain the BP Refinery at Grangemouth on full throughput for about eight days. By 1910,

* In 1913 more shale was mined but less oil was produced – 3,280,142 ton of shale from which 264,935 ton of oil were obtained

petrol, which had been almost valueless in the early years of oil refining, was now much in demand due to the innovation of the motor car at the turn of the century, and commanded a price of 1s to 1s 6d/gal.

It was about this time that the British Government started to tax the fuel used by motor vehicles – at the rate of 3d/gal. Production from the world's oil fields was 44m ton/year and there were 500,000 ton of ocean-going shipping equipped to burn fuel oil. Lord Fisher, the First Sea Lord, had foretold away back in 1880 that oil would replace coal as fuel for the Royal Navy.

It was, however, Winston Churchill who, in 1914, made the momentous decision to make the Royal Navy almost wholly dependent on oil. As First Lord of the Admiralty, he persuaded Parliament to make the British Government a stockholder in the Anglo-Persian Oil Company – and it was the Anglo-Persian Oil Company which later took the shale oil industry under its wing.

In the 1914–18 war the shale industry made a valuable contribution to the country's oil supplies; providing 250,000 ton of oil/year, but the end of this war saw the shale oil works in financial trouble, and, to reduce marketing costs, the Scottish Oils Agency was formed in 1918 to market products from the remaining shale oil companies.

These products were stated to be:

1   Motor spirit of most excellent quality
2   Naphtha for dry cleaning and india rubber manufacture
3   Lamp oils with a 75 year record of safety
4   Power oil for the farm tractor and fishing boat
5   Lighthouse and long burning oil for the important duties of lighthouse and railway signal lamps
6   Fuel oil for furnaces and diesel engines
7   Gas oil for the manufacture and enrichment of gas
8   Batching oil for the spinner, the weaver and rope maker
9   Cleaning and lubrication oils for machinery
10   Paraffin wax for candles, tapers and matches, for water proofing and electrical installation
11   Candles of every kind
12   Sulphate of ammonia to manure our fields in peace time and provide explosives in war
13   Paraffin coke, the smokeless fuel

This is a wide range of products – comparable with those produced by a modern oil refinery today.

It is interesting note the claim of a 75-year record of safety for lamp oils. Before the advent of the motor car, many oil producers ran into trouble by having too high a proportion of low flash point distillate in their lamp oil. This was the cause of many lamp accidents in the home. In the London area in 1895 it is recorded that 25 per cent of the deaths caused by fires were due to lamp accidents.

Sulphate of ammonia, one of the other products listed by the agency, is also interesting. The ammonia was derived from the nitrogen in the shale. The retorting process involved the use of steam and the nitrogen in the shale combined with the hydrogen in the steam to form ammonia. At first the evil smelling ammonia water which condensed along with the oil was thought to be a nuisance and was separated from the oil and pumped to waste. Then it was noticed that the grass grew better in the areas affected by this water and it was realised that a valuable fertiliser was being wasted. Most shale oil works, therefore, built sulphate of ammonia plants in which ammonia gas was released from the crude ammonia water and bubbled into lead-lined vats containing sulphuric acid to form crystals of ammonium sulphate.

The formation of the Scottish Oils Agency, however, was not the complete answer to the oil companies' financial difficulties, and in 1919 they were reorganised to form Scottish Oils Ltd, a subsidiary of the British Petroleum Company (then the Anglo-Persian Oil Company). BP thus became firmly established in Scotland.

In 1928 the name of Winston Churchill comes on the oil scene once again. As Chancellor of the Exchequer he granted shale oil and other indigenous oils a tax preference of 4d/gal. As the tax on imported oil increased over the years, this duty preference was also increased. This, however, was not sufficient to prevent the decline of the shale oil industry, and by the middle of the present century there were only four crude shale oil works left, these supplying a central refinery at Pumpherston. In 1962 the refining of shale oil ceased. (The duty preference was withdrawn then as a result of the EFTA agreement). This was, of course, only the end of one part of the industry. The other part, the refining of imported oil which now completely dominates the oil scene in Scotland will be referred to later.

So far this paper has been concerned mainly with the pioneer of the oil industry, Dr James Young, but there were others who followed in his footsteps by introducing his methods of producing and refining oil into other parts of the world. Some of them went to Australia, some to South Africa and some were building shale retorts in parts of Europe. While Young was busy at Bathgate and at the same time considering expanding his business by refining shale, a man called William Fell, from West Calder, left Scotland to join his brother, James Fell, a coffee planter in Ceylon. When he got there he discovered that there was a slump in the coffee market, and to obtain fresh outlets for coffee a sailing ship was chartered to take a full load of coffee to New South Wales, Australia, where there was a gold rush. But, when the ship arrived in Sydney, the crew deserted the ship for the gold diggings, leaving only the captain and William Fell, who was in charge of the consignment aboard. As they obviously were unable to work the ship on their own, the pair decided that they might as well also go to the gold diggings, which were near a place called Bathurst. After a few weeks they decided the work was too uncongenial and they set out to return to Sydney. One evening, when they were about to camp for the night in a valley called Hartley Vale, they saw a shepherd's cottage and decided to put up there. It was winter time and there was a fire burning in the hearth which appeared to be neither wood nor coal. In fact, William Fell was sure that it resembled Scottish oil shale. The shepherd showed him where he obtained his fuel and Fell loaded the shale onto the pack horses and got it to Sydney. When he eventually arrived back in Scotland, William had the shale analysed and found that the yield of oil was 180gal to the ton.

No time was lost in forming a company with capital from the UK. The company, which became known as the Australian Kerosine & Oil Company, had William Fell as managing director. Scottish shale miners and craftsmen, including bricklayers, were enlisted, and with their families filled two sailing ships bound for Australia to start the shale Oil Industry there – an industry which flourished on and on for years under the direction of Fell and his descendants.

In 1949, while working in South Africa, the author visited the torbanite mine and crude oil works near Ermelo, about 140 miles east of Johannesburg. There the torbanite seam, about 3ft thick in places, was being mined and the torbanite processed in horizontal retorts to produce crude oil for the refinery at Boksburg near Johannesburg. Both the operations at Ermelo and Boksburg were under the direction of ex Scottish Oils men, Messrs Forbes and Robertson.

No reference to the people in the oil industry would be complete without mentioning the oil workers of the Lothians of Scotland – the men who worked for Young's Company and the other shale oil companies, mining, retorting and refining the shale oil. At one time there were as many as 10,000 employed, half of them being miners. Many of them came from Ireland, indeed at one time the Uphall oil plant near Broxburn was known as Paddy Mulhern's Oil Works, because the foreman's name was Mulhern. He was the man who gave you a job if you came from the Emerald Isle.

In 1922 some of the shale oil workers were sent to South Wales to help start up the BP oil refinery at Llandarcy. Descendants of the original shale oil men are employed in the modern refinery there today – Scotsmen with Welsh accents! Then, in 1924, there was another new oil refinery to be commissioned by shale oil men. The year before, in 1923, it had been decided to start building an oil refinery at Grangemouth to refine imported crucle oil, although it was not the first Scottish oils plant to do so.

In 1921 the Uphall oil works were refining Persian crude oil. In that year an 8in crude line had been laid from Grangemouth to Uphall, a distance of 14 miles, so that imported crude oil could be pumped from the port of Grangemouth to the shale oil refinery at Uphall. This must have been the longest crude oil line in the UK and it was not until 1951 that a longer one came into operation, when a 12in pipeline from Finnart on Loch Long, in the West of Scotland, was laid to the refinery at Grangemouth, in the east. This line still exists and is 57 miles long. However, it has recently been superceded by a 20in diameter pipeline, following nearly the same route as the original 12in line, through which the oil is pumped across Scotland to Grangemouth at a rate of more than 1,000 ton/h.

In the space of 120 years the processing of oil in Scotland has jumped from a few thousand ton/year to over 9m ton/year which is the present capacity of the oil refining plant at Grangemouth. In the same period the art of oil refining has made tremendous strides, although the principles have not changed that much from those employed by Young. In Young's day however, the plant was not so complicated. When he started the Bathgate works he built horizontal retorts grouped in 21 benches for processing the cannel coal. The oil vapour from the retorts was condensed to crude oil and distilled in horizontal boiler stills, 11ft long and 4ft in diameter. In later years, six egg-ended pressure stills 29ft long and 7ft 6in in diameter were built for cracking the heavier distillates to produce 'burning oil'. This was a process patented by James Young junior in 1865. The oil vapour from the stills was condensed in atmospheric and water-cooled condensers. In 1862 A.C. Kirk, who was Young's engineer, developed refrigerating plant for chilling the waxy oil distillate to remove the wax for candle manufacture. Treatment plants for refining the distillates and crude wax by using sulphuric acid and soda ash or caustic soda were also designed by Young and his staff. The basic refining processes of a modern oil refinery were therefore present at Bathgate and also at Addiewell, which at one time was reputed to be the biggest oil works in the world.

For many years the distillation process in the oil works in Scotland was carried out in boiler stills, at first batchwise, and then continuously, by coupling a number of stills together so that each redistilled the residue from the previous still. In fact the first crude oil distillation unit built at Grangemouth in 1923 was on this principle and there was a bench of steam heated stills to separate the gasoline from the kerosine. The boiler stills were eventually superseded by pipe-still units.

In 1936 a crude oil distillation unit, consisting of a pipestill heater, fractionating column with associated heat exchangers, and condensers, was designed by Scottish Oils staff and installed at Pumpherston. In 1941, a second larger unit was constructed because by this time Pumpherston was processing oil from wells in England. The first consignment of English crude oil arrived from Formby in Lancashire in 1939. The 1941 crude unit had a capacity of 140,000 ton/year – in comparison the crude oil distillation unit brought on stream earlier this year at Grangemouth has a capacity of 4.5m ton/year.

The egg-ended cracker stills of Young's day were followed by thermal pipe-still crackers, built at Uphall, Pumpherston, and Grangemouth in the 1920s. Those at Grangemouth were converted to crude oil distillation units and their cracking duty taken over by a new fluid catalytic cracking plant, erected in the early 1950s, which was more efficient than its predecessors at breaking down the heavier oils to gas and motor gasoline. A hydrocracker is now being built at Grangemouth which embodies the latest techniques in cracking. A wax distillate from vacuum distillation is contacted with hydrogen in the presence of catalysts, at an operating pressure of more than 2,000 lb/in^2 above atmospheric, to crack the heavier products to gas, gasoline and feedstock for petroleum chemicals.

From the days of Young, the oil industry has kept in the forefront of technology. For a brief period the main use of oil was for lubrication. Then it became a fuel to burn. Some people have always said it was too precious to burn. Today the oil production at Grangemouth in Scotland is not all burned. Over a million ton of light distillate go to the production of petroleum chemicals each year. Even Young foresaw that oil could be used for purposes other than lubrication and fuel. He predicted that synthetic detergents could be made from it. This prediction was not realised until the early 1940s when research work showed that the alkyl sulphate type of detergent could be manufactured from shale oil olefins. The first plant was built at Pumpherston refinery in 1948. Today Pumpherston produces more than 100 different products from its detergent plant, although none of them is now produced from shale oil.

The detergents manufactured now are more effective than the cleaning product produced by Pumpherston in 1889. In that year a material called 'Laundrine' was made which was supposed to purify and bleach soiled clothes. When Mr and Mrs Gladstone visited the works in 1890, Mrs Gladstone was presented with a case of 'Laundrine'. It appears to have consisted of small cubes of wax.

The history of Pumpherston, the last of the shale oil refineries, is one of diversification. It was not originally built with a view to oil being its main product, and it was not originally one of Young's works, although it now operates under the name of Young's Paraffin, Light and Mineral Oil Company Ltd. The production of ammonium sulphate was the primary objective. The Pumpherston Oil Company was born in 1882, the year before Young died, and was founded by Mr Williarn Fraser who had been manager at the Uphall works of the Uphall Mineral Oil Company. Mr Peter McLagan, the owner of Pumpherston Estate, had asked him to test the shale on his property. It was found to be very suitable for sulphate of ammonia production. A company was floated with Mr Fraser as managing director, the other directors being Messrs James Wood, James Craig, Robert Tennant and John Paterson. Incidentally, Mr Craig was one of the partners in J. & A.F. Craig Engineers in Paisley, who are still supplying the oil industry with processing plant.

Mr Fraser's son, also William, eventually took over from him. He, like Dr James Young, received his technical education at Anderson's University, or rather the Royal Technical College, as it was called when he was there. He became managing director of Scottish Oils Ltd when it was formed in 1919, and subsequently chairman of the British Petroleum Company. He never forgot the works where he originally learnt the oil business and when he received a title he chose to be known as Lord Strathalmond of Pumpherston. Latterly he was not able to visit Pumpherston Works very often, but when he did he liked to reminisce about early days and to point out the plant and buildings he remembered, including the stable where the horses were kept, which incidentally, was only recently demolished. Lord Strathalmond's son, who is a director of the British Petroleum Company, succeeded to the title on his father's death this year.

At one time the spent shale from which the oil had been produced served no useful purpose. But in 1934 a brick plant was set up at Pumpherston to produce building bricks from the used shale, and the output eventually reached 20m bricks/year. Spent shale is now being used in large quantities for road construction and for land reclamation on the Grangemouth refinery site.

Today Young's Paraffin Light and Mineral Oil Company Ltd still exists to remind us of its founder, Dr James Young. If he were to step out of the past now, he would find that the shale oil industry which he knew, and which flourished for over 100 years in Scotland, has been superseded by the vast oil and chemical complex at Grangemouth, where 9m ton of imported oil are being processed annually to satisfy an ever expanding market. Oil consumption in Scotland last year increased by 8.6 per cent and is currently running at 8.5m. ton/year, and the consumption of petroleum products in the UK as a whole is likely to be in excess of 100m ton this year. New products from petroleum are constantly being evolved, the latest being protein; a protein-from-petroleum plant, the first of its type in the world, is in operation at Grangemouth to produce 4,000 ton/year of protein from a normal paraffin feedstock. The research work was carried out in France and at Grangemouth.

No supply of indigenous oil to supplant shale oil has been found in Scotland, although there is a small production of oil from oil fields in England. The last well drilled in Scotland was at Pumpherston in 1963. There was a small gas flow, initially about 15,000ft3/d which was used to supply the burner on a drier for drying spent shale for brick manufacture. The supply became exhausted after a few months. However, the oil find by Phillips Petroleum in the Norwegian sector of the North Sea, and the recent oil strike by BP, 110 miles east north east of Aberdeen, at a depth of 11,231ft in the British sector of the North Sea, raise fresh hopes of a new supply. The rate of flow from the BP test well was 4,700 bbls/d of low sulphur crude and the first cargo of 233 barrels of North Sea oil from the test bore was off loaded at Grangemouth on Thursday 19 November 1970. A lot more exploratory work has to be done to establish the extent of the field before it can be said to be a commercial proposition. In addition to its exploration work in the North Sea, BP, in conjunction with the Gas Board, has recently been carrying out seismic surveys in the Minch and off the Orkneys to ascertain whether there are locations in these areas where gas or oil may be found.

In conclusion, there is little doubt that Edwin L. Drake made history when he struck oil in Pennsylvania in 1859, but he himself made no impact on the oil industry. In fact, after the original strike, nothing more is heard of him – but not so Dr James Young. It was he who made use of his scientific training to establish the basic principles of refining oil and it was his zeal, business ability and technical skill which set a standard for future generations of oil men to follow.

You know what gundy is? – working in the oil works
Thomas: oilworker, born 1904, Pumpherston

I worked in Pumpherston Works, actually,
for fifty one and a half years,
and I was never outside the Work.
I never worked anywhere else in my life
bar Pumpherston Work.
And I thoroughly enjoyed it.
I had some good times.
I had a connection with the Union.
I was on the Executive Council for a long while.
I was the Secretary of that and Treasurer forbye,
by the way,
with the Scottish Shale Miners and Oil Workers Union.
In fact,
I've still got the desk ben there
in the room
that Joe Heaney went into Edinburgh and bought.
And I've still got it ben there yet.

In the Works at that time
all the stuff came in from the different Works,
crude Works, you understand.
They had no refineries.
They were crude Works.
They only made crude.
They just had retorts and that.
They couldn't make lubricating oil
or paraffin oil
or anything like that
or candles
or wax.

They just sent in the raw crude oil to us. And it came in in tanks.
And you had to put in a long rubber hose.
And there was a pipe on the end of it with wee holes in it,
perforated with holes,
and you stuck this into the tank
and turned on the steam,
you see.

And when I was about eighteen.
Old Duncan McIntyre wanted me to go over to the Refinery.

Well, the Flemings were actually managers of the Refinery but,
at this time,
a lot of the personnel at Pumpherston had flitted down
to Grangemouth to work in Grangemouth, you see.
The Flemings went along with them too.
The families of the Flemings went down to Grangemouth too
about Twenty-three or Twenty-four even.

I worked in the cooperage then,
painting the barrels.
They used to have a big pail, you know,
those whitewash brushes.
And there were maybe three or four of us maybe painting barrels.
And big Pat Smith, he cut out the stencils.
Oh, they would be going to Buenos Aries
and all over the world,
you know.
Well,
these barrels would go out of here,
hundreds and hundreds every week,
forbye tanks.
And it was mostly paraffin in them,
paraffin and lube oil, lubricating oil.
At one time they used to have five gallon tins too.
We had to solder the caps on the top of them.
And they went away abroad too,
all over the world really,
and blacks too.
Sulphate of ammonia too.
Sulphate of ammonia at that time was costing a colossal sum –
away in about sixty or seventy pounds a ton.
Sulphate of ammonia!
They were getting a hundred and odd pounds a ton for it
in the latter end there too.
The sulphate of ammonia was put in bags.
It was dried.
It goes into the same kind of system as a washing machine,
you know, the spins.
It went into spinners, you see,
and the spinners spun the water out of them.
And then they were taken away to a conveyor
and it went into a big box.
And the boy at the bottom of the box used to get

– there were two hundredweight bags of sulphate came out –
and they made an awful lot of that.
And then, of course, they made all the different kinds of oil.
And gundy.
You know what gundy is?
Well, they used to make gundy as well.
And they used to have a market for it.
They would just coup it out!

That went for making certain plastics?

That's right, plastics and things like that.
Oh aye.
And then they made miners wax.
There were special machines for it.
There was about four or five machines.

(Wife talking): And there was Tam Dick.
He used to come up from East Calder too.
And Tam cleaned the stills, along with Andrew Chapman
and a few more of those boys.
And Tam, you know, was like a wild man.
All he had on was a pair of trousers with holes in them.
Holes all over them, in fact, and a blooming old torn jacket.
And how they used to get bathed at that time was,
they had a steam thing at the top and they had it open a wee bit,
it leeked a wee bit, it dripped,
it came down a wee bit of rhone pipe into a barrel,
and it came down from there into another barrel!
And that's where the still cleaners washed themselves
until they put up stills baths for them
down near one of the roundalls
next to the crude stills.
I mind of one of the Managers saying to Duncan McIntyre one day,
he says, 'What in goodness is that? A wild beast?'
'Och', Duncan says, 'It's only Tam Dick', he says,
'He's just getting himself down, going away to get washed.'
Tam used to go in and fill coal for the Co-operative in the morning
after he was finished down there cleaning his stills.

(Thomas): And I've seen them going into the stills,
and I'm not exaggerating any,
I've seen them going into those stills
and coming out with their clogs on fire,
it was that hot.

How they did it I don't know.
But that's what they used to do.
That was the coking stills.
Aye, the coking stills.
Oh aye.

In the Refinery I was on the making of paraffin for a while,
you see.
And you got the raw paraffin
and you gave a treatment of so much acid
and then you settled it for a few hours
and then you ran the tar off it,
the acid.
It was a strong strong smell on the acid tar.
And after you settled it for a while
you dropped it into containers down below that again.
And you treated it with soda then, caustic soda,
and you kept putting the soda in it.
Well, once you were used to it,
you know,
you had to measure it,
but once you got used to it like,
like I was,
I could tell by the smell of it,
the lovely smell it had,
the sweet smell of it!
And then you settled it down
and then you pumped it away into storage tanks,
you see.
They took it out of there.
Of course,
they treated the naptha and that different.
They treated that with lead and some of these things.
I just can't mind all what else they put into it.
They could put it in engines too, you know.
It was that light, you see,
petrol and naptha,
you could put both into engines.
And there were some – old Bob Bell –
used to run his old motor bike on naptha.
Aye, he used to run his motor bike on naptha!

(Wife Talking): Aye, they could use it for car engines
but it was mostly for cleaning, I think,

for a lighter, you know,
a cleaning job.
You know, a cleaning job!
It made a lovely job of cleaning anything.

(Thomas): And I was on the wax for a long while
treating the wax.
And wax was a very special thing, you know.
When I got the wax
– it actually came from paraffin sheds, you know –
and you'll know what like,
you'll have seen it,
it was just like chewing gum.
Aye well, it was thicker,
and slobby,
and, well,
they put it into presses, you see.
What they done was they put down a square,
maybe about three feet square,
and they put in a big sheet on the top of that square,
you see.
Then they filled up the wax onto that sheet.
And then they folded the sheet across so that it was all closed in.
And then they put it into the presses.
Well, the presses pressed all the oil out of it, you see,
all the stuff that the Company was really wanting,
all the valuable oil that was coming out of it.
And what was left
the boys had to go up there and knock them out.
They were just like cakes of wax.
Knock them out with their scrapers,
and they went into melters down below.
Well, that was the stuff that I got,
you see, to treat.
I had two huge stacks.
We had what they called hard wax
and soft wax
and I never knew the difference,
even yet,
what they were.
But I was told that one was hard,
and one was soft,
and I had to treat them accordingly.

Would that be like different melting points?

Aye, it would likely be a flashpoint, maybe,
of some kind.
It flashed it, you know,
when you've seen up in the lab there,
you are trying something,
and the wee thing,
and you flicked it out,
and it flashes!
Well, that's what they called the flashpoint.
And I know I was very good at knowing these mechanical things.
Well,
we treated the wax the very same with acid
and then soda.
And the soda that came off it at the bottom, it was
– oh, it was used for some other purpose after that again.
It was used in the tar boxes for neutralising the tar!
That's what it was used for.
It was used in the tar boxes.
And old Jimmy Bell from Kirknewton
used to work on the tar boxes.
He was one of the boys that came down from Oakbank Work
when it shut down.

Now,
don't ask the year [1932],
because I don't know.

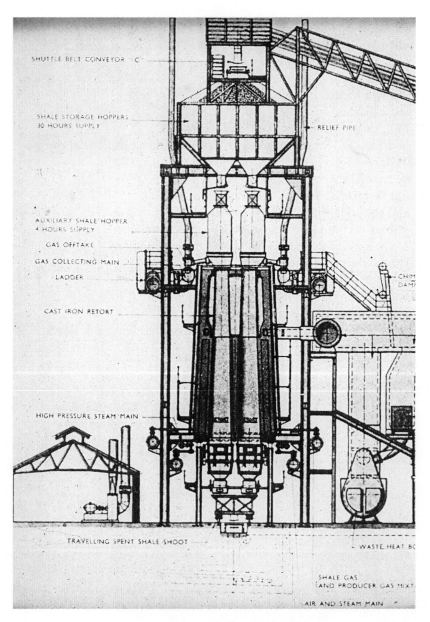

SHUTTLE BELT CONVEYOR 'C'

SHALE STORAGE HOPPERS
30 HOURS SUPPLY

RELIEF PIPE

AUXILIARY SHALE HOPPER
4 HOURS SUPPLY

GAS OFFTAKE

GAS COLLECTING MAIN

LADDER

CHIM
DAM

CAST IRON RETORT

HIGH PRESSURE STEAM MAIN

TRAVELLING SPENT SHALE SHOOT

WASTE HEAT BO

SHALE GAS
AND PRODUCER GAS MIXT

AIR AND STEAM MAIN

Section drawing of a Westwood Retort, 1951

Shale worldwide

The address by Fraser Cook, General Manager of BP Grangemouth, on 20 November 1970 commemorating the centenary of the Young Chair of Chemical Technology at the University of Strathclyde, mentions that the establishment and development of shale oil industries in Australia and South Africa owed much to james Young's discoveries and to the experience and skills of former Scottish Oils oilmen.

The Institute of Petroleum published two volumes entitled *Oil Shale and Cannel Coal* in 1938 and 1950 which cover international gatherings, organised by Robert Crichton, aimed at analysing the shale oil industry around the world. The Soviet Union was not represented on either occasion. Estonia (Gulf of Finland) and Czechoslovakia attended the first conference in 1938 but not the second in 1950. Giving potentially valuable economic information to the West, presuming he was invited to do so, when he could purchase theirs from the Institute of Petroleum in two bound volumes in London, was probably unlikely to sound like a good idea to Stalin at these particular times. Both conferences discussed countries with significant deposits of shale and their potential for development alongside matters of production, industrial techniques and so on. Specialists from different countries presented papers analysing their own situation and then invited questions and comments. The following is a very brief summary. More recent information can be had in David Kerr's *Shale Oil Scotland* (1994, second edition due shortly):

Australia: Torbanite was discovered in 1815 in the Hartley Valley, a few miles east of Lithgow, New South Wales. It was not until Young's pioneering work on extraction methods in the 1850s in Scotland that production became possible on a wider scale, first in 1865 at Mt. Kembla (American Creek) near Wollongong, and Hartley (80 miles from Sidney) which became the main refining centre in the 1870s. Capertree Valley had deposits of torbanite which were worked in 1896, the small village of Torbane being built for the purpose, the crude oil being sent some 43 miles to Hartley for refining. Between 1873–1900, torbanite was mined and refined at Joadja, 18 miles from Mittagong, by the Australian Kerosene Oil & Mineral Co. In 1866 rich deposits were opened up by the McKenzie Bros. at Marangaroo, nine miles from Lithgow, and sent to Bathgate Oil Works for retorting. The sample revealed 240 Imp. gal. of oil per long ton, which made it the richest oil shale in the world. Incidentally, Lithgow seems very like a contracted form of Linlithgow, known locally in West Lothian as 'Lithgy'. One wonders whether Lithgow was named by some earlier

emigrants from Linlithgow? During the Second World War, petrol
rationing led to operations starting once more in Marangoo by The
Lithgow Oil Proprietary Ltd. In 1937, National Oil Proprietary Ltd
was formed following public tender and Government capital assistance
to obtain petrol from oil shale. The site was at Glen Davis, Capertree
Valley, 27 miles north of Lithgow. Mining difficulties, compounded by
an acute shortage of skilled miners in Australia and increased pay
rates, meant that insufficient quantities of shale were available to allow
full production at the oil plant. The intention in 1950 was to raise,
within two years, the production rate to seven million gallons from three
million gallons in 1949. The Glen Davis refinery produced 10 million
gallons of motor fuel in 1947. It closed down in 1951. The main shale
deposits are in New South Wales, Queensland and Tasmania. Research
is thought to be continuing.

South Africa: The mining of torbanite began on a commercial scale
in 1935. The deposits being worked in 1949 were at Mooifontein in
the Ermelo district of the Transvaal, 140 miles east of Johannesburg
and 5,750 feet above sea-level. A section on 'labour and welfare' is
included here in view of the racist regime prevailing at the time.
Some old shale workers, reading this, might well have found ironic
resemblances to their own conditions of employment and dependency
on 'Company' housing, social faciltites and so on. Many of the oral
testimonies, especially of shale miners, described their own lot in
terms of 'slavery'. Of course, this related to the nature of the work
and primitive living conditions they felt burdened with. So called
'native? South African shale workers had this and the additional
oppression of living and working under Apartheid. The following
report describes institutionalised racism as a basic fact of life, unwor-
thy of explanatory comment.

> The administration of the mine falls under the mining manager, who has
> to assist him a mine overseer, and shift bosses, each of whom has under
> his control three European miner's sections. The operation of coal-cut-
> ters and drills and the lashing and tramming of products are done by
> natives under the supervision of the European miner, who personally
> carries out blasting operations. The natives work in gangs, each gang
> being supervised by a European assisted by a trained native boss 'boy'.
> The total labour employed in the mine at present numbers 630, dis-
> tributed 466 in sections and 104 on haulages, and 60 on general work
> such as brushing, haulage extensions, etc., on the 'off' shift. The high
> haulage figure is required due to the necessity for operating lengthy (up
> to 12,000 ft) and widespread haulages on account of variations in
> deposit values. Housing is provided on the mine property for all native
> employees and approximately one-third of the European employees. In
> the European quarter, recreation is provided by a recreation hall and

club with adjacent sports fields. The native compound is divided into two portions for married and single employees. In the case of the former a free house, coal, water, and food are provided. The single quarters consist of rooms or dormitaries, with a central ablution block and kitchen from where free meals are supplied. Native recreation mainly takes the form of tribal dancing, and sports fields are available for those who have become accustomed to European games.

(Vol 2, 184–5)

France: France dates their industry back to 1838, though it never fully developed its shale deposits. In 1909, representatives from the Societee Lyoness des Schistes Bitumineux visited Uphall, Oakbank, Broxburn and Pumpherston Oil Works before building a retorting plant and refinery at Autun, Saône-et-Loire. Another significant deposit was in the Aumance basin at Allier. In 1937, 111,000 tons of shale was produced at Autun and 18,400 tons at Allier. There was also workings at St Hilaire. The papers for the 1950 conference are written in French. Following the War, the industry in Autun was reorganised to take account of fuel imports which was not possible during the German Occupation. Other comments indicate that at least four plants were in production in the Wurtemberg area.

Sweden: Experimental plants at Rockesholm and Launa in Nerike were started but failed between 1916–18. In 1925, a shale oil plant for the Swedish Navy was built at Kinne-Kleva, owned by the Government and run by the Naval Board. It was the only plant operating in 1938. In 1950, the Swedish Shale Oil Company Ltd operated the Kvarntork shale oil works, production estimated at 550,000 brl/year.

America: With the discovery of petroleum in Pennsylvania in 1859, the small shale oil industry fell apart. There was no commercial oil shale operations of much consequence from that time although field surveys and laboratory work was undertaken between 1916–29 in Colorado. The American Government, through the Bureau of Mines, constructed an Oil Shale Demonstration Plant near Rifle, Colorado and a research centre at Laramie, Wyoming, both in 1944, in response to concern about the depletion of petroleum resources during the War. The Americans examined every facet of mining and refracting, but the availability of petroleum meant that shale oil remained uncommercial. Shale oil was clearly viewed, however, as a 'standby' for the day when the petroleum would 'run out'. The following table details the estimates of oil recoverable from oil shales within America in 1939:

State	Total Oil	Recoverable Oil (Thousands of barrels of 42 US gallons)
Colorado	79,625,998	47,625,598
Nevada	6,039	3,623
Utah	48,800,000	25,680,000
Wyoming	3,044,000	1,826,400
Indiana	7,680,000	6,912,000
Kentucky	10,978,560	9,880,704
Pennsylvania	13,800	8,280
West Virginia	13,800	8,280
Total:	144,162,197	92,144,985

If my maths is correct, to obtain final figures in gallons, then 92 billion barrels of recoverable shale oil would need to be multiplied forty-two thousand times (42,000). In comparison, the Scottish shale oil industry mined 164 million tons of shale during its century of existence, basically by pick and shovel. It is perhaps worth noting too that over 80 per cent of the world's recoverable oil shale reserves were said to lie in Colorado alone. One analyst, L.M. Fanning, warned that if all the oil shales of western Colorado, eastern Utah, and south western Wyoming were mined, a desert 200 miles long and 150 miles wide would be created (Vol 2, 81). This sounds uncomfortably close to the dimensions of a small country – Scotland perhaps? In some parts of West Lothian, of course, shale mining has indeed led to ground level falling by some 30 feet.

Manchuria (Japan & China): Oil shale was discovered at Fushun in 1909, covering the whole surface of the coal deposits there, an area of 11 square miles with a recoverable quantity of 540 million tons. The shale would have needed to be removed in any case to get at the coal deposits. In 1938, production was 150,000 tons of oil per annum. In 1923, the owners of the mine, The South Manchurian Railway Company, sent 500 tons of shale to the Oakbank Oil Company in Scotland to assess its industrial possibilities. They built a plant in 1924 having a capacity for treating 10 tons per day and reached a capacity of 150,000 tons of oil per year from 1934. Their visit to Oakbank is described in graphic terms in one of the oral histories, *The Japanese Shale*, by an oil worker from Oakbank, Adam. Manchuria has since been returned to China. It has been estimated that 70 million tons of shale per year was being mined there in the 1970s (Kerr, 92).

Czechoslovakia: The Parmian seam of the Kladno coal basin in Western Bohemia. Shale oil used for gas-making and general fuel purposes.

Estonia (Finland): Production for illuminating gas began during the Great War. Commercial production began in the early 1920s. By 1937, production of shale oil reached 109,358 tons with 6,000 men being employed by eight Companies. The shale bed is described as parallel with the south shore of the Gulf of Finland in an unbroken line extending 70 miles between Tallin in Estonia and Leningrad in the USSR. In 1971, 18 million tons of shale was mined.

Canada: An embryonic shale industry happened in 1859 at Collingwood, Ontario and in 1862 near Rosevale, New Brunswick. However, since then Canada has depended on foreign sources of oil and petroleum. The richest deposits are in New Brunswick, Nova Scotia, and Quebec. Small experimental and test plants were erected in 1921 near Rosevale, in 1928 at Turtle Creek and between 1928–30 at McLellan Brook and New Glasgow.

Brazil: Despite having large shale deposits, Brazil had not achieved successful commercial production by 1938. The first plant was set up in 1891 and operated only a few months. In 1938, a German firm, Julius Pintsch, planned to build an experimental plant in the State of Bahia, hoping to produce 3,500 tons of oil and 400 tons of gasolene in the first year. Brazil still had a significant shale oil industry in the 1980s.

Russia (USSR): In 1950, it was stated that despite vast deposits, the shale oil industry had been slow to develop. The current five-year plan anticipated an annual production rate of three million tons of oil. The principal shale deposits are near the Volga River, in the provinces of Leningrad, Oblast, Gorky, Saratov, Kuibyshev, and in the Republics of Tatar and Chuvash. In the 1980s, Russia was said to have one of the last remaining significant shale oil industries along with China and Brazil.

New Zealand (1900) and **Switzerland** (1915) were reported as having had 'embryonic' shale oil industries.

* * *

It is interesting to read the 1950 conference papers because these show just how worried the American Government was about diminishing supplies of natural petroleum. This makes it clear that the shale oil industry was still viewed as strategically vital to the world economy, an available source of oil to turn to when necessary, the operative word here being 'when' rather than 'if'. Yet a decade later, its hub, the shale oil industry in Scotland, had closed down. However, the oil scare of the 1970s caused American Oil Companies like Esso and Union Oil to make large investments during the 1980s in shale plants in Colorado. The Esso plant closed in 1982. The Union Oil Company built the largest commercial shale oil plant in the USA at Parachute Creek, Colorada. It closed too in 1991 despite having a Government subsidy of 26 dollars a barrel when world crude stood about 20 dollars. Their own production costs were 57 dollars a barrel. Little wonder, then, that David Kerr quotes a Research Director for the US Bureau of Mines, P.L. Russel, (a Scots sounding name to be sure), as declaring in 1980 – *the Scottish oil industry may well have been the most successful to date* (Kerr, 94). Of course, the oil continued to flow in Scotland when BP struck oil in the Fortes Field in 1970. Twenty years later, BP was pumping 17.5 million gallons of oil per day out of the North Sea. Today the amount of oil coming out of the North Sea is 70 million gallons per day, with the refinery at BP Grangemouth processing half of it.

But it all started with shale. In view of the significant industries that still persist in China, Russia and Brazil, and the research interest that continues to this day in Australia and America, it is perhaps tempting to wonder in what form shale might yet stage a come-back if the black, black oil ever does run out. Certainly, 75 million tons of workable shale are estimated to remain under the fields of West Lothian, with about one billion tons of unproved reserves. How prepared my generation would have been, or future ones for that matter, to howk the stuff out themselves, by hand, five days a week and every Saturday morning (sometimes Sundays as well, if you were an oil worker) must remain open to conjecture. But what is not is that the shale is still there should anyone wish to try. And if they do, they would no doubt begin to understand better the endurance, and the enduring legacy, of the generations written about in these pages.

No Smoking

Robert: drawer, born 1914, Brigend

I remember Walter Nellies,
he was in hospital,
and John Mallon,
he was the shop steward at No.6,
and he went into hospital to see Walter Nellies,
and he had pneumoconiosis, you know.
And we were sitting in the corridor
waiting on the visiting hours starting
and,
of course,
automatically,
I pulled out my cigarettes,
you see.
And I gave John Mallon one
and I lit one myself.

Along came the sister,
in the corridor,
and she says,
'There's no smoking here!
So please put your cigarettes out!
Smoking is not allowed here!'
And she was right!
You know!
I thought a lot of her for that.
And she was right!

But when we went into the ward
to see Walter Nellies,
he was smoking his pipe!
And so were all the old chaps
that had pneumoconiosis.
They were allowed to smoke
during the visiting hours,
but they weren't allowed to smoke
at other times, you know.

We weren't allowed to smoke at all.

Some truths can only be told as stories

The laziest man in Winchburgh, according to my father, sat in front of a blazing fire, crying his eyes out. His mother rushes in and asks what's wrong? 'I'm burning', he says. My father would then laugh like a pooch.

* * *

Culture is not about the dead, but what gave them life, and meaning. A century from now, these voices and their preoccupations will sound as strange and wonderful as Henry Mayhew interviewing the Victorian working class, had we any such recordings. Already, in my lifetime, the people and places in this study have disappeared from common memory.

And what will we say if we are asked who they were, and what made them tick? Certainly not the brutal and physically demanding work; not bigotry; not the basic nature of the housing, sanitation and living conditions, all of which were attested to frankly and without the remotest tinge of regret or sentiment – none of that at all – but that their children should not go through what they did.

And the rising above it all – the value and place accorded individual character and ability, especially if it reflected credit on the whole community. For Jock Murray, Jock Wardrope, John Wilson, Walter Nellies, Sarah Moore, Robert Crichton and many lesser known figures were hailed as folk heroes, much more so than national political figures like Shinwell or Lord Roseberry. Because these had captured not only the imagination of the shale community but came to represent, even to themselves, and in the midst of sometimes desperate circumstance, their own best virtues – integrity, grace and worth.

And the sense throughout, even as they were telling their stories to the tape-recorders of their modern interviewers, just 'chaffing' they might have said, that theirs had been a different world, one a million years away from the lighter, better paid but soulless assembly line jobs some had gone on to at British Leyland, or the constant shifts of the BP plant at Grangemouth when the shale industry finally closed down in 1962.

And we may say that what ended then was not just a way of life, a certain kind of community, but an outlook, a manner, a certain kind of being.

Brithers

Alistair Findlay

When we meet noo, thegither,
we nod and say Ay. Ays meet,
then look away or doon,
silent bearers o' a terrible secret,
we miss him, oor faither.

Withoot lookin we can see him in
each others' face and voice and hair.
He's there, in that silence between us,
listenin, in that pause, waitin for the moment
when he'll go wi' us for a pint,
oor faither, who lives in oor silence.

Sometimes he'll sit between us,
listenin tae his stories,
watchin weel kent faces scratchin ears,
lookin roon or lightin up,
laughin like a pooch at the funny part,
at art and politics and religion, and bloody eejits,
oor faither, comin alive in oor laughter and talk,
reverent only of fitba', poetry and back breaking work.

We create oorsels as he did, and MacDiarmid,
wi' words and terrible talk and a' the slavers
o' the scottish workin-class, an aristocracy o' havers
pissin wi the poor against the same bloody wa', the collective
unconsciousness o' a big team ba', batterin at a' the doors o'
the universe tae see if the cosmos, oor faither, is in –
an gaun tae th'gemm.

How they wid laugh tae see
the reduction o' oor history
tae buildin an extension, or worse,
a conservatory!

Ancient footsteps clatter doon echoin stairs,
and eerie memories fa' tae where we whisper here,
thegither, terrible men, makin love in the dark.

Oor mother, waitin till we all come hame,
openin her door on beery breath and singin weans
creatin, and creatin again, that quiet mellow voice
in the hall, oor faither, who sings nae mair.

NOTES

Preface

(1) R.I. Moore in J. Fentress & C. Wickham, *Social Memory*, Blackwell, Oxford, p.viii, 1992

(2) Cairns Craig, *Out of History*, Polygon, 1996, p.206

Beginnings

(1) Sybil Cavanagh, *The Shale Oil Industry*, WLD Library, 1992

(2) David Kerr, *Shale Oil: Scotland*, Self-Published, 1994, p.8, 9

(3) O.L. Dick, *Aubrey's Brief Lives*, Secker & Warburg, 1971

Shale Talk

(1) Leon McAuley, *The Fountain*, Londonderry Verbal Arts Centre, 1993, Foreword

(2) Sara Randall, *Studies of Scottish Shale Oil Industry*, Institute of Occupational Medicine, WLD Library, 1984

(3) Tom Leonard, *Reports from the Present*, Cape, 1995, p.43

(4) Tom Leonard, *Radical Renfrew*, Polygon, 1990, p.xvii,

(5) Peter Sansom, *Writing Poems*, Bloodaxe Books, 1994, pp.38, 39

(6) Ibid p.41

(7) Burngrange Mine Inquiry, *Scotsman*, WLDL, 26/3/1947

(8) Bob Findlay, Winchburgh Language Survey, WLC, 8/2/1952

(9) Duncan Glen, personal correspondence, 3/11/1994

Unmapped Workings

(1) William McIlvanney, *Scotland on Sunday*, 26/6/1994

(2) Bob Findlay, Tribute, *West Lothian Courier*, 6/2/1959

(3) Obituary, John Findlay, *Linlithgow Gazette*, 15/11/1963, p.10

(4) Obituary: John Findlay, WLC, 15/11/1963

(5) Obituary: Robert Findlay, *Linlithgow Gazette*, 5/1/73

(6) John McKay, op cited pp.662, 665, 667

(7) Robert Grey, *The Labour Aristocracy in Victorian Edinburgh*, Clarendon Press, p.8, 1976 see also A. McKinlay & R. Morris, *The ILP on Clydeside*, Manchester University Press, 1991, p.7

(8) Michael Lynch, *Scotland: A New History*, p.416

(9) Ibid pp.419, 420

(10) William Donaldson, *The Language of the People*, Aberdeen University Press, 1989, pp.2, 4

(11) Ibid pp.47, 48

(12) Ibid p.1

(13) Ibid p.35

(14) John Foster, *Class Struggle & The Industrial Revolution*, Methuen, 1974

(15) Tom Gallagher, *Glasgow: The Uneasy Peace*, Manchester University Press, 1987

(16) Tom Gallagher, *Edinburgh Divided*, Polygon, 1987

(17) A.B. Campbell, *The Lanarkshire Miners*, John Donald, 1979

(18) T. Gallagher & G. Walker, *Sermons & Battle Hymns*, Edinburgh University Press, 1990, pp.180, 181,

(19) Stephen Knight, *The Brotherhood*, Granada, 1984, p.247

(20) See also: T. Gallagher in T.M. Devine, *Irish Immigrants & Scottish Society in 19th & 20th Centuries*, John Donald, 1991, p.21

(21) Patrick Gallagher, *Paddy the Cope*, WLDL.

(22) See T. Gallagher, and D. McCrone (below) – also Alan Findlay, Under The Microscope, WLC, 19/9/80:

> No serious student of politics in West Lothian would deny that in the minds of most non-members the Labour Party is closely related with the Catholic sector of the electorate. In Queensferry, the Party is referred to as the Catholic Party. A prominent ex-official and councillor from Bathgate recently confessed that he could never in his 20 years experience in the local branch recall any more than a 10 per cent non-Catholic membership. Fauldhouse, with one of the biggest branches in the county, has less than five per cent of its members drawn from the non-Catholic sector of the community. (Non-Catholic sector means people who do not send their children to Catholic schools.)

(23) Obituary of Bob Findlay, WLC, 13/10/1978

(24) D. McCrone, *Understanding Scotland*, Routledge, 1992, pp.157, 158

(25) Jock Wardrope, in George Garson, op. cited, p.5

(26) W.S. Marshall, *The Billy Boys*, Mercat Press, 1996, p.66

(27) Ibid p.57

(28) Ibid p.141

Eejits and bloody eejits

Inscription: John Montague, *The Rough Field*, Bloodaxe Books, 1990

(1) Letters, *Midlothian Advertiser*, WLDL, 27/2/1948

(2) Ibid, John Fairley, *Memories of the Stage*

(3) Rob Roy Production, *Midlothian Advertiser*, WLDL, 20/4/1923

(4) Paul H. Scott, *Scotland: A Concise Cultural Study*, Mainstream, 1993, p.151,

(5) Ibid

(6) Obituary: Robert Findlay, *Linlithgow Gazette*, 8/7/1927

(7) Bulleteers, Bob Findlay, WLC, 5/5/1961, p.5

(8) B. Hollingworth, *Songs of the People*, Manchester University Press, 1982, p.6

A community exists in its anecdotes

(1) A.P. Cohen, *Whalsay*, Manchester University Press, 1987, p.3

(2) Bob Findlay, Humour in the Shalemines, WLC, 17/8/1951

(3) George Orwell, *Inside the Whale*, Penguin, 1986, pp.54,77

(4) Bob Findlay, Bathgate Brevities, WLC, 31/7/1959, p.5

Births, deaths and marriages

(1)   John Benson, *British Coalminers in the 19th Century*, Longmans, 1980, p.125

(2)   Ibid p.133

(3)   Ibid pp.137, 138

(4)   Ibid p.161

(5)   Ibid p.171